Pocket Book of Marine

and Aeronautical...

Pears Book of Meats
and Accompaniments

BEE NILSON

Pears Book of Meats and Accompaniments

Pelham Books

Published in Great Britain by
PELHAM BOOKS LTD
52 Bedford Square
London WC1
1971

7207 0530 4

Printed in Great Britain by
Western Printing Services Ltd, Bristol
in Ten on Twelve Point Times
and bound by the Dorstel Press, Harlow

Contents

Foreword

This is the first in a series of four cookbooks which, while each is complete in itself, together will make a comprehensive book of home cooking. Some of the material first appeared in *Pears Family Cookbook*, published in 1964; this has been revised and brought up-to-date.

Pears Book of Meats and Accompaniments tells how to choose and cook meat and offal, sausages, poultry and game, with well-tested recipes for traditional and foreign dishes. There are also recipes for stuffings, sauces and other accompaniments, and a suitable choice is suggested with most recipes.

A section on the selection and preparation of vegetables and salads is a feature not usually found in books of meat cookery; but the vegetable accompaniment is just as important as the sauce or garnish in making a pleasing whole.

All recipes are given in both British and metric weights and measures, while, wherever appropriate, an alternative cup or spoon measure has been given as well as the weight. Temperatures are in both Fahrenheit and Centigrade.

Other books in this series will include:

Pears Book of Cakes and Puddings
Pears Book of Light Meals
Pears Book of Kitchen Management

1   Introduction

HOW TO USE THE RECIPES

1. Read the recipe right through to make sure you have all the ingredients and utensils needed.
2. Assemble the ingredients. The method used here, of writing the recipes in stages, shows which ingredients will be needed together and in what order they will be used.
3. Do as much preparation as possible before actually starting to cook, for example, weigh out the ingredients, prepare vegetables, cut up or otherwise prepare the meat.

ABBREVIATIONS

tsp.	level teaspoon/s	gran.	granulated
Tbs.	level tablespoon/s	in.	inches
c.	level cup	E.	electric
pt.	pint/s	G.	gas
qt.	quart/s	g.	gramme/s
oz.	ounce/s	kg.	kilogramme/s
lb.	pound/s	dl.	decilitre/s
min./s	minute/s	l.	litre/s
hr./s	hour/s	mm.	millimetre/s
S.R.	self-raising	cm.	centimetre/s

TEMPERATURES

° degrees Fahrenheit   °C. degrees Centigrade

WEIGHTS AND MEASURES

ALL MEASURES USED IN THIS BOOK ARE LEVEL MEASURES

They have the following capacities:

1 cup (c.)   = ½ an Imperial pint or 10 fluid ounces.
           = 284 millimetres (when using millilitre measures count it a scant 300 millilitres).

INTRODUCTION

1 tablespoon (Tbs.) = 15 millilitres or the size of a medicinal table-spoon.

1 teaspoon (tsp.) = 5 millilitres or the size of a medicinal tea-spoon.

IMPERIAL WEIGHTS AND MEASURES

16 ounces	= 1 pound	
20 fluid ounces	= 1 pint	
2 pints	= 1 quart	
8 pints	= 1 gallon	

AMERICAN MEASURES

1 American cup = 8 fluid ounces or approximately 230 milli-litres (British 284 ml.)

1 American tablespoon = ½ fluid ounce or approximately 14 milli-litres (British 15 ml.)

1 American teaspoon = ⅙ fluid ounce or approximately 5 milli-litres (British 5 ml.)

1 American pint = 16 fluid ounces (British 20 fl. oz.)

If standard American cups and spoons are used with this book, the spoons can be taken as being the same size as those used in the recipes, but count 1 cup as equivalent to 1¼ American cups.

METRIC WEIGHTS AND MEASURES

In all recipes British weights, and many of the measures have been converted to the metric system. This has not been done with table-spoons and teaspoons, because these are the same size as spoons used in many countries who use the metric system.

The conversion has been adjusted to give practical metric weights and measures which are still sufficiently accurate to give good results. The following figures have been used:

1 ounce	= 25–30 grammes (g.) (real value 28·35 g.)	
1 pound	= ½ kilogramme (kg.) (real value 453·6 g.)	
	= 500 grammes	
2 pounds	= 1 kilogramme (real value 2·2 lb.)	
	= 1,000 grammes	
1 pint	= ½ litre (1) (real value 568·2 millilitres)	
	= 10 decilitres	
1 inch	= 2½ centimetres (cm.) (real value 2·54 cm.)	
	= 25 millimetres (mm.)	

INTRODUCTION

1 fluid ounce = 25–30 millilitres (ml.) (real value 28·41 ml.)
1 litre   = 1,000 millilitres or 10 decilitres

OTHER USEFUL APPROXIMATIONS
¼ pint = 1½ decilitres or 150 millilitres
½ pint = ¼ litre or 250 millilitres or 2½ decilitres
¼ pound = 125 grammes
½ pound = 250 grammes or ¼ kilogramme

2 Meat—General Notes

QUALITY IN MEAT

This depends on a number of factors and choosing, and handling good-quality meat is a highly skilled job. When you are lucky enough to find a butcher who knows his job and, more important, puts his knowledge into practice, stick to him. Quality in meat starts with the breeding and feeding of the animals to produce the best proportions of muscle, fat, and tendon in the right places. The ideal amount of fat is very important to quality. There should be a layer under the skin, and the very best meat has fat within the fibres called 'marbling'. This makes the meat tasty and tender and is specially important with beef.

Meat consists of cells held together by fine connective tissue to make meat fibres. These in turn are bound together to form the muscles which are attached to the bones by tough connective tissue or tendons. Muscles which have a great deal of use such as leg muscles have more and stronger connective tissue than the less-used ones and are tougher, requiring slower and longer cooking.

When meat is cooked the connective tissue shrinks and exerts a squeezing effect on the cells, like a sponge, squeezing out water and nutrients. The higher the temperature and the longer the cooking, the greater the shrinkage and therefore the greater the losses. Only the most tender cuts of meat can remain palatable when subjected to very-high-temperature cooking such as grilling, frying, and high-temperature roasting.

The age of the animal also affects quality, the older the tastier (veal has less flavour than beef, but it is more tender).

The way in which the animal is treated before killing affects quality and the subsequent hanging is also important.

Meat needs to be hung up in a cold dry store or cold room for periods of from 3–4 days to a week to make it more tender. If meat is eaten immediately after it is killed and before *rigor mortis* sets in it is tender but later becomes tough and needs hanging to allow chemical changes to take place. These are mainly the production of lactic acid in the muscle which has the effect of softening connective tissue, the tissue largely responsible for toughness. Some people hang game until it is so soft that it falls off the hook and is then 'high' or 'gamey'.

MEAT TENDERISERS

These are devices for making tough meat tender.

A metal meat tenderiser consists of a heavy base to which are attached thick metal needles. The meat is prodded all over with the needles and this breaks up the connective tissue and makes it more tender. It is quite an effective measure. The other useful method is to paint or sprinkle the meat with a liquid or powder containing lactic acid and papain enzymes which digest and soften protein. Care must be taken not to exceed quantities and times recommended by the makers or the meat will fall to pieces and be tasteless.

ROASTING

This is a simple method of cooking meat which was used before the days of efficient ovens. The meat was hung before an open fire and cooked by radiant heat. In order to prevent burning and scorching before it cooked through, the meat had to be kept moving and the rotating spit was invented to do this. Recent times have seen a revival of this method. Enthusiasts claim that the meat is better than when oven roasted which they label 'baked' and inferior. See *Rôtisserie*, page 15.

However, oven roasting is still the simplest method, and has the advantage that other things can be cooked at the same time and less expensive cuts of meat can be made succulent and tender, by means of slow oven roasting.

Another modern development in roasting is the use of a covered roasting pan or the wrapping of meat in aluminium foil which is removed towards the end of cooking to allow the meat to brown. Some would say that this is not roasting but braising or steaming. The advantage of using foil is that, when the meat is roasted at fairly high temperatures, the inevitable spluttering of fat is confined to the cover and the oven kept clean. In addition, if the joint is not top-quality meat, the cover helps to provide moist heat, and make the meat more tender. It should be remembered that the shiny surface of the foil reflects instead of absorbing radiant heat from the oven walls and, unless temperatures and times are adjusted to compensate, the meat will not cook in the expected time. A much simpler solution to the problem of the splashed oven and less tender cuts of meat is to cook uncovered meat at a low enough temperature to prevent splashing of fat and at the same time to render tough meat tender. See *Slow Roasting*, below. Modern polyester cooking films have the advantage of containing moisture without reflecting heat and there is no need to use higher temperatures as with foil.

The following are methods of oven roasting commonly in use today with their advantages and disadvantages:

High-Temperature Short-Time Roasting E.425° (220°C), G.6–7. Only suitable for tender cuts of meat and used chiefly by those who like meat to be well browned outside and under-done inside. Potatoes roast very well with this method. The oven is splashed with fat unless the meat is covered.

High Initial Temperature and Moderate Heat for the rest of the time E.450–475° (230–250°C), G.8–9 then E.350° (180°C), G.4. This method belongs to the days of belief in the theory that sealing the outside of the meat prevented subsequent loss of juices, a theory which has been proved incorrect. The only advantage of this method is that it cuts the cooking time slightly by heating the meat more quickly but at the same time it causes splashing of fat, and loss of weight.

Moderate Hot Temperature throughout E.375–400° (190–200°C), G.5–6. Suitable for all tender roasting joints and the best to use for a covered pan. Potatoes brown well round uncovered meat or in a separate pan. Considerable splashing of fat and shrinkage of the meat if uncovered.

Slow Roasting E.325–350° (160–180°C), G.3. Suitable for all joints, including the less tender cuts. No splashing of the oven.

The temperature is too low for good roast potatoes unless the oven has a steep temperature gradient where the potatoes can be put in the hottest part. It is difficult to over-cook meat by this method so cooking times are not very critical.

Use of a Meat Thermometer This is a thermometer which is pushed into the thickest part of the joint (not on to bone) and records the internal temperature, whether it is rare, medium done, or well done.

It is the most trouble-free way of roasting. The cooking times depend on the method of roasting and the oven temperature.

Some modern ovens have a meat thermometer as part of the fittings.

General Recommendations Many people vary roasting temperature and times to suit their convenience and to fit in with other food being cooked at the same time. If a roasting thermometer is used, the guesswork is taken out of the cooking. Cooking times required will always vary even for joints that look the same. The amount of bone, the distribution of fat, the composition of the muscle all have an effect on the cooking time.

Whether fat needs to be added to the meat during cooking depends on whether the meat is lean or not. Very lean meat like veal needs some protection against drying and is usually covered with fat bacon or suet or else a piece of foil.

Basting is not necessary unless for purposes of flavour, *e.g.* basting with wine, spirit, or fruit juice. Many meats are improved by the addition of herbs and spices, see *Herbs and Spices in Meat Cookery*, page 20.

Most meat is better raised up from the juices by placing it on a low grid. This applies specially to pork if the crackling is to be crisp.

For details of roasting individual meats see *Roast Beef, Roast Lamb*, etc.

RÔTISSERIE

A modern spit roaster, either a separate portable appliance or an attachment for fitting under the eye-level grill of a cooker. A method of cooking any good-quality roasting meat which is a suitable shape for fixing on the rotating spit. Also very good for poultry and for small pieces of meat such as Kebabs. With big pieces, the boned and rolled joints are the easiest to handle. Meat does not need basting unless it is very lean and then the better method is to tie a piece of fat over the lean surface to act as a self-baster. It can be removed at the end to let the meat brown. Otherwise brush the meat with melted butter or oil at the beginning of cooking and during cooking too if it seems necessary to keep the meat moist.

Cooking Times Joints, 20–30 mins. per lb. ($\frac{1}{2}$ kg.); medium-sized broiler chicken, 60 mins.; pheasant, 15–20 mins. per lb. ($\frac{1}{2}$ kg.); stuffed turkey (small one), 20 mins. per lb. ($\frac{1}{2}$ kg.); duckling, 15–20 mins. per lb. (½ kg). For smaller pieces of meat, times are similar to grilling over a moderate heat.

POT ROASTING (for meat, game, poultry)

Cooking Time 40–45 mins. per lb. (½ kg.)

This is an old-fashioned method of cooking which is a combination of frying and stewing or steaming. It requires a heavy pan and a gentle heat if it is to be done on top of the stove. Pot roasting can equally well be done in the oven, after the preliminary frying on top, and modern covered roasting pans and the practice of wrapping meat in foil achieve similar results. The method is used for tougher cuts of meat which are not suitable for roasting at high temperatures.

The meat is first fried in a little hot fat until it is brown all over, then covered with a tight-fitting lid and cooked slowly until tender, turning the joint over occasionally. Potatoes and vegetables may be cooked round the meat but will not be the same as if roasted or baked because of the large amounts of steam present. When the meat is cooked, gravy is made in the pan in the usual way. If the meat is cooked in the oven use E.325–350° (160–180°C), G.1–2.

The modern thermostatically-controlled oven achieves the same result of making tough meat tender simply by cooking it at a very low temperature (see *Slow Roasting*, page 14), a method that was not possible in former times. See also *Beef, Lamb,* etc.

CASSEROLE COOKING

Any oven-proof dish can be used as a casserole, either with its own lid or one of foil. Any food which is suitable for cooking in a sauce-pan can equally well be cooked in the oven in a casserole. The temperature will vary with the recipe but is usually in the range of 250–350° (120–180°C), G.½–4. It should be remembered that a cas-serole takes time to heat through and the thicker it is the longer it takes before the contents actually start to cook. To bring the contents to simmering point on top of the stove cuts down the cooking time, otherwise you need to add anything up to ½ hr. on to the cooking time to allow the contents to heat up. Alternatively, the casserole can be put in a much hotter oven than is required for the actual cooking and the heat at once turned down to the correct cooking temperature.

CARVING

To become a good carver requires a certain amount of experience but to start right is important. The knife should be really sharp, the kind of knife being less important than its sharpness. It should be sharpened every time it is used and if the knife is stainless steel be sure you have the correct kind of sharpener for it.

Most meat should be carved across the grain, that is, across the meat fibres. If cut the other way, with the fibres, the shape of the fibres can be clearly seen. The reason why across the grain is considered to be the best way is that, unless the meat is very tender, it will be difficult to chew the long fibres. In most cases cutting across the grain means cutting at right angles to the bone. In rolled joints it usually means carving across the already cut ends. Carving should be a sawing action with long light strokes backwards and forwards, and on as even a plane as possible so that the surface remains flat, otherwise the carver pretty soon finds that only little scrappy bits are coming off each time because of the bumps and hollows formed by the crooked carving.

Use a fork with a thumb guard and if possible do the cutting away from yourself.

Exceptions to the rule for cutting across the grain are with

Saddle of mutton which consists of two loins joined in the middle. In this case the carving is done in slices parallel with the backbone.

Legs of lamb or mutton are also sometimes carved parallel to the bone.

Game and Poultry. See Chicken, p. 137.

With a calf's and pig's head the cheek is the meaty part and should be carved from mouth to ear.

REHEATED MEAT

Reheated meat needs very carefully handling otherwise food poisoning may result. Any left-over meat should be cooled rapidly, stored in a refrigerator and used up as soon as possible. Reheated meat must be brought to the boil to make it safe and it needs plenty of seasoning to make it palatable. Some very popular traditional dishes use leftovers and are good dishes to serve if these precautions are taken. Meat does not lose any significant nutritive value through being twice cooked.

STOCK

Stock is an important aid to making good sauces, and stews of all kinds. Ready-prepared stocks are available as meat extracts, meat and chicken cubes, and canned and bottled *consommé*.

In the days of universal solid-fuel cookers a stock pot was usually to be found in continuous use at the back of the stove and into it went bones and trimmings of all kinds. Some people still do this but for the majority the ready-prepared stock is more practical. But it is always worthwhile using a carcase of a chicken or other bird to make stock, and also to use any veal bones and trimmings. The pressure cooker is the simplest way of making it because the cooking time is so much less.

When the stock is cold, cover it, and store it in the refrigerator. It is wasteful to use meat for stock unless the meat is going to be eaten as a separate course or left in the soup. Protein is the most nutritionally valuable part of the meat and this is not dissolved out into the stock.

BONE STOCK

Cooking Time 2–3 hrs, or ¾ hr. in a pressure cooker.
Use any kinds of bones, cooked or raw. Chop or saw them into convenient pieces to fit in the pan, cover with cold water, and bring to the boil. For each pint (½ 1) of water add 1 carrot, 1 onion, and a *bouquet garni*. Cover the pan and simmer the stock or pressure cook it. Strain into a bowl and when it is cold remove any fat from the top of the stock.

MUSHROOM STOCK

Cooking Time 10–15 mins.
Use the stalks and peelings of mushrooms. Wash them well and put them in a pan with cold water to cover. Boil for 10–15 mins. and then strain.

VEGETABLE STOCK

Cooking Time 20–30 mins. or 5–10 mins. pressure cooking.
Use any mixture of vegetables such as the outside leaves of cabbage, cauliflower stalks, outside celery stalks and leaves, the green tops of leeks, watercress stalks, mushroom stalks and peelings, and any other

vegetables available. Chop or shred them finely, add boiling water to come three-quarters of the way up. Add a few bacon rinds or bones, a *bouquet garni*, a few peppercorns and 1 or 2 cloves. Cover and boil for 20–30 mins. Strain and use.

ASPIC JELLY

A clear savoury jelly made from meat stock, or vegetable stock, and gelatine to make it set. It is used for masking cold meats and other savoury dishes, for cocktail savouries, for lining moulds for savoury jellies, and in many other ways.

Aspic jelly may be purchsed ready made in crystal form but this is not generally of very good quality. It can be improved by the addition of Madeira or brandy. Better than this are the aspic jellies sold in jars, in jelly form, to be melted and used as needed. They are usually fairly expensive but so is home-made aspic jelly using a good meat stock, and the latter is hardly worth while in the average home when only small quantities of the jelly are needed at a time.

Quite a good jelly for the same purpose is made using any of the *bouillon* cubes which can be relied on to give an absolutely clear liquid. Set it with gelatine in the proportions recommended by the manufacturer. In the same way a tin of *consommé* can have gelatine added to it and be used as aspic. As the *consommé* already contains enough gelatine to make it set when chilled, only a little more (about ¼ the usual amount), need be added.

Vegetable aspic is made in the same way using clear vegetable stock and gelatine.

ASPIC JELLY WITHOUT STOCK

1 Tbs. gelatine   ½ tsp. salt
½ pt. boiling water (¼ l.)   2 Tbs. tarragon vinegar
2 tsp. sugar   2 Tbs. lemon juice

Dissolve the gelatine in the boiling water. Add the remaining ingredients and cool.

3 Herbs and Spices in Meat Cookery

These are important to those who look for variety in the flavour of meat dishes. Some cooks only use a few of the traditional British flavourings such as sage and onion or mint, and every country has its own traditional flavourings, largely governed by what grows where. The majority of herbs will grow in the United Kingdom, others can be purchased dry, and spices are available everywhere.

There are no rules about the use of flavourings; personal taste should be the deciding factor.

The following are just some suggestions.

FOR ROAST MEATS

Use chopped fresh, or powdered dry herbs, to sprinkle over or rub into cut surfaces before cooking; use fresh or dried in stuffings and in gravies and sauces to serve with the meat. Garlic, marjoram, rosemary, sage, caraway, fennel and thyme.

FOR BOILED MEATS

Add to the cooking liquid and/or use in accompanying sauces. Whole allspice, bay leaves, fennel, rosemary, whole cloves, chives (in sauce).

FOR GRILLS AND FRIED MEATS

Use finely chopped fresh, or powdered dry, to sprinkle on during cooking or afterwards; to flavour basting sauces and for compound butters. Basil, bay leaves (on skewers with kebabs), fennel, marjoram, rosemary, sage, lemon juice, tarragon.

FOR CASSEROLES, STEWS, MINCED MEATS, MEAT LOAVES, etc.

Paprika pepper; ground cinnamon, cloves, ginger, cumin; garlic; chervil; bay leaves (casseroles and stews); ground mace or nutmeg; tarragon, thyme, caraway, savory, lemon juice and rind, celery seeds.

FOR VEGETABLES

To add during cooking, before serving, or to an accompanying sauce.

Potatoes—mace, nutmeg, fresh dill, chives, parsley.
Sauces—mace, nutmeg, marjoram, tarragon, chives, parsley, savory.
Tomatoes and salads—basil, fresh marjoram, tarragon, sage, chervil and parlsey.
Cabbage, cauliflower, sprouts—caraway, dill seeds, mace, nutmeg.

BOUQUET GARNI

Is used for flavouring stocks, sauces, and many other savoury dishes. The one most commonly used consists of a bay leaf, a sprig of thyme, and a sprig of parsley, all tied together with cotton or, if dried ones are used, tied in a small piece of muslin. As the bouquet is always removed before serving, it is a good plan to leave the tying thread long enough to hang over the edge of the cooking vessel. Mixtures that are strained obviously can have the ingredients put in loose.

A wide variety of other herbs are used and also sometimes a small piece of celery is tied with the herbs.

GARLIC or *ALLIUM SATIVUM*

It belongs to the same family as the onion. Each garlic bulb consists of a number of segments or 'cloves'. The flavour is very pungent and, unless very lightly used, is disagreeable to many people, both the 'after taste' in their own mouths and the smell of it on the breath of others. Some mistakenly think they can't do 'gourmet' cooking unless they put garlic into everything.

The flavour is most subtle when a cut clove is used for rubbing on food before cooking, *e.g.* a slice of meat or a chop; or for rubbing round a bowl before mixing a salad in it. Otherwise garlic should be used in minute amounts and very finely chopped or crushed. Alternatively a garlic press can be used to give juice for flavouring; garlic salt, dried garlic and garlic vinegar are all readily available ($\frac{1}{8}$ tsp. dried garlic equals 1 clove).

Garlic goes particularly well with lamb or mutton and with most of the vegetables that normally grow in a hot climate where garlic is a traditional seasoning. The best way of using it with lamb or mutton is to insert a small piece between the bone and flesh and this will flavour both meat and gravy.

21

4 Glossary of Meat-Cooking Terms

BARDING

Is tying a thin sheet of fat bacon or fat salt pork over meat, usually the breast of a bird, to act as a self-basting device. It also adds flavour. It is usually removed before serving but sometimes left on small game birds like woodcock and pheasant.

BASTING

Is keeping the surface of food moist by spooning liquid or melted fat over it at frequent intervals. A process used in cooking many kinds of food, chiefly when grilling, baking, or roasting. Basting roasted meat is not as important today as it used to be because ovens can be controlled at low temperatures which do not cause undue drying of the surface of food, and aluminium foil or cooking film put over meats which might be dry, avoids the necessity for basting. It still is important, however, as a device for giving the outside layer of meat or other food a good flavour, e.g. basting with wine or a sauce as in barbecues.

BLANC

A French cookery term used for a variety of different cooking liquids, e.g. a court bouillon or a white stock.

BLANCHING

Is a preliminary to the cooking of many foods, used to help remove skins of fruits, to remove a strong or bitter taste, or too much salt, or to help keep the food a good colour. Two methods are used. The food may simply be dipped in boiling water and then into cold water. This is the method used for peeling fruit. After this treatment the skins come off very easily. Also used to shrink fruit so that it packs more readily into preserving jars.

The second method is to put the food in cold water, bring to the boil, and boil for a few minutes before straining and continuing the cooking.

BLANQUETTE

A white stew where the meat and vegetables are cooked in a white sauce. Cream or egg is added to the sauce just before serving. See *Veal Blanquette.*

BONING

This is cutting the flesh away from bones either before or after cooking. Special thin pointed knives are used and skill and experience are needed to do it without damaging the flesh. Most butchers will do boning for you if you ask them. If you want to do it for yourself the most important thing is to know the shape and position of the bones and to cut close to the bone with a scraping action which does not tear the flesh. To watch an expert do it is the best way of learning.

BROCHETTE

Fine long skewers for threading small pieces of food on for grilling, the food being sent to table still on the *brochette.* Some of them have very lovely ornamental heads. See *Kebabs, Kidney-Brochette, Lamb-Kebabs, Liver Kebabs.*

BROWNING

Liquid browning is made from caramelised sugar dissolved in water and is used for colouring meat dishes and sauces. A brown *roux* does the same thing with a better flavour but it is not always practicable to use it.

BUTTERED CRUMBS

Used for gratin dishes and as a topping for other savoury dishes. Most quickly made by putting pieces of buttered bread in a blender to make crumbs. Alternatively, melt ½ oz. butter (15 g.) for each cup of crumbs and stir to mix well. Will keep in refrigerator or freezer.

CURING

A process which involves salting, drying, and smoking in order to preserve meat and fish, *e.g.* bacon, ham, kippers, and bloaters. The degree of salting usually determines how long the cured food will keep. The smoking is mainly important for imparting flavour.

DEVILLED

A method of grilling when the meat is treated with a mixture of oil, mustard, and other seasonings. It is similar to some modern barbecues. See *Devilled Turkey*.

EXTRACTIVES

These are the substances which give meat its distinctive flavour. They are water-soluble and are responsible for the flavour of meat soups such as *consommé*. They stimulate appetite and the flow of gastric juices. See also *Meat Extracts*.

GALANTINE

A preparation of meat, usually spiced or stuffed, rolled up and tied into a thick sausage shape. It is then wrapped in a cloth (modern ones in foil), and boiled in stock made from the bones of the meat. It is then removed from the stock and pressed under a heavy weight until it is cold. The stock is strained and allowed to set, when it is used for garnishing the galantine, and sometimes a little of it is melted and used as a glaze. See *Veal Galantine*. A boned boiling fowl is also sometimes used to make galantine in the same way as the veal. The name is also used for various types of minced meat mould. See *Sausage Galantine and Liver Galantine*.

JARDINIÈRE, À LA

Garnished with fresh vegetables cut in small balls or dice or fancy shapes. They are cooked separately and arranged round the dish of meat in heaps. The vegetables usually included are carrots, turnips, peas, cauliflower, and French beans.

JUGGED

A method of cooking game in a jar or jug, nowadays in a casserole. See *Hare, Rabbit, and Venison*.

KEBOB, KABOB, KEBAB

Different spellings of Persian, Turkish, and Indian methods of cooking small pieces of meat on skewers, usually grilled. Mutton or lamb are the meats most commonly used. In Turkey this is known as *Shis Kebab* and in Russia as *Shashlik*. The meat is usually served with a traditional rice dish and in Britain is often garnished with such items as mushrooms, tomatoes, sweet peppers, bacon, ham, or onion.

Other meats can be cooked in the same way, especially kidneys, liver, beef-steak, sausages, and pieces of young chicken.

In France a similar method of cooking is called '*en Brochette*'. Today it is a popular method of cooking out of doors for picnics or barbecues. See also *Lamb Kebabs, Liver Kebabs, Grilled Kidneys*.

KNUCKLE

The lower part of the leg of an animal, very lean meat and a lot of bone. Calf's knuckle is sold as a separate joint. See *Veal*. With lamb and mutton the knuckle is usually left attached to the rest of the leg or shoulder and when this is roasted the knuckle forms a very tasty morsel. See *Shank*.

LARDING

A process whereby strips of pork fat are threaded through lean meat to give it moistness and flavour during cooking. A special needle is used for the purpose called a 'larding needle'. Barding is an easier method of preparing meat than larding but not quite so good for large thick joints of very lean meat. See *Barding*.

MARINADE

A highly seasoned liquid used to give flavour to meats by steeping them in it before cooking and then by basting them with it during cooking. The liquids used are oil, vinegar, wine, fruit juices. See *Marinated Beef Steak, Lamb Kebabs, Barbecue Basting Sauces*.

MEAT EXTRACTS

These are the water-soluble constituents of meat and contain a small quantity of protein and mineral salts and some vitamins of the B complex, chiefly nicotinic acid and riboflavin. They also contain the flavouring substances of meat (see *Extractives*), and this is the chief reason for their use in cooking.

Meat extracts are an important by-product of the corned-beef industry. The liquid left after the meat has been pressed for canning is evaporated to give a thick brown meat extract which keeps indefinitely. A similar product can be made in the kitchen by boiling old beef and then concentrating the resultant stock. It takes a lot of meat to make a little extract which is one of the reasons why pure meat extract is so expensive. Very little, however, is required to give flavour to stocks and sauces and it is cheaper to buy it than make it. Products such as meat cubes which are used for the same purpose as meat extract contain other cheaper ingredients. As well as a little meat extract they contain ingredients such as hydrolysed protein, flour, yeast extract, caramel, fat, dried meat, and flavourings.

PAR-BOIL

To boil for part (about half) the cooking time. The cooking is then finished by some other method.

PÂTÉ

French for 'pie'. In many restaurants the term is used for what is in fact a 'terrine'. A French pie is shaped like an English raised pie, but the pastry is more edible, containing butter and egg. Sometimes it is made like a large plate pie or a turnover.

RAGOUT

A French term used for a wide variety of preparations made from meat, fish, and poultry and similar to many stews and casseroles.

SCORE, TO

To mark with cuts, e.g. the rind of pork before roasting.

SEASONED FLOUR

1 Tbs. salt   4 oz. flour (¾ c. or 125 g.)
¾ tsp. pepper

Sift these together and keep in a dredger for dusting meat and fish before cooking.

SHANK

The part of a leg from knee joint to foot, most often of lamb. Shank-end is the lower half of a leg and is more meaty than the shank alone. See Knuckle.

GLOSSARY OF MEAT-COOKING TERMS

SIMMERING

Cooking below boiling point, about 183°. The surface of the liquid is agitated but not bubbling.

SINGE

To pass through a flame and burn the surface to remove hairs, *e.g.* with poultry. It is done either with a gas flame or a lighted taper or with a spirit lamp.

SMOKING, see *Curing*, p. 23

TENDONS

Dense, compact tissue in the legs and necks of animals and birds. It joins muscles to bones and is very tough. It does not soften with ordinary cooking methods, but under pressure produces gelatine. For removal of tendons from the legs of poultry, see *Chicken Preparation*.

TERRINE

Heat-resistant earthenware dishes with lids. Used for cooking certain meat dishes. See *Liver Terrine, Veal Terrine.*

5 Beef

Is the name given to the flesh of ox, bull, or cow when it is killed and prepared for food. The most famous beef in Britain comes from Scotland from Aberdeen Angus cattle, small animals, bred and fed to produce prime meat. Large amounts of beef are imported, especially chilled meat.

Beef varies a great deal in quality. There are about fifteen bovine species, ranging from those suitable only for sausage manufacturing to the very best quality ox or bullock. Breeding, age, sex, and type of feeding all influence quality. After killing, the length of time the meat is hung influences the quality and, with frozen meat, the time allowed for it to thaw is also important.

CHILLED BEEF

Is beef kept in cold storage (−1°C) which is not a low enough temperature to freeze it solid. It is also stored in 'gas' or an atmosphere containing 10–15 per cent carbon dioxide, which inhibits the growth of microbes. Chilled meat does not keep as long as frozen, but is of a better quality and commands a higher price. It comes from Australia, New Zealand, and the Argentine.

FROZEN BEEF

This is meat which is kept cold enough to freeze it really solid. The old method of freezing produced a result which was not as good as chilled meat because of the large losses of juice when the meat thawed and the consequent dry result when the meat was cooked. Modern deep freezing, on the other hand, produces results which are excellent and can be used for both raw and cooked meat.

Times required for thawing frozen joints in a refrigerator are 3–5 hrs. per lb. (½ kg.) up to 4 lb. (2 kg.), and 5–7 hrs. per lb. (½ kg.) if larger.

For thawing at room temperature allow about half these times.

CHOOSING BEEF

Good-quality beef is a light bright red and the fat creamy colour and firm in texture. Old, inferior, or stale beef is dark in colour and the fat often yellow and oily.

BEEF CUTS AND THEIR USES

Roasting High-temperature roasting—only sirloin or a large piece of rump steak suitable.

Low-temperature roasting—topside, thick flank, top rib, fore rib, back rib, leg of mutton cut, brisket.

Anonymous boned and rolled cuts—roast slowly or braise or pot roast.

Grilling or frying Rump, fillet, or upper cut of sirloin.

Pot roasting and braising Flank, silverside, top rib, back rib, leg of mutton cut, chuck, brisket.

Stewing, Goulash, Curries, Casseroles Thin flank, leg, shin, blade, chuck, sticking, clod, skirt, shoulder steak.

Boiling (Fresh meat) Brisket, silverside, topside. (Salt meat) Silverside and sometimes topside.

Puddings and Pies Flank, chuck, skirt, shoulder steak.

AITCHBONE

A large joint at the top of the hind quarter, containing the ischiopubic bone, or aitchbone. When this bone is removed the remaining meat is known as topside or silverside, depending on the part. The joint called aitchbone is such a large one that it is seldom sold as such today, but it makes a good economical joint for roasting, and was much used in the days of larger households.

BARON

Two sirloins of beef joined together at the backbone and cooked that way. A very large joint not often cooked today except for a banquet.

BRISKET

This consists of the six lower ribs of the beast. It has a fair amount of bone and fat and can be cooked with or without the bone. It is used either fresh or salted. Fresh, it can be slow roasted, braised, pot-roasted, or boiled and always requires long slow cooking. Salted it is usually boiled and served hot, or cold as cold pressed beef. See *Boiled Beef*, page 45.

BLADE BONE

Is a shoulder bone (part of the *scapula*), hence blade-steak. It is a cut which needs slow cooking, either slow roasting, pot roasting, or braising and is a cheap and good cut.

CHATEAUBRIAND

A thick slice of beef fillet, usually grilled or fried.

CHUCK STEAK

Is steak from the back of the beast, just below the neck. It is a good lean cut for braising, stewing, pies and puddings, and any recipe recommending long, slow cooking.

CLOD

Is meat from the *humerus* or upper bone of the front leg. It needs long, slow cooking and is suitable for pies, puddings, minced beef, stewing. It is a good cut to pressure-cook because this softens the rather large amount of gristle it contains.

ENTRECÔTE

Is cut from the upper part of a sirloin and either grilled or fried, usually without the bone, but a thick one may have the bone left in. After cooking it is then divided into portions.

FEET—called Cow Heel

Suitable for boiling or stewing when the meat becomes very pleasant and tender. Not very often available in the shops as they are used by manufacturers of gelatine, and for boiling with other meats to provide the gelatine for meat moulds like brawn.

FILLET STEAK

A steak taken from the undercut of a sirloin. It is the most expensive steak and very tender, though some contend that it has not the flavour of rump steak.

BEEF

Fillet steak is served under a variety of names: *chateaubriand*, *tournedos*, fillet steak, *filet mignon*. It is usually grilled or fried but large pieces are sometimes roasted in which case it needs larding with fat to keep it moist.

Fillet steak is known in the U.S.A. as tenderloin.

When you buy a sirloin you see the fillet as the smaller of the two pieces of muscle either side of the bone. When it is to be cut into steaks the butcher removes the whole fillet of the animal in one piece. If you buy a large sirloin joint you can remove the fillet and use it separately as steaks.

Fillet steak is also suitable for cutting into pieces and grilling on skewers as in *kebabs*. See *Grilled Steak* and *Fried Steak* for cooking methods suitable for fillet.

FLANK

A cut from the belly of the beast which varies in thickness to give thick flank and thin flank as well as just flank. It is a lean cut which needs slow cooking. Thick flank is suitable for slow roasting, the others for braising, pot roasting, or stewing.

LEG

The name is usually only applied to the hind leg (fore leg is shin). It is a lean gristly meat and needs very long slow cooking, but as a result it produces an excellent gravy. Best used for stewing (3hrs. cooking), or for pressure cooking (1 hr.).

LEG OF MUTTON CUT

Is a cut from the shoulder of the beast, more usually boned and sold as shoulder steak. Suitable for any long slow cooking, slow roasting, pot roasting, braising, and stewing. It is usually cheap and is very good value.

MINUTE STEAK

A very thin piece of steak which cooks in a minute. See *Fried Beef Steak*, page 35.

PLATE

A similar cut to brisket but from a bit further down the belly of the

31

BEEF

animal. It is sometimes salted but is also suitable for pot roasting and braising. Sometimes this cut forms part of thick flank.

RIBS

All are good roasting joints. They include sirloin, wing rib, top rib, fore rib, and back rib. Some have quite long bones and others very short ones, but the long bones are often cut off to make separate joints.

Sirloin The characteristic feature of this rib cut is that the underside of the bone has a small piece of very tender muscle attached to it, the fillet. See *Fillet*. Sirloin may be cooked on the bone, or boned and rolled.

Wing Rib is the next cut to sirloin but has no fillet attached. It is best-cooked on the bone, and is particularly easy to carve. The other ribs can all be roasted on the bone, or boned and rolled. If you buy them on the bone you are sure you have a genuine rib roast.

RUMP STEAK

It comes from the hind quarters of the animal, round about the pelvis. It is a first-class steak for grilling and frying, not quite as tender as fillet steak but often of better flavour.

SHANK. See *Leg* (same thing)

SHIN

Is the fore leg. See *Leg*.

SILVERSIDE

Comes from the thigh of the hind quarters and contains no bone. It is the joint most frequently salted and used for making 'Boiled Beef and Carrots'. See *Boiled Beef*. Also suitable for cooking as fresh meat, boiled or braised. It needs long, slow cooking.

SIRLOIN. See *Ribs*

SKIRT

A thin lean steak from inside the animal, e.g. the diaphragm. It is sometimes classed as offal. It has a good flavour and gives a very rich gravy. Excellent for pies, puddings, and stews.

32

TOPSIDE

Comes from the thigh of the animal, is a lean cut and contains no bone. Best braised, pot roasted, or slow roasted and is sometimes boiled, either fresh or salted.

ROAST BEEF

Method see *Roasting* page 13.

High-temperature Roasting. For under-done meat and the better cuts such as sirloin and rump E.425° (220°C), G.6–7.

Cooking Times. 15 mins. per lb. (½ kg.) and 15 mins. over for under-done meat; 20 mins. per lb. (½ kg.) and 20 mins. over for medium done.

Moderate-temperature Roasting. E.375–400° (190–200°C), G.5–6.

Cooking Times. Sirloin and ribs on the bone and thin pieces, 25 mins. per lb. (½ kg.) medium to well done. Boned and rolled and thick pieces, 30 mins. per lb. (½ kg.) medium to well done. For under-done meat use the lower temperatures in each case.

Slow Roasting. Suitable for all cuts including brisket and leg of mutton cuts, E.300–325° (150–160°C), G.2–3.

Cooking Times. Ribs unboned and thin pieces 40 mins. per lb. (½ kg.) medium to well done. Boned and rolled and thick pieces, 45 mins. per lb. medium to well done. For under-done meat use the lower temperature.

Using a Meat thermometer. Internal temperature of meat 140° (60°C) under-done; 160° (70°C) medium done; 170° (75°C) well done. Times as above depending on the oven temperature.

Quantities. With bone allow ½–¾ lb. (¼–½ kg.) per person; no bone allow 4–6 oz. (125–175 g.) per person.

Accompaniments. Thin or thick gravy. See *Gravy*. Fresh grated horse-radish or horseradish sauce; Mustard; Yorkshire pudding; Roast potatoes; Green vegetable.

YORKSHIRE PUDDING

Cooking Time 30–45 mins.   *Temperature* E.450° (230°C), G.7.
Quantities for 4–6.

   4 oz. plain flour (¾ c. or 125 g.)   ½ tsp. salt

Sift into a basin and make a well in the centre.

   2 eggs   About ½ pt. milk (¼ l.)

Break the egg into the well and start stirring from the centre gradually working in the flour and adding half the liquid. Beat very thoroughly and then add the rest of the liquid to make a thin batter. Alternative method, put egg, flour, milk and salt in the blender goblet and mix at high speed for 1 minute.

1 oz. dripping (30 g.)

Put the dripping in an oblong meat tin about 8 in. × 10 in. (20 × 25 cm.) and, when it is hot, pour in the batter. Put near the top of the oven and bake until risen and brown. If you like it a bit under-done in the middle give it the shorter time and if liked crisp, the longer.

BATTER PUDDING is a more solid pudding made in the same way but with twice the amount of flour to egg and liquid.

TOAD-IN-THE-HOLE

1 lb. skimmed pork sausages (½ kg.)

Put these in the baking tin and cook for 5 mins. before adding the batter. Cook as before.

MEAT IN BATTER

1 lb. small cutlets or chops or
1 lb. beef steak cut in pieces (½ kg.)

Cook the meat in the pan for 5 mins. before adding the batter. Finish as before.

GRILLED BEEF STEAK

A better method than frying except for all the very thin steaks, Cooking Time. 10–15 mins. depending on the thickness and whether it is liked well-done or rare.

Quantities. Allow 6–8 oz. per portion (175–250 g.).

Cuts used are fillet, rump, sirloin, porterhouse, tournedos, chateau-briand, mignons. Brush the steak with melted butter or oil. Heat the grill thoroughly or have a clear red fire. Cook the steak with a fierce heat for 1 min. each side, then reduce the heat slightly or move the meat further away and continue cooking, turning every 2 min. Put on a hot dish with the chosen garnish and pour any juices in the grill pan over it. Sprinkle with salt and pepper and serve at once.

Garnishes. Parsley or *maître d'hôtel* butter, grated fresh horseradish, fried potatoes, fried onions, green salad, watercress, grilled tomatoes, grilled mushrooms, French or English mustard.

GRILLED MARINATED BEEF STEAK

For each 1 lb. (½ kg.) of steak allow 1 Tbs. olive oil, 1 Tbs. vinegar, salt, and pepper. Mix these together and let the steak soak in them for 24 hrs., turning once or twice. Then grill as above.

FRIED BEEF STEAK

Cooking Time. 5–15 mins. depending on the thickness of the steak and whether you like it well done, medium, or rare. 'Minute' steak, 2 mins.

Quantities. 4 oz. (125 g.) per person if cut thin or as *tournedos*; 6–8 oz. (175–250 g.) if cut thick.

Suitable cuts are fillet, rump, and slices from the sirloin. Heat a little fat or oil in a heavy frying pan and when it is hot put it in the steak. Brown for 1 min. on each side. Keep cooking over a fierce heat turning every minute or two but avoid over-cooking or the meat will be tough and dry. Even when well done it should still feel springy to the touch. Serve on a hot dish.

Swill out the pan with a little liquid such as stock, wine, or lemon juice. Let the liquid boil for a minute or two to dissolve all the tasty sediment from the bottom of the pan and pour this over the meat.

FRIED STEAK AND ONIONS

Cooking Time. 10–15 mins. for the onions and 5–15 mins. for the steak, depending on its thickness and whether you like it well done or rare.

Quantities for 4.

1–2 *lb. rump steak* (½–1 *kg.*) *Salt and pepper*
1½ *lb. onions* (¾ *kg.*) *A little butter*

Have the meat cut in 4 portions which will be fairly thin if you are using the smaller amount of meat. Peel the onions and cut them in ⅛ in. (3 mm.) thick slices. Trim excess fat off the meat and cut the fat in small pieces. Salt and pepper the meat. Put the chopped fat in a heavy frying pan and heat until the fat begins to run. Remove fat and add the onions. Reduce the heat and cook gently, stirring frequently until the onions are tender and lightly browned. Remove and keep hot. Add a small nut of butter to the pan and turn up the heat. When the butter begins to brown turn up the heat and add the steaks. Brown each side quickly and continue cooking over a good heat until they are done as required. Turn every minute or two. Serve on a hot dish with the onions. Add a little water or stock to the pan and stir and simmer until the sediment in the pan is dissolved. Pour this over the steak.

FILET MIGNON OF BEEF WITH MUSHROOM SAUCE

Cooking Time 20 mins.   *Quantities for 4.*

1 oz. butter (25 g.)
4 pieces of fillet steak cut 1 in. thick (2½ cm.)

Heat the butter in a deep frying pan or shallow stew pan. Put in the steaks and brown them very quickly 2 mins. each side. Remove them from the pan.

½ oz. flour (1½ Tbs. or 15 g.)
½ pt. stock (1 c. or ¼ l.)   Salt and pepper

Add the flour to the fat and mix well, cooking for a few minutes. Add the stock and stir until it boils. Season well.

8 oz. mushrooms (250 g.)

Wash and slice the mushrooms (no need to peel or de-stalk culti-vated ones). Add them to the sauce and boil gently for 10 mins. Add the steaks and simmer for 5 mins.

Watercress

Serve the steaks garnished with watercress.

TOURNEDOS

Small thick slices of fillet of beef weighing about 4 oz. (125 g.) each. Usually grilled or fried and served with a variety of accompaniments.

TOURNEDOS SAUTÉ

Cooking Time. About 15 mins.   *Quantities for 4.*

1 lb. (½ kg.) fillet steak cut into 4 pieces each about 1¼ in. (3 cm.) thick

Butter for frying

Heat enough butter to cover the bottom of the frying pan, and when it is hot fry the *tournedos* quickly, turning every minute or two for about 8 mins. Lift out and keep hot.

> More butter if needed   ¼ pt. stock (1 c. or ¼ l.)
> ½ oz. flour (1½ Tbs. or 15 g.)   Salt and pepper
> ¼ pt. madeira or sherry (½ c. or 1½ dl.)

If necessary, add more butter to the pan to give about 1½ Tbs. fat. Add the flour and mix and cook until it begins to brown. Gradually add the stock and wine and stir until it boils. Boil hard until it is the desired thickness, season to taste, and pour over the *tournedos*.

BEEF STEAK WITH LEMON

Cooking Time 45 mins.   *Quantities for 4.*

> 1½ lb. rump steak (750 g.)

Trim off surplus fat and cut it in small pieces. Cut the meat into 4 portions. Heat the fat in a shallow stewpan until it begins to melt. Remove the bits of fat and add the steak.

> 8 thin slices of lemon

When the steak is brown on one side, turn and add the pieces of lemon, cover the pan and stew very slowly for 10–15 mins.

> 4 Tbs. marsala or port wine   4 Tbs. water
> 1 meat cube   Salt and pepper

Add to the meat and simmer for a few minutes without the lid, to allow some of the liquid to evaporate.

> 1 Tbs. lemon juice

Add to the pan. Serve the steak with the sauce poured over it. If preferred, the liquid may be thickened with a little blended potato flour or cornflour. Serve with

> *Baked jacket potatoes.*

STEWS AND CASSEROLES

The following 8 recipes are suitable for cooking either on the hot plate or in a casserole in the oven at E.300° (150°C), G.2. The recipes for braising, pages 43–44, and for boiling, pages 45–46, are also suitable for oven cooking.

BEEF GOULASH

Cooking Time 2–3 hrs.　　*Quantities for* 4.

> 1 *lb. lean stewing steak* (½ *kg.*)
> 1 *oz. dripping or oil* (2 *Tbs. or* 25 *g.*)

Cut the meat in 1 in. (2½ cm.) cubes and fry it brown in the hot fat, in a saucepan or casserole.

> 2 *onions*

Slice the onions and add them to the meat towards the end of browning and continue cooking until the onions begin to brown.

> ¼ *pt. stock* (1½ *dl.*)　　2 *tsp. paprika pepper*
> 1 *tsp. salt*　　　　　　Pinch *of carraway seeds*
> 2 *Tbs. tomato paste or* 2 *tomatoes*

Add these to the meat, cover, and simmer for 2–3 hrs., adding a little more stock if needed.

> 4–6 *medium potatoes*

Peel the potatoes and cut them in quarters. Boil them for 15–20 mins. and then add them to the goulash for the last 10 mins. of the cooking time. Serve on a hot dish, accompanied by

> *Boiled cabbage.*

BEEF OLIVES

Cooking Time 1½–2 hrs.　　*Quantities for* 4.

> *Veal forcemeat recipe (see Stuffings, page* 260) *or packet veal stuffing*
> 1 *lb. topside or rump steak cut in very thin slices* (½ *kg.*)

Make the stuffing. Cut the sliced meat into pieces about 4 in. by 3 in. (10 by 8 cm.). Lay them out on a flat surface and put a little stuffing

38

on each. Roll up tightly and secure with thick white cotton or fine white string.

Skin and slice the onion and fry it and the meat in the fat until brown.

1 onion   1 oz. fat or oil (2 Tbs. or 25 g.)

1 carrot   1 bay leaf
½ tsp. salt   Pinch of pepper
½ pt. stock (¼ l.)

Peel and slice the carrot and add it to the pan together with the other ingredients. Cover and simmer 1½–2 hrs. or until the meat is tender. Remove the cotton ties and place the olives on a serving dish. Remove any excess fat from the top of the gravy and, if desired, thicken this with a little potato flour or cornflour (½ Tbs. to ½ pt. or ¼ l.), blended smooth with a little cold water. Pour into the stock and stir until it thickens and boils. Pour over the olives.

BEEFSTEAK STEWED WITH OLIVES

Cooking Time 1½–2 hrs.   *Quantities for 4.*

1½ lb. stewing steak (¾ kg.)   1 onion
1 oz. fat or oil (2 Tbs. or 25 g.)

Cut the steak in small pieces. Skin and chop the onion. Fry them both in the hot fat or oil.

3 oz. stuffed olives (75 g.)   1 tsp. salt
½ a red or green pepper, fresh or canned
About ½ pt. canned tomato juice (¼ l.)

Slice the olives and chop the pepper. Add to the meat together with the salt and enough tomato juice to almost cover the meat. Put on the lid and cook gently until the meat is tender, adding more tomato juice if needed. This can be cooked in a casserole in the oven. E.300° (150°C), G.2.

Accompaniments. Boiled macaroni or noodles or boiled potatoes. Green beans or peas or a lettuce salad.

BEEF *BOURGUIGNON*

Cooking Time 2¼ hrs.   *Quantities for 4.*

2 oz. butter (50 g.)   3 rashers bacon
1 medium onion

Skin and slice the onion. Remove rinds and cut bacon in small pieces. Heat the butter and fry the onion and bacon in it gently until brown.

1 lb. stewing beef (½ kg.)

Cut the meat in small pieces. Remove the bacon and onions from the pan using a perforated spoon, and fry the meat until it is brown.

2 Tbs. flour

Sprinkle over the meat and cook until it browns.

½ pt. stock (1 c. or ¼ l.)   1 Tbs. red wine
2 oz. mushrooms (50 g.)   Bouquet Garni
1 tsp. salt   ¼ tsp. pepper

Stir the stock into the pan, return bacon and onion and add the other ingredients. Cover and cook slowly for 2 hrs. If more convenient, continue the cooking in a casserole in a slow oven.

CARBONNADES À LA FLAMANDE
or Beef with Beer

A famous Belgian dish which is stewed beef and onions, with beer as the liquid.

Cooking Time 2–3 hrs.   Temperature E.300° (150°C), G.2.
Quantities for 4.

1½ lb. beef steak (¾ kg.) cut in ½ in. thick (1 cm.) slices
2 oz. dripping (50 g.)

Cut the meat in suitable portions for serving. Heat the dripping and fry meat until it is thoroughly browned. Lift out and put in a casserole.

8 oz. onions, skinned and sliced (250 g.)

Put the onions in the fat and fry golden brown. Add them to the meat.

1 oz. flour (3 Tbs. or 25 g.)   2 tsp. salt
½ pt. beer (1 c. or ¼ l.)   ¼ tsp. pepper
1 tsp. brown sugar   Bouquet Garni
1 small bit of garlic, chopped

Mix the flour with the remaining fat in the pan. Stir and cook until it browns and then add the beer, sugar, and the seasonings. Stir until it boils and all the sediment has been dissolved from the bottom of the pan. Pour this over the meat, cover, and cook slowly until the meat is tender.

1½ *Tbs. vinegar*

Add vinegar just before serving,

BEEF ROLLS

Cooking Time 1 hr. *Quantities* for 4.

4 *rashers bacon* 8 *sage leaves, fresh or dried*
1 *lb. topside or rump steak cut very thinly* (½ *kg.*)

Cut the sliced meat into 8 or more small pieces. Remove rinds and put a piece of bacon on each piece of meat, having it slightly smaller than the meat. On this put a sage leaf. Roll up tightly and secure with thick white cotton or fine white string.

1 *oz. fat or oil* (25 *g.*)

Heat the fat or oil and fry the rolls in it until they are brown. Lift out the rolls and pour off any surplus fat.

⅛ *pt. wine* (¼ *c. or 1 dl.*)   ½ *tsp. salt*
¼ *pt. stock* (½ *c. or 1 dl.*)   ¼ *tsp. pepper*
1 *Tbs. tomato paste*

Pour the wine and stock into the pan and stir well to dissolve all the sediment. Mix the tomato with 2 Tbs. water and add, together with the seasonings. Cover, and simmer gently until the meat is tender. Remove the strings before serving the rolls. If preferred, the rolls may be put in a casserole and cooked in a slow oven.

CURRIED BEEF

Cooking Time 2–3 hrs. *Quantities* for 4.

1½ *lb. stewing beef* (¾ *kg.*) 2 *tsp. salt*
1½ *oz. flour* (4½ *Tbs. or 45 g.*)

Cut the meat in cubes. Mix flour and salt and coat the meat with it by shaking them together in a paper bag.

2 *medium-sized onions* 2 *apples*
½ *clove garlic*   1 *tomato*

Peel and chop the onions, garlic, and apple. Chop the tomato.

2 *oz. dripping* (50 *g.*) 2 *Tbs. curry powder*

Heat the dripping in a pan or fireproof casserole, fry the meat in it, and then the vegetables. Add the curry powder and fry a few minutes longer.

½ pt. stock (¼ l.)   Rind and juice ¼ lemon
1 tsp. brown sugar   1 Tbs. desiccated coconut
                    2 Tbs. raisins or sultanas

Stir in the stock and add the remaining ingredients. Cover and simmer for 2½–3 hrs. The longer cooking gives the better flavour. If preferred, it may be cooked in a casserole in a slow oven, E.300° (150°C), G.1.

Serve the curry with boiled rice and any of the garnishes listed.

8 oz. rice (1c. or 250 g.)   Sliced green or red peppers
Chutney   Chopped spring onions
Minced cashew nuts   Bombay duck
Grated fresh coconut   Slices of lemon or lime

BEEF AND SAUSAGE CASSEROLE

Cooking Time 2 hrs.   Temperature E.300° (150°C), G.2.
Quantities for 4–5.

1 lb. stewing steak (½ kg.)   1 oz. dripping (25 g.)

Cut the steak in small pieces and fry it brown in the hot fat.

1 onion   1 turnip
1 or 2 leeks   2 carrots

Peel and slice the onion, carrots, and turnip. Wash and slice the leeks. Add these to the meat in the pan and continue cooking until the vegetables are a little browned.

¼ tsp. pepper   ¼ tsp. salt   ½ pt. stock (1 c. or ¼ l.)

Add stock and seasonings to the pan, cover, and cook gently for 1 hr. If the casserole has not been suitable for frying in, transfer the meat and vegetables to the casserole at this stage.

2 sausages   Flour
1 lb. potatoes (½ kg.)

Cut the sausages in small pieces and coat them in flour. Peel potatoes and cut them in quarters. Add both these to the casserole and continue cooking for another hour, or until the potatoes are done. Add more stock if required.

BRAISED BEEF

Braising is a good method of treating some of the less tender cuts of beef, such as flank, rib, chuck, silverside, leg of mutton cut.

Cooking Time. Less than 3 lb. (1½ kg.) 2 hrs.; 3 lb. and over 20 mins. per lb. (½ kg.) and 20 mins. over.

Temperature E.350° (180°C), G.4.

Quantities. Without bone allow 4–6 oz. (125–175 g.) per portion; with bone allow 6–8 oz. (175–250 g.) per portion.

Beef in one piece
Mixed vegetables in season
Fat for frying
Salt and pepper

Bouquet Garni
Stock, or half stock and
half wine or beer

Prepare the vegetables in the usual way and slice or chop them coarsely. Any mixture can be used or just one kind. There should be enough to make a layer at least 2 in. (5 cm.) deep on the bottom of the pan. Heat a little fat and fry the piece of meat until brown all over. Lift it out, pour off any surplus fat, put in the layer of vegetables, and season well. Put the meat on the vegetables and add enough stock to come almost to the top of the vegetables. Cover and simmer on top of the stove or in a casserole in the oven.

When the meat is cooked, lift it out, and slice it. Arrange on the dish with the vegetables as a garnish and serve the liquid, skimmed of surplus fat, as a sauce. Alternatively, sieve the vegetables and use them to thicken the sauce, or put vegetables and liquid in the electric blender.

BRAISED BEEF WITH GREEN PEAS

Cooking Time 2 hrs.   *Temperature* E.325° (165°C), G.3.
Quantities for 4.

1½ oz. butter (45 g.)   1½ lb. braising steak in one piece (¾ kg.)

½ tsp. salt   ¼ tsp. pepper
1 lb. shelled peas, fresh or frozen (2 c. or ½ kg.)

Heat the butter and fry the meat until it is brown all over. Pour off any surplus butter.

Add the peas, salt, and pepper, cover and cook gently on top of the stove or in the oven. Lift out the meat, slice it, and serve with the peas and gravy as a garnish.

SWISS STEAK

Cooking Time 1½–2 hrs. *Temperature* E.300° (150°C), G.2.
Quantities for 3–4.

> 1 lb. flank, blade or chuck steak (½ kg.) cut about
> 1 in. (2½ cm.) thick
> 1 oz. flour (3 Tbs. or 25 g.) ½ tsp. salt Pinch of pepper

Mix flour and seasonings and rub into the meat.

> 2 onions 1 oz. fat or oil (2 Tbs. or 25 g.)

Skin and slice the onions and heat the fat. Fry the meat and onions until brown. If possible do this in a casserole, otherwise transfer the meat and onions to the casserole at this stage.

> Little chopped or dried marjoram Good pinch of sugar
> ½ pt. cooked or canned tomatoes (1 c. or ½ l.)

Add these to the meat, cover, and cook very gently until the meat is tender. Cut it in portions and serve it on the dish with the cooking liquid.

> Cooked mixed vegetables or green peas or beans

Serve with cooked vegetables as a garnish.

BOILED FRESH BEEF

Cooking Time. Allow 20 mins. per lb. (½ kg.) plus 20 mins., but if the joint is 3 lb. or under (1½ kg.) allow 1½–2 hrs. Pressure cooking allow ¾–1 these times.

Quantities. Allow 4–6 oz. (125–175 g.) per portion without bone, ½–¾ lb. (250–375 g.) with bone.

> A piece of brisket, 1 bay leaf
>   silverside, or topside 3 cloves
> 1 onion ½ Tbs. salt
> 1 carrot Hot water
>   Sprig of parsley

Wipe the meat with a damp cloth. Peel the onion and stick the cloves into it. Peel the carrot and wash the herbs. Choose a pan just large enough to hold the meat and vegetables. Heat in it enough water to come half way up the meat. Get the water boiling before adding the meat, then put it in with the vegetables and seasonings. Immediately reduce the heat to simmering and cook until it is tender. On no account should the water be allowed to boil as this causes the meat to shrink a lot and be tough and dry instead of tender and moist. Slice the meat and serve it on a platter together with additional vegetables which may be cooked with the meat or separately. Serve with a sauce made from some of the stock, e.g. parsley sauce. Strain the stock and use it for making soups and sauces.

If the meat is to be served cold, put it on a plate in a cold place to cool as quickly as possible and then store in the refrigerator. To cook additional vegetables with the meat, choose root vegetables and cut them in fairly large pieces, adding them for the last hour of cooking. They will take longer than normal to cook as the liquid is simmering and not boiling.

BOILED BEEF AND HORSERADISH SAUCE

Cooking Time 2 hrs.   *Quantities for 8.*

> ½ Tbs. salt   1 stalk celery
> 1 carrot   1 onion
> 1 parsnip   5 whole allspice
> 2–2½ lb. lean brisket (1 kg.)

Choose a pan just large enough to hold the meat and vegetables. Put in enough water to come half way up the meat, bring it to the boil and add the other ingredients together with the meat. Turn down the heat and simmer until the meat is tender. Just before it is ready remove some of the stock to make the horseradish sauce.

> 1½ oz. butter or margarine (45 g.)
> 2 tsp. dry mustard   ½ pt. meat stock (¼ l.)
> 1½ oz. flour (4½ Tbs. or 45 g.) ½ pt. milk (¼ l.)

Melt the fat and add the mustard and flour, stirring and cooking until it looks crumbly. Remove from the heat and gradually stir in the liquid, whisking until free from lumps. Return to the heat and boil for 5 mins. or cook longer over hot water or in a *bain-marie.*

> *Salt and pepper to taste* 6 Tbs. vinegar 1 tsp. sugar
> 3 oz. grated horseradish or more if you like it hot (1 c. or 75 g.)

Add these to the sauce and heat to boiling. Serve hot with the sliced hot meat and cold with any left overs.

BOILED SALT BEEF

Many butchers will salt a piece of beef especially for you, others salt their surplus pieces and offer them for sale as mid-week joints. Silver-

45

side is the cut usually salted, but others are sometimes used. As well as salting the meat by steeping it in brine, some saltpetre is added and this has the effect of turning the meat deep pink when it is cooked. Salted raw meat has a grey look on the outside. The favourite ways of serving it are boiled with dumplings and vegetables, or cold and pressed. For the latter purpose the larger the joint the more succulent the meat will be and one can often buy better-quality ready-cooked silverside than it is possible to produce in the home when cooking only small pieces of meat.

BOILED SILVERSIDE OF BEEF WITH DUMPLINGS

Cooking Times. 1 lb. (½ kg.) or less 1 hr.; 2–3 lb. (1–1½ kg.), 2–3 hrs.; 4–5 lb. (2–2½ kg.), 3–4 hrs.; more than this 20 mins. per lb. (½ kg.) plus 20 mins.

Quantities. Allow 4–6 oz. (125–175 g.) per portion.

Soak the meat in cold water to cover for 3–4 hrs., or overnight.

1 onion   1 bay leaf

3 or 4 cloves   6 peppercorns

1 sprig parsley

Skin the onion and stick the cloves into it. Wash the herbs. Put the meat in a pan large enough to hold it and the vegetables together. Bring meat and water to the boil, add the other ingredients, turn down the heat to keep the liquid just simmering.

4 oz. carrots per person (125 g.)

Peel or scrape the carrots, cutting large ones in half. Add them to the pan 1 hr. before the end of cooking.

8 oz. S.R. flour (1½ c. or 250 g.)   ½ tsp. salt

3 oz. prepared suet (¾ c. or 75 g.)

Sift the flour and salt into a basin. If fresh suet is being used, grate it coarsely. Add suet to flour and mix well. Stir in enough water to make a soft dough. Use a knife and mix quickly. Flour the hands and divide the dough into 4–6 small balls. Drop these into a pan of boiling water and cook with the lid on for 15–20 mins. Do not lift the lid during cooking or they may be heavy. Drain and serve with the meat.

Slice the meat and serve with the dumplings and carrots and some of the cooking liquid as a sauce. Sprinkle with

Chopped parsley

Pressed beef. Put the cooked meat in a basin with stock to cover and put a plate and weight on top. Cool as quickly as possible and then store in the refrigerator.

MINCED BEEF

Butcher's mince is made from trimmings left when preparing joints. You can soon learn to tell by the look of it whether it has a high percentage of fat in it or not, and a fatty mince is usually cheaper than a lean one. Many recipes require lean mince and most butchers will mince lean steak for you if you ask them. It is quite easy to do for yourself if you have a good mincer, hand operated or electric. They are not expensive and are very useful items of kitchen equipment for many jobs, in addition to mincing raw meat. It is important to use the blades the manufacturer recommends for mincing raw meat otherwise you will make very heavy work of the mincing and may even find the meat will not go through at all.

Mince should be used as soon as possible because it very quickly goes bad. If you do have to keep it, do not leave it in a heap, but spread it out as thinly as possible, put a piece of aluminium foil lightly on the top, and store it in the refrigerator.

Mincing is a useful way of making the tougher cuts of meat tender without long slow cooking, and most countries have traditional ways of using mince, *e.g.* Scotch Mince Collops, American Hamburgers and Meat Loaves, Swedish Meat Balls.

Any cuts of meat listed as suitable for stewing can be minced, except shin and leg, which are too gristly. Cut the meat into largish pieces, removing any visible streaks of gristle, and any surplus fat.

MINCED BEEF BALLS
Cooking Time 20–30 mins.   Quantities for 4–5.

1 *lb. lean raw beef* (½ *kg.*)

Mince the meat 3 times to make it very smooth.

2 *Tbs. chopped onion   Little dripping*

Fry the onion in a little dripping until it begins to brown.

1 *tsp. salt   1 large boiled potato*
¼ *tsp. pepper   4–8 Tbs. milk or water*
¼ *tsp. ground mace or nutmeg*

Mash the potato and mix all the ingredients together thoroughly. Shape into about 20 small balls, rolling each in the hands, moistened in cold water if the mixture tends to stick.

Oil or fat for shallow frying

Heat the fat and put the balls in leaving plenty of space between them. Keep shaking the pan and turning the balls as they fry to keep them a good shape. When they are brown all over put them in a hot dish. Pour 2–3 Tbs. water in the pan and stir and boil to dissolve the sediment. Pour over the balls.

MINCED BEEF COLLOPS

Cooking Time 5–10 mins.   *Quantities for 4.*

1 lb. minced lean beef ($\frac{1}{2}$ kg.)   1 shallot or small onion

1 oz. butter or dripping (25 g.)

Mince the beef, peel, and chop the onion. Fry the onion in the fat until it begins to brown, then add the mince.

Salt and pepper to taste $\frac{1}{4}$ pt. stock (1$\frac{1}{2}$ dl.)

1 Tbs. fresh breadcrumbs or rolled oats   Pinch of nutmeg

1 Tbs. mushroom ketchup or a few chopped mushrooms

Add the other ingredients and simmer very gently until the meat is just cooked (i.e. changes colour).

Serve the mince on a dish decorated with the toast and parsley.

Chopped parsley   Small triangles crisp toast

Slices of hardboiled egg

An optional extra for garnishing.

MINCED BEEF LOAF

Cooking Time 1 hr.   *Temperature* E.375° (190°C), G.5. *Quantities for* 4–6.

1 lb. lean beef ($\frac{1}{2}$ kg.)

Put the meat through the mincer twice to make it fine enough to hold together well otherwise the loaf will be hard to slice.

1 small onion   Fat for cooking

Peel and chop the onion and fry it in a little fat.

1½ oz. fresh breadcrumbs (½ c. or 45 g.) or 6 Tbs. rolled oats
1 tsp. salt   ¼ tsp. ground mace or nutmeg
¼ tsp. pepper   4–8 Tbs. milk or stock or 1 beaten egg
A little chopped garlic or garlic juice if liked
Chopped fresh herbs or dried herbs, to taste

Mix all the ingredients together using enough liquid to make the mixture bind together easily. Turn it on to a floured board. Flour your hands and shape the mixture into a loaf about 2 in. (5 cm.) deep. Melt a little fat in a roasting pan, add the loaf, and cover the top with a piece of aluminium foil. Bake, removing the foil for the last 10 mins. to allow the loaf to brown. Serve on a hot dish. Make thickened gravy in the pan or serve the loaf with tomato or other sauce poured over it. When serving, cut the loaf in thick slices.

Alternative method. Pack the mixture into a greased loaf tin, bake as before, allowing longer if the mixture is more than 2 in. (5 cm.) deep in the tin. Turn out and serve as before.

HAMBURG STEAKS
Cooking Time 20–25 mins.
Quantities. Allow 4 oz. steak per portion (125 g.).

Minced beef steak (no gristle or fat)   Salt and pepper

Season the steak and shape it into flat cakes about 3 in. (8 cm.) in diameter and ¾–1 in. thick (2 cm.). Grill under a medium heat, turning once, and cooking until they are brown and cooked through. They can be served with a wide variety of accompaniments, including brown gravy, parsley butter, grilled tomatoes, mushrooms, potatoes and vegetables, watercress, pickles, a slice of cheese grilled on top until it melts, bacon rolls, and any savoury sauce.

Alternative mixture. To each lb. (½ kg.) of steak add 4 oz. (125 g.) minced lean bacon and 4 oz. (125 g.) stale bread soaked in milk, squeezed dry, and beaten smooth. Mix well, season, and shape as before. These are sometimes served on fried or baked onion rings.

MOUSSAKA

A famous central and south-eastern European dish using minced meat, cheese sauce, and potatoes. A time-consuming dish to make, but inexpensive and enjoyed by most people.

Cooking Time 1 hr. *Temperature* E.375° (190°C), G.5.
Quantities for 4 or more.

> ¾ *lb. raw minced meat* (375 g.)   2 *oz. butter* (50 g.)
> 8 *oz. onion* (250 g.)   8 *oz. tomatoes* (250 g.)
>   4 *Tbs. chopped parsley*

Peel and chop the onion, or mince it with the meat. Chop the tomatoes. Heat the butter and fry the other ingredients in it. Season well with salt and pepper.

> 1½ *lb. potatoes* (¾ *kg.*)

Peel and slice potatoes. Grease an 8 in. (20 cm.) cake tin or straight-sided oven dish.

Put a layer of potatoes in the bottom, add a layer of meat mixture and repeat layers finishing with potatoes.

> 4 *Tbs. wine*

Sprinkle the wine over the potatoes.

> ½ *oz. butter* (15 g.)   ¼ *pt. milk* (¼ *l.*)
> ½ *oz. flour* (1½ *Tbs. or* 15 g.)

Melt the butter in a small pan, add the flour, and stir and cook for a few minutes. Stir in the milk, and stir until it boils. Cook for 1 min.

> 1 *egg*   4 *Tbs. grated cheese*

Beat the egg slightly. Remove the sauce from the heat, stir in the egg and cheese. Pour this over the potatoes and meat. Bake in a moderate oven. Turn out of the tin and cut in wedges for serving.

ABERDEEN SAUSAGE

A home-made sausage about the size of a breakfast sausage. It is usually sliced cold and served with salad or pickles and it makes a pleasant change from canned and other ready-cooked meats. Old recipes recommend making it with oatmeal instead of rolled oats and boiling it in a pan of beef stock. The following modern version is simpler to make and produces an excellent sausage.

Cooking Time 2 hrs., either boiled or steamed or baked in a slow oven.
Temperature E.300° (150°C), G.1 or 2.
Quantities for 8 to 10.

1 small onion   8 oz. streaky bacon (250 g.)
1 lb. lean beef steak (½ kg.)

Peel the onion. Remove any gristle from the beef, and the rinds from the bacon. Mince all three together twice to give a smooth texture. If the meat is too coarse the sausage won't slice properly.

4 oz. rolled oats (1 c. or 125 g.)   1 Tbs. Worcester sauce
1 egg, beaten   1 tsp. salt
                          ¼ tsp. pepper

Add these to the meat and mix well. Shape into a long thick sausage like a breakfast sausage and wrap carefully in aluminium foil, sealing the ends well. If it is to be baked, place the sausage on a baking tray or in a tin. To boil, put in boiling water to cover and then reduce to simmering.

After 2 hrs. cooking, remove the foil carefully and roll the sausage in

Dried breadcrumbs.

Leave until cold and store in the refrigerator or in a cold larder. Serve thinly sliced.

BEEF STEAK AND KIDNEY PIE

Cooking Time 2 hrs.
Temperature E.450° (230°C), G.8 for the first 10 mins., then reduce to E.350° (180°C), G.4 for the remainder of the time.
Quantities for 6–8.
Flaky or short crust pastry using 8 oz. flour (1½ c. or 250 g.) or use ¾ lb. (375 g.) ready-made pastry.

2 lb. stewing steak (1 kg.)   1 tsp. salt
8 oz. kidney, any kind (250 g.)   ¼ tsp. pepper
1 Tbs. flour   Water

Cut the steak in small pieces removing any surplus fat. Cut the kidney in small pieces. Roll both meats in the flour and seasoning mixed together. Easiest to do by shaking flour and meat together in a paper

51

bag. Pack the meat into a 2 pt. (1 l.) size pie dish having it well filled. Add water to three-quarters fill the dish.

Roll out the pastry to a piece about 1 in. (2 cm) longer than the top of the pie dish. Cut off strips to go round the edge of the dish and stick them in place with cold water. Lift the main piece of pastry on top of the pie and stick it to the edging pastry with cold water. Crimp the edges and cut a hole in the centre to let out steam.

Beaten egg or milk

Brush the top of the pie with egg or milk and bake. When the pastry is browned to your liking cover the pie with a piece of greaseproof paper or aluminium foil. Serve hot or cold.

Accompaniments. For the hot pie, serve a green vegetable or peas or green beans. It is nicer without potatoes because the pastry is already a starchy food. Cold pie is served with a green or mixed salad or tomato salad.

BEEF STEAK AND KIDNEY PUDDING

Cooking Time 4 hrs.   *Quantities for* 4–6.

1 lb. stewing steak (½ kg.)   1 tsp. salt
1 oz. flour (3 Tbs. or 25 g.)   ¼ tsp. pepper
8 oz. ox or veal kidney (250 g.)

Cut the steak in cubes and the kidney in small pieces. Mix flour and seasoning and put in a paper bag with the meat. Shake together to coat well.

2 small onions

Peel and slice them finely or chop coarsely.

8 oz. S.R. flour (1½ c. or 250 g.)   3 oz. prepared suet (¾ c. or 75g.)
1 tsp. salt
Cold water to mix

Sift the flour and salt into a basin and add the suet. Mix to a soft dough with cold water, using a knife for mixing and adding the water as quickly as possible. Cut off a quarter of the pastry and roll the rest to a circle big enough to line a 1½–2 pt. (1 l.) basin. Lift the pastry into the basin and mould it to fit the sides with a little overhanging the top. Add the meat and onion in layers and enough cold water to come half way up the meat. Roll the remaining piece of pastry into a circle to fit the top of the basin and place it on top of the meat. Seal top and bottom by pressing gently.

Cover with a lid of aluminium foil pressing the edges down well. Put in a saucepan with hot water coming half way up the sides of the pudding and keep the water boiling gently all the time the pudding is cooking. Watch occasionally to be sure it is not boiling dry, and, if necessary, add a little more boiling water.

The pudding is usually sent to table in the basin but may be turned out on a deep hot dish. Left-over pudding can be steamed again for 1 hr.

Accompaniments. Because the suet pastry is starchy this is nicest served with a green vegetable or two vegetables as long as one is not potatoes, *e.g.* serve cabbage and carrots.

POTTED BEEF

This is the beef which is cooked slowly until very tender and then pulverised to a paste and used as a meat spread. The method of cooking used to be to put the beef in a pot and stand that in a saucepan of water, cooking it very slowly until the meat was quite soft. It was then pounded in a mortar to make it into a paste. The following is a modern version of potted meat.

Cooking Time 2–3 hrs. Pressure cooker 20 mins. and another 15–20 mins. for reduction of the liquid.

Temperature for casserole cooking E.300° (150°C), G.2.

Quantities for 6–8 depending on the size of the knuckle of veal.

8 oz. boneless shin beef (250 g.)   1 knuckle veal (bone and meat)

Wash the knuckle and remove all the meat. Cut veal and beef into small pieces. Put the meat and bones in a pan or casserole with 1 tsp. salt, cover, and simmer gently until the meat is tender. For the pressure cooker use 1 pt. water (½ l.).

Strain. Remove the meat and chop or shred it.

6 allspice   A piece of bay leaf
6 peppercorns   2 tsp. salt

Put the bones back in the liquid with seasonings and boil hard to reduce the liquid to about ½ pt. (¼ l.). Strain the liquid and pour it over the meat which you have shredded and put in a mould or in several small pots. Leave to set and store in the refrigerator. Slice and use as a sandwich filling or on toast or serve cold with salad or pickles.

53

Modification for an electric blender. Put cooked meat and unreduced liquid in the blender in small instalments and mix until smooth. Flavour with ground spices and set in moulds. The texture is similar to canned luncheon meats.

COLD BEEF

Best cuts for serving cold are boiled silverside or roast beef, but both need to be from a large joint, preferably cooked specially to be served cold and not cut until it is cold. It is always more juicy and tasty than some left-over from a hot joint. Most people prefer cold roast beef to be under-done but there is a certain amount of risk with this especially if the joint has been boned and rolled. If the meat is under-done it will not have reached a high enough temperature in the middle to destroy microbes which will continue to multiply during cooling.

Meat to be served cold should always be cooled as rapidly as possible and then stored in a refrigerator until it is required.

Braised or boiled beef is also suitable for serving cold, the former having a very good flavour from the vegetables cooked with it.

Accompaniments for cold beef are: pickles (especially mustard pickles), cold horseradish sauce, chutneys, and salad, including potato salad.

CANNED BEEF

On sale in wide variety, including cured meat such as corned beef, stewed beef, mince loaves, curries, *chilli con carne*, and many others. Some are for use as cold meats, others require heating. If the sealed can is kept in a cool dry place, the meat will keep up to five years or more. It is a waste of space to keep it in the refrigerator, although in warm weather meat like corned beef slices more easily if it is first chilled thoroughly. It is a good idea to keep one can in the refrigerator as an emergency supply for this purpose.

After a can has been opened, the contents will not keep longer than freshly cooked meat.

Because all canned foods are carefully controlled for quality, there is inevitably a certain monotony of flavour but, by using the contents for a basis and adding other ingredients of your own choice, a can of meat will be vastly improved.

CANNED BEEF AND MACARONI
(using canned stewed steak)

Cooking Time about 30 mins.   *Quantities for 4.*

2 oz. macaroni (50 g.)

Boil the macaroni in plenty of salted water until it is just tender. Strain.

Heat the fat in a saucepan and fry the onion in it until it browns.

1 oz. fat or oil (25 g.)   1 onion, sliced

Pinch of ground mace or nutmeg   *1 Tbs. flour*
½ lb. raw or canned tomatoes (250 g.)   ¼ pt. stock (1½ dl.)

Add the flour to the onions and mix and cook for a minute or two longer. Add stock, tomatoes, and mace. Boil gently for 5–10 mins.

1 lb. can stewed steak (½ kg.)

Add the steak and heat thoroughly without boiling.

Salt and pepper   Gravy browning
2 oz. grated cheese (⅔ c. or 50 g.)

Season to taste with salt and pepper and add gravy browning if necessary to make a good colour. Just before serving, stir in the grated cheese or, if preferred, hand the cheese separately.

CORNED BEEF

Is pickled meat which is compressed before it goes in the can. This squeezes out considerable amounts of the juices. After packing in the cans it is sterilised at high temperatures. This treament very much reduces the amount of B vitamins left in the meat, especially of vitamin B1 or *thiamine*, but also of *riboflavin* and *niacin*. If corned beef were to replace fresh beef it would be necessary to supplement the diet with foods rich in vitamin B. Meat is one of the important sources of all three of the main B vitamins. Corned beef does, however, contain more iron than fresh beef and is valuable for this and for the protein it contains.

It is most commonly eaten cold with pickles and salad but many appetising dishes can be cooked with it.

CORNED BEEF AND EGGS *AU GRATIN*

Cooking Time 40 mins. *Temperature* E.350° (180°C), G.3.
Quantities for 4–6.

1½ oz. *butter or margarine (45 g.)*

1½ oz. *flour (4½ Tbs. or 45 g.)* 1 pt. *milk (½ l.)*

Melt the fat in a saucepan and add the flour. Stir and cook until it looks crumbly. Remove from the heat and gradually stir in the milk, whisking until smooth. Return to the heat and stir until it thickens and boils.

4 oz. *grated cheese (1 c. or 125 g.)* Salt and pepper

Add the cheese to the sauce, stirring until it melts. Season to taste.

4 *hard-boiled eggs* 12 oz. *diced corned beef (375 g.)*

Place the beef and eggs in layers in a fire-proof dish. Cover with the sauce.

Dried breadcrumbs or cracker crumbs or cornflake crumbs

Cover the top with a layer of the crumbs and bake in a slow oven for about ½ hr. or until well heated through.

CORNED BEEF HASH

Cooking Time 10–15 mins. *Quantities* for 4.

12 oz. *corned beef (375 g.)* 1 lb. *boiled potatoes (½ kg.)*

Dice the beef and potatoes and mix them together.

1 *small onion, chopped* 1 Tbs. *milk*

Fat for frying Salt and pepper

Heat enough fat to cover the bottom of a frying pan and, when it is hot, fry the onion until it begins to brown. Add the meat and potatoes, spreading out flat and sprinkle with the milk and salt to taste. Stir well and then leave over a very low heat to become brown underneath, and hot through. Turn out on to a hot plate. Serve hot.

6 Lamb and Mutton

The majority of lamb eaten in Britain is imported frozen lamb from New Zealand. Home-produced English, Scottish, and Welsh lamb and mutton are also available. The quality of all these is good and it is seldom that one buys poor-quality lamb. Lamb comes from an animal less than one-year-old, older than that it is mutton. Mutton is not very plentiful today as the smaller joints of lamb are preferred. When it is for sale it is usually home-produced. Many people dislike the flavour of mutton but others think it is one of the finest meats available.

In general, mutton needs longer, slower cooking than lamb but the chief difference is in the size of the joints.

In appearance, lamb should be red with white fat and the bones should be moist and red at the joints. Mutton should be bright red with yellowish fat and the bones white.

FROZEN LAMB

Frozen joints are generally better if completely thawed before cooking. Quick frozen chops and cutlets are better if cooked without thawing, allowing approximately double the time needed for fresh meat. For thawing times, see *Beef*, page 28.

LAMB AND MUTTON CUTS AND THEIR USES

BREAST

This is the belly of the animal and is fairly fatty but also contains a considerable amount of tender, sweet meat and a few small bones. It is usually either chopped into portions before cooking or else left in a piece and boned and rolled. Surplus fat should be trimmed off before it is cooked. Breast is suitable for pot roasting, braising, boiling, stews, and casseroles.

CHOPS

These may be loin chops which are from the lower part of the spine of the animal and have short T-shaped bones, or chumps chops which come from the top of the leg. Loin chops are more tender but a good chump chop can be very tender and has more meat on it. Poorer quality chump chops are better for casserole cooking than for frying or grilling.

CUTLETS

These come from the ribs of the animal and are smaller than chops with less meat on them and longer bones. The cut from which they come is called 'neck' but it is, in fact, well down the back. 'Best end of neck' is the part which is usually divided into cutlets. When the appearance of the cutlets is very important the bone is usually trimmed of meat and fat down to the main meaty part or 'eye'. After cooking, the bare bone may be decorated with a cutlet frill made of paper and sold for this purpose.

LEG

This is sold either as a whole leg or it may be cut in half. The lower end is called 'shank end' and the upper end the 'fillet'. The shank end is suitable for braising, stewing, boiling, and pies, while the fillet end is mainly roasted whole but may be sliced or cubed and grilled or fried. Whole legs of lamb are usually roasted and legs of mutton boiled or roasted.

LOIN

This is the part of the animal lying between the lower ribs and the top of the legs. It consists of short T-shaped bones to which is attached very tender meat, ending in a boneless flap of mixed meat and fat. The kidneys are attached to the underside of the loin and are sometimes sold with it and can be roasted still attached. Loin may be separated into chops (see *Chops*), or sold in a piece for roasting. The butcher will chop through the bones so that carving will be easy.

NECK

The true neck of the animal is usually known as scrag end and is a lean bony cut best separated into pieces and used in stews and casseroles.

Middle neck is the top of the rib cage and is used with the neck. Best end of neck is the main rib cage and is usually cooked as a piece. Or it may be separated into portions. See *Cutlets*. When the cut is being prepared for roasting, ask the butcher to 'chine' it for you. He slits the meat away from the end bone but leaves the bone still attached. This simplifies carving. A best end of lamb usually has 6–7 cutlets and weighs about 1½–2 lb. (¾–1 kg).

SADDLE

This is more or less the whole of the back of the animal, *i.e.* the best end of neck and the loin together. It is roasted in one piece and makes a very large joint.

SHANK BONE

The end bone of a leg or shoulder, usually sold attached to the more meaty part. When a leg or shoulder is divided into smaller joints the bit with this bone attached is called the 'shank end'.

SHOULDER

The foreleg and the muscles with which it is attached to the body. It contains a very high proportion of bone but is very good-quality meat. The weight varies from 3½–5½ lb. (1½–2 kg). Large shoulders are often cut into 3 smaller joints. With a whole shoulder the shank bone is sawn through so that it can be turned back and make the shoulder occupy less space. Shoulders are frequently boned and rolled or stuffed.

ROAST LAMB OR MUTTON

For methods, see *Roasting*, page 13.

Leg, shoulder, loin, and best end of neck are the best joints for roasting. Mutton requires a little longer to cook than lamb and the joints are usually larger. Both mutton and lamb are usually preferred well done.

Both leg and shoulder are sometimes boned and stuffed. Suitable stuffings are veal forcemeat, rice stuffing, lemon stuffing. See *Stuffings*, pages 258–60.

Moderate Temperature Roasting E.375–400° (190–200°C), G.5–6. Allow 30 mins. per lb. (½ kg.).

Slow Roasting E.325–350° (160–180°C), G.3. Allow 45 mins. per lb. (½ kg.).

Roasting Thermometer. Internal temperature 175–180° (80–85°C).

Quantities. Leg, allow ¾ lb. (375 g.) per portion; saddle, shoulder and loin, 1 lb. (½ kg.) per portion; best end of neck and breast ½–¾ lb. (250–375 g.) per portion.

Accompaniments. Thick or thin gravy. Sprinkling the meat and pan with flour before cooking begins helps give a good colour to the gravy. Red currant jelly, or mint, or onion sauce; Roast, boiled, or mashed potatoes; Green peas or beans; Carrots; Turnips; Haricot beans; Green vegetable.

GRILLED LAMB CHOPS

Cooking Time 10–20 mins. *Quantities.* Allow 1 per portion.

Loin chops are the best for grilling. Trim off surplus fat and brush the chops with oil or melted fat. Turn frequently during grilling so that browning and cooking are finished together. Garnish and serve at once.

Garnishes. Parsley Butter or Watercress Butter, a small pat on each chop. Or serve separately a sauce such as Mushroom or Onion. Serve fried or mashed potatoes and a second vegetable.

For those who like meat and fruit together, put a slice of pineapple or orange on top of the chop when it is half-cooked, brush fruit with oil or melted fat, and continue grilling.

STEAMED LAMB CHOP

Cooking Time 20 mins.

Quantities. Allow 1 loin chop per portion.

Trim all the fat from the meat except for a very thin layer on the outside. Season with salt and a little pepper. Take a piece of foil and put the chop in the centre. Draw the foil up to the top and seal the edges well. Cook in the top of a steamer and serve with the juices as a sauce. If no steamer is available, put the chop in a plate over a pan of boiling water and cover it with the saucepan lid. This way it will take up to 5 mins. longer to cook.

BAKED LAMB CHOPS WITH MUSHROOM SAUCE

Cooking Time about 1 hr.   *Temperature* E.350° (180°C), G.4.
Quantities for 4.

    4 *chump chops*   2 *Tbs. flour*
    Pinch of pepper   ½ *tsp. salt*

Trim excess fat from the chops. Mix the flour and seasoning in a paper bag and shake the chops in this to coat them.

    1 *oz. butter (25 g.)*

Heat in a frying pan and brown the chops in it. Transfer them to a baking dish. Pour off excess fat.

    Stock or wine

Use a little to swill out the frying pan and pour the liquid over the chops.

    Pinch of dried garlic   2 *Tbs. water*
½ *of a can of condensed cream of tomato soup (10½ oz. or 300 g. size)*

Mix together and pour over the chops. Bake, uncovered, until the meat is tender. Serve with

    Boiled pasta or rice and a green vegetable.

BAKED LAMB CHOP *AU GRATIN*

Cooking Time 1½ hrs.   *Temperature* E.325° (160°C), G.3.
Quantities for 4.

    4 *lamb chops cut about 1 in. thick*   1 *oz. fat (25 g.)*

Trim fat off the chops and remove the bones. Heat the fat and fry the chops in it until they are brown.

    2 *onions*

Peel and slice onions. Place the chops in a large shallow casserole in a single layer and put several slices of onion on top of each.

    ¾ *lb. canned tomatoes (375 g.)*   ½ *tsp. salt*
    ¼ *tsp. pepper*   1 *tsp. sugar*

Pour tomatoes over the chops and add seasoning.

    2 *oz. grated cheese* (½ *c. or 50 g.*)
    2 *oz. fresh breadcrumbs* (⅔ *c. or 50 g.*)

Mix these together and sprinkle them over the meat. Cover and bake slowly.

FRIED LAMB CUTLETS

Trim off all fat and clean the bone down to the 'eye' of meat. Dip in egg and breadcrumbs and fry in deep fat for 5–10 mins. Serve with any vegetables and with a sauce such as onion, tomato, brown, or mushroom.

GRILLED LAMB CUTLETS

As for *Grilled Lamb Chops* but they only need 7–10 mins. cooking.

STEAMED LAMB CUTLETS

As for *Steamed Lamb Chops* but they only need 10–15 mins. cooking.

LAMB CUTLETS IN ASPIC

Cooking Time 30 mins.   Quantities for 4.

8 lamb cutlets

Trim off all fat and clean the bones down to the 'eye' of meat. Bake the cutlets in a moderate oven for about 30 mins. or steam them for about 15 mins. Press them between two plates with a weight on top and leave to become cold. Chill before coating with the aspic.

Vegetables or herbs for garnishing

Prepare either mint leaves, pieces of sweet pepper, slices of olives, or small sprigs of chervil.

1 oz. gelatine (3 Tbs. or 25 g.)	1 tsp. salt
1 pt. boiling water (½ l.)	2 tsp. sugar
4 Tbs. tarragon vinegar	4 Tbs. lemon juice

Dissolve the gelatine in the boiling water and add the other ingredients. Leave to cool and begin to thicken. Place the chilled cutlets on a wire rack over a large dish or tray and pour over enough jelly to coat them. Leave this to set and arrange the garnish on it. Pour over more jelly to mask the garnish. Chill. Serve with the surplus jelly as a chopped garnish.

GRILLED LAMB CHOPS WITH HERBS

Cooking Time 15–20 mins. plus 1 hr. marinading.
Quantities for 4.

4 lamb chops   1 tsp. salt
1 tsp. dried rosemary 1 tsp. dried marjoram
1 tsp. dried thyme

Pound the herbs and salt together to make a fine mixture. Rub well into the chops on both sides. Put in a covered dish in the refrigerator for an hour. Grill in the usual way.

GRILLED LAMB STEAKS WITH RED CURRANT JELLY

Cooking Time 25 mins. *Quantities* for 4.

1½–2 lb. lamb steaks (¾–1 kg.) cut 1 in. (2½ cm.) thick
from the top of a leg

4 Tbs. red currant jelly

Grill the steaks under a moderate heat or on the lowest runner, allowing about 12 min. each side.

Melt the jelly in a small pan and brush the steaks with it during the last few minutes of cooking. Season the steaks with salt and pepper and serve at once with more jelly if liked. Serve with sauté or mashed potatoes and a green vegetable or salad.

PAPRIKAS OF LAMB

Cooking Time about 20 mins. *Quantities* for 4.

2 onions, sliced finely 2 oz. butter (50 g.)

½ tsp. paprika pepper

Add to the onions and cook a little longer.

1 lb. boned shoulder of lamb (½ kg.)
1 Tbs. flour ½ tsp. salt

Heat the butter and brown the onions in it, using a sauté or frying pan or a shallow saucepan.

Cut the meat in 1 in. (2½ cm.) cubes and sprinkle it with the flour and salt. Add it to the onions and mix. Cover the pan with a lid or with foil and cook gently until the meat is tender.

A little stock, sherry or marsala

Add enough to the pan to make a very little gravy. Stir until it boils and simmer a few minutes. Serve with

Sauté or boiled potatoes and a salad.

CURRIED LAMB OR MUTTON (using raw meat)

Cooking Time 1½ hrs. on top or in the oven.
Temperature E.325° (160°C), G.3.   *Quantities* for 4.
1½ lb. (¾ kg.) *lean meat without bone* (3 *lb.* (1½ *kg.*) *with fat and bone*) Cut the meat into small pieces.

Peel and slice the onions.

       4 small onions

Heat this and fry the onion in it until it is just beginning to colour.

       2 oz. butter or oil (50 g.)

       1 *Tbs. curry powder*   1 *tsp. salt*

Add to the onion, together with the meat, and continue frying until the meat is well browned.

1 *lb. tomatoes, fresh or canned* (½ *kg.*)   ¼ *small clove garlic*

Peel and chop the garlic and add it and the tomatoes to the meat. Add a little water if it seems necessary. Simmer until the meat is tender. Serve with boiled rice and chutney.

NAVARIN OF LAMB

Cooking Time 2 hrs. on top or in the oven.
Temperature E.300° (150°C), G.1–2.   *Quantities* for 4.

       1½ *lb. lamb or mutton without bone* (¾ *kg.*)
       1½ *oz. fat or oil* (45 g.)   ¼ *tsp. pepper*
       Pinch of sugar   1 *tsp. salt*

Remove fat and cut meat into pieces weighing about 2 oz. (50 g.) each. Heat fat or oil and fry the meat until it is brown adding the seasoning and sugar during frying. When it is well browned, pour off excess fat.

       2 *Tbs. flour*

Sprinkle it over the meat and continue cooking until the flour browns.

       1 *pt. water* (½ *l.*)

Add to the meat and stir until it boils.

1 clove garlic (optional)

Peel and crush the garlic and add it to the meat. Cover, and simmer for 1 hr.

8 small onions

Peel, and fry in fat saved from the first frying, or in a little fresh fat or oil. Fry until the onions are brown. Drain them well on kitchen paper, add to the meat.

1½ lb. small potatoes (new if possible) (¾ kg.)

Prepare and add potatoes to the meat. Simmer until the vegetables are cooked, about another ¾ hr. Before serving the navarin, skim off any surplus fat. Serve with a green vegetable.

RAGOUT OF LAMB OR MUTTON
Cooking Time 2 hrs.   Quantities for 4.

4 oz. butter beans (125 g.)

Wash the beans and soak overnight with cold water to cover. Alternatively, cover with boiling water and soak for 4–5 hrs.

2 lb. piece of shoulder of lamb or mutton (1 kg.)

Cut the meat off the bone and then cut it into small pieces.

1 tsp. salt   1 tsp. paprika pepper

Sprinkle these over the meat.

2 Tbs. oil

Heat the oil in a saucepan or casserole and fry the meat until brown.

6 shallots or small onions   2 Tbs. chopped parsley
¾ pt. canned tomatoes (5 dl.)

Peel and chop the shallots or onions and add them to the meat together with the tomatoes, soaked beans, and parsley. Cover, and simmer until the meat and beans are tender.

1 Tbs. cornflour   ¼ pt. yoghurt (1½ dl.) (1 small jar)

Blend cornflour to a cream with a little cold water and stir it into the meat. Bring back to the boil and boil for a few minutes. Stir in the yoghurt and serve at once.

LAMB WITH RICE

Cooking Time 1 hr.   *Quantities for 4.*

1 lb. lean lamb (½ kg.) without bone (2 lb. (1 kg.) with bone)

2 Tbs. oil

Cut the meat into 1 in. (2 cm.) cubes. Heat the oil and brown the meat in it for about 8 mins.

1 medium onion

Peel and slice the onion and add it to the meat. Cover and cook gently until the onion is soft.

| 1 tsp. salt | 3 Tbs. tomato paste |
| ¼ tsp. pepper | ¼ pt. water (1½ dl.) |

Add seasoning to the meat, mix tomato paste with the water, and add. Cover, and cook gently for about 45 mins. or until the meat is tender.

6–8 oz. long grain rice (¾–1 c. or 175–250 g.)

Boil the rice (see Rice, page 224) and arrange it on a hot serving dish in a ring. Put the meat in the centre.

LANCASHIRE HOT POT

Cooking Time 2½ hrs.   *Temperature* E.300° (150°C), G.1–2.
Quantities for 4.

| *Seasoned flour* | 1 oz. fat or dripping (25 g.) |
| 1½ lb. best end of neck of mutton or lamb (¾ kg.) |

Trim surplus fat from the chops and coat them with seasoned flour. Heat the fat and fry the chops in it until they are brown. Arrange the chops upright in a deep casserole with the meat end at the bottom.

| *Pinch of sugar* | 1 onion |
| 1 oz. mushrooms (25 g.) | 2 kidneys |

Sprinkle the sugar over the meat. Chop the kidneys and add to the meat. Peel and chop the onion. Wash and chop the mushroom and add both to the meat.

1 lb. potatoes (½ kg.)

Peel and slice these and arrange in an overlapping layer on top of the meat. Sprinkle them with salt and pepper.

½ pt. stock (¼ l.)

Pour in the stock, cover, and cook slowly for 2 hrs. Remove the lid and cook another ½ hr, allowing the potatoes to brown. Serve with

Pickled red cabbage.

DEVILLED NECK OF LAMB OR MUTTON

Cooking Time 1½ hrs. on top or in the oven, or 15 mins. pressure cooking.

Temperature E.325° (160°C), G.3.   *Quantities for 4.*

2 *lb. neck of lamb* (1 *kg.*)   1 *oz. fat or oil* (25 *g.*)

Cut the meat into 1 in. thick pieces. Heat the fat or oil and fry the meat in it until it is brown.

2 *stalks celery*   2 *tomatoes*   1 *onion*

Wash and chop the celery. Peel and chop the onion. Skin and chop the tomatoes. Add them to the meat and continue frying for a few minutes.

2 *tsp. dry mustard*   2 *tsp. salt*
1 *tsp. Worcester sauce*   ¼ *tsp. pepper*
¼ *pt. vinegar* (1½ *dl.*)   ¼ *pt. stock* (1½ *dl.*)

Mix the seasonings smooth with the sauce, stock, and vinegar and add them to the meat. Mix well. Cover and cook until the meat is tender. Serve with

Boiled potatoes or rice; green vegetable or salad.

NECK OF LAMB CASSEROLE

Cooking Time 1½ hrs.   *Temperature* E.350° (180°C), G.4.
Quantities for 3.

2 *lb. neck of lamb* (1 *kg.*)

Trim off any fat and put the meat in a casserole.

1 *can Scotch Broth* (10½ *oz. or* 300 *g. size*)
1 *tsp. salt* 4 *small carrots, halved*
1 *onion, cut small*
1 *can of butter beans plus liquid* (15½ *oz. size* 450 *g.*)

Add to the meat, cover and cook until tender.

Chopped parsley

Serve with plenty of parsley sprinkled over it. This makes a complete dish on its own but for more bulk, serve some boiled potatoes with it.

IRISH STEW

Cooking Time 1½–2 hrs.   Quantities for 4–6.

   2 lb. neck or breast of lamb or mutton (1 kg.)
   2 lb. potatoes (1 kg.)   2 large onions

Trim surplus fat from the meat and cut it into joints. Peel and chop the onions. Peel and cut the potatoes into thick slices or rough pieces.

   1 Tbs. salt   ¼ tsp. pepper

Put a layer of meat in the bottom of a casserole or saucepan, add a layer of potatoes, and then of onions, and finally seasoning. Repeat the layers. Add water to come three-quarters of the way up the meat. Cover and simmer until tender. This may be done on top of the stove or in the oven at E.300–325° (150–160°C), G.2–3, but in the latter case it is advisable either first to bring the stew to the boil before putting it in the oven, or else allow an extra 20 mins. for the casserole to heat up and cooking to begin.

   Plenty of chopped parsley

Serve with the parsley sprinkled on top.

BOILED LAMB OR MUTTON

Mutton is considered a better boiling joint than lamb and the leg is the cut usually preferred, but shoulder is also boiled, as well as boned and stuffed breast of lamb or mutton.

BOILED BREAST OF LAMB OR MUTTON

Cooking Times and Quantities. See Boiled Leg.

Ask the butcher not to chop the breast in pieces. Remove surplus fat and cut out the small bones. (The butcher will do this if you ask him.)

Make a stuffing such as veal forcemeat, mint stuffing, or lemon stuffing. See *Stuffings*, pages 258–60.

Place the meat out flat, skin side down, and spread the stuffing over it. Roll up tightly and tie with fine white string or coarse white cotton. Boil as for Leg.

Serve hot with a sauce made from the cooking liquid, parsley, caper, fennel, or tomato sauce.

If it is to be served cold, put it between two plates with a heavy weight on top and leave to cool. This presses it into a suitable shape for slicing.

BOILED LEG OF MUTTON

Cooking Time 30 mins. per lb. ($\frac{1}{2}$ kg.) and 30 mins. over, or 10 mins. per lb. in a pressure cooker.

Quantities. Allow $\frac{1}{4}$-$\frac{3}{4}$ lb. per person raw weight (250-375 g.). Use a pan which is just large enough to take the meat comfortably. Add water to barely cover (hot or cold). Add an onion stuck with a few cloves, a *bouquet garni*, and 2 Tbs. salt. Bring the water to the boil and then reduce the heat to simmering and cook for the required time. After it has reached simmering point the pan may be transferred to a slow oven for the rest of the cooking time.

Vegetables such as parsnips, carrots, more onions, turnips, or swedes may be cooked with the meat for the last hour. Use the cooking liquid to make a sauce to serve with the meat, parsley sauce or caper sauce. Cook boiled potatoes separately. Other vegetables which go well with boiled mutton are green beans or butter beans. Cold boiled mutton is delicious with pickles and/or salad. Trim off as much fat as possible because most people do not enjoy cold mutton fat.

BOILED SHOULDER OF MUTTON WITH FENNEL SAUCE

Cooking Time 2 hrs.　*Quantities for 4-6.*

　　3 lb. shoulder mutton (1$\frac{1}{2}$ kg.)　2 Tbs. salt
　　A few sprigs of fennel　　3$\frac{1}{2}$ pt. water (5 l.)

Put in a pan and bring to the boil. Simmer for 2 hrs. Serve with the sauce.

　　1 oz. butter (25 g.)　1 oz. flour (3 Tbs. or 25 g.)
　　　　　　　1 pt. mutton stock ($\frac{1}{2}$ l.)

Melt the butter and stir in the flour. Stir and cook until crumbly. Stir in the stock and stir until it boils. Boil for about 5 mins.

　　1 Tbs. sugar　1$\frac{1}{2}$ Tbs. vinegar
　　1 egg yolk　4 Tbs. chopped fennel

Mix the egg and vinegar and add to the sauce together with the sugar and fennel.

Do not allow to boil again. Serve at once as fennel loses flavour if kept waiting.

LAMB KEBABS

Cooking Time 15 mins. plus time for marinating.   *Quantities for 4.*

1½ lb. leg or shoulder of lamb without bone (¾ kg.)

(3 lb. with bone) (1½ kg.)

Cut the meat into pieces about 1¼ in. (3 cm.) square, trimming off most of the fat.

1 onion

Peel and slice and put in a bowl with the meat.

¼ tsp. salt	Juice of 1 lemon
Pinch of pepper	2 Tbs. wine or cider

Add to the meat and leave to stand in the refrigerator for several hours or overnight.

8 small tomatoes   8 mushrooms

Thread the meat on skewers alternating it with mushroom and tomato. Grill for 15 mins., basting with any liquid from the bowl. Turn once during cooking. Serve on skewers with

Boiled rice or risotto or green salad.

MINCED LAMB PATTIES

Cooking Time 20–25 mins.   *Quantities for 4.*

1 lb. lean lamb (½ kg.) (2 lb. with fat and bone) (1 kg.)

¼ tsp. salt   ¼ tsp. pepper

Mince the lamb twice and mix with the seasoning. Shape into four flat cakes about 1 in. (2 cm.) thick.

4 rashers streaky bacon

Remove the rinds and wrap one rasher round each patty. Secure with a cocktail stick. Grill slowly under a medium heat, turning once during cooking. Serve hot with vegetables and Parsley Butter or a sauce.

LAMB AND APPLE PIE

Cooking Time 1¾ hrs.
Temperature E.450° (230°C), G.8. for 15 mins., then E.350° (180°C),
G.4. for rest of time.
Quantities for 4.

4 oz. flour (125 g.) made into short crust pastry
or use 6 oz. ready-made (175 g.)

Make the pastry and put it in a cool place.

1 lb. lean lamb or mutton without bone (½ kg.) or 2 lb. with bone (1 kg.)

8 oz. cooking apples (250 g.)   3 oz. onions (75 g.)
Salt and pepper

Cut meat into small pieces. Peel and slice the apples and onions.
Put these into a pie dish in layers, seasoning well with salt and pepper.
Add cold water to come half way up the dish. Cover with the pastry
and cut a hole in the centre. Brush with

Beaten egg or milk

Bake until the meat is tender. Serve hot or cold.

SMALL LAMB OR MUTTON PIES

Cooking Time 1 hr. for stewing the meat (or ¼ hr. pressure cooking),
then 25–30 mins. for baking the pies.
Temperature E.425° (220°C), G.7. *Quantities* for 12–18 small pies.

1 lb. lean boneless lamb or mutton (½ kg.) or 2 lb. with bone (1 kg.)

3 onions   1 tsp. salt   Pinch pepper

Cut meat into small pieces. Peel and chop onions and put all in a
pan with the seasoning and water barely to cover (½ pt. (¼ l.) pressure
cooking). Cook until the meat is tender.

Flour or cornflour

Mix a little to a smooth paste with cold water and add enough to
the meat to thicken the liquid.

2 Tbs. chopped parsley

Add parsley to meat mixture and turn into a flat dish to cool
quickly.

8 oz. flour (250 g.) made into short crust pastry
or use 12 oz. ready-made (375 g.)

Make the pastry. Roll it out thinly and cut rounds large enough to line the bottoms of deep bun tins. Cut an equal number of rounds for the tops. Put a little of the cold meat mixture into each tin and cover with the lid. Seal the edges well. Brush the tops with

Beaten egg or milk

Bake until the pastry is brown top and bottom. Serve hot or cold.

COLD LAMB

The lean of roast or boiled lamb or mutton is delicious served cold with any kind of salad. Specially good with it is a salad of cucumber, watercress, and spring onions or a potato salad flavoured with mint. Mint sauce, red currant jelly, sweet pickled fruit, chutney, or pickle are all suitable accompaniments. See also *Lamb Cutlets in Aspic, Small Lamb Pies* and *Lamb and Apple Pie.*

SHEPHERD'S PIE

Cooking Time $\frac{1}{2}$–$\frac{3}{4}$ hr.   *Temperature* E.400–425° (200–220°C), G.7. *Quantities* for 4.

12 oz. lean cooked lamb or mutton (375 g.)

Mince the meat.

1–1½ lb. potatoes ($\frac{1}{2}$–$\frac{3}{4}$ kg.)

Peel and put on to boil.

2 *medium onions*	1 *oz. flour* (25 g.)
1½ *oz. fat* (45 g.)	$\frac{3}{4}$ *pt. stock* (5 dl.)

Peel and chop the onions. Heat the fat and fry the onions until they begin to brown. Add the flour and stir and cook until crumbly. Add the stock and stir until it boils. Boil gently until the onions are tender.

Salt and pepper

Season the sauce to taste. Add the meat and bring to the boil again.

1 *oz. butter* (25 g.)	1–2 *Tbs. milk*

Heat together. Drain and mash the potatoes and beat in the butter and milk. Put the meat in an oven-proof dish and spread the potatoes over the top, roughing the top with a fork, or piping the potatoes through a forcing bag. Bake or grill until brown on top.

Variation. Add Worcester sauce, chopped gherkins, tomato ketchup, or chutney to the sauce.

CURRIED LAMB OR MUTTON (cooked meat)

Cooking Time 40 mins.   *Quantities for 4.*

2 oz. butter (50 g.)   2 medium onions

Peel and chop the onions. Heat the butter and fry the onion in it until golden.

2 Tbs. curry powder

Add to the onion and mix well.

1 lb. cooked lean lamb (½ kg.)

Cut the meat in small pieces, add to the pan, and fry for 2 or 3 mins., stirring frequently.

¾ pt. canned tomato juice (5 dl.)

Add to the meat and simmer for ½ hr., stirring frequently.

2 tsp. salt   2 Tbs. lemon juice

Add to the meat, stir, and serve with

Boiled rice and chutney.

7 Pork

Pork is the fresh meat from a pig. Salted and cured pig meat is either bacon or ham. Fresh pork is chiefly used for roasting, frying, grilling, and for making sausages of all kinds, brawns, and pork pies, while the rendered fat (lard) is a valuable cooking fat. Pork is a fatty meat and the dry methods of cooking like roasting and grilling which allow fat to drip away from the meat are usually more palatable than braising or stewing. Pickled or salt pork is usually preferred for boiling though fresh leg of pork is sometimes boiled and used cold.

CHOOSING PORK

Pork is a meat which can go bad quickly if it is not stored properly, therefore care is needed in buying it, especially in warm weather. Under these conditions never buy pork unless it is kept in refrigerated cabinets. Good-quality pork should be firm and smooth and in a younger animal the flesh is pink and fine-textured. In an older animal it is a deeper pink or rose colour and in very old is darker and coarse-grained. A brownish dry look indicates either poor quality or staleness. There should be a good layer of firm white outside fat. The skin of a young animal is thin and elastic while with the old one it is rough and tough.

PORK CUTS AND THEIR USES

BELLY

This is a thin cut of alternate layers of lean and fat (bacon, called 'streaky'). It is frequently salted and then boiled. Sometimes the fresh belly is sold cut in thick slices suitable for frying and grilling and is cheaper than using chops.

BLADE

A cut from the top part of the foreleg, usually roasted.

CHOPS

This is the most expensive way to buy pork. The chops come from the loin or ribs and are usually fried or grilled.

CUTLETS

Chops cut from the spare rib, cheaper than rib chops but cooked in the same ways.

FILLET

A slice from the top end of the leg, or the meat from boned loin. Suitable for grilling and frying.

HAND AND SPRING

The foreleg. Used for roasting and boiling. Usually cheaper than hind leg.

LEG

This means the hind leg. Usually roasted and often cut in two to make smaller joints. Sometimes boiled to serve cold. Pickled or salted leg is boiled and used hot or cold.

LOIN

The most expensive joint. It is either roasted as a piece or cut into chops for frying or grilling. Either the whole loin or individual chops are sometimes stuffed.

SPARE RIB

This is a curious-looking joint with a small amount of skin and a large cut surface showing where the foreleg was attached. The spare rib cut is above the foreleg and behind the head. It is a good roasting joint and also used for cutlets (chops). It is a cheaper cut than loin or leg.

ROAST PORK

For methods, see *Roasting*, page 13.

Cuts used are: loin, leg, hand and spring, spare ribs.

Moderate Temperature Roasting E.375–400° (190–200°C), G.5–6;

spare ribs and loin 30–35 mins. per lb. (½ kg.); leg 35–40 mins. per lb. (½ kg.).

Meat Thermometer. Internal temperature 185° (85°C).

Quantities. With bone ½–¾ lb. per portion (250–375 g.), no bone 4–6 oz. per portion (125–175) g.

Cook pork very thoroughly, over-, rather than under-cooking. To get crisp crackling make sure the rind is raised above the level of the drippings in the pan. It helps either to rub salt into the rind or to brush it with oil.

Accompaniments. Boiled, roast, or mashed potatoes; Gravy and Apple Sauce; Sage and Onion Stuffing; Celery; Onions; green vegetable; Red Cabbage.

ROAST PORK WITH ORANGE SAUCE

Roast a 3½–4 lb. piece of pork. Lift out when cooked and keep hot. Pour off the fat from the pan.

Juice of 2 oranges

Add to the pan and stir to dissolve any sediment. Serve this in place of gravy, adding a little stock if more gravy is required.

ROAST LOIN OF PORK WITH APPLES AND PRUNES

Cooking Time. See *Roasting.*   *Quantities* 1 chop per portion.

For about 3 lb. of loin (1½ kg.) allow 6 prunes and 1 apple

Pour boiling water over the prunes and leave to stand until soft enough to remove the stones.

Peel and chop the apple.

Using a sharp knife, separate the meat from the rib bone for part of the way down, to make a pocket for the stuffing. Put in the prunes and apples and sew up or tie up to keep the stuffing in place. Remove the ties before serving.

Roast potatoes   Red cabbage

Serve with the meat.

GRILLED OR FRIED PORK CHOPS

Cooking Time 15–20 mins., depending on the thickness.
Quantities 1 per portion.

Spare rib or loin chops

Trim off surplus fat.

Grilling. Cook fairly slowly under a moderate heat, turning once during cooking. Cooking and browning should finish together. Pork meat should always be thoroughly cooked, but if the heat is too fierce it will become hard and dry in the process.

Frying. Use just enough melted lard or oil to cover the bottom of the frying pan. When it is hot, brown the chops quickly on each side and then reduce the heat to continue the cooking. To cover the pan with a lid at this stage helps to keep the meat moist. When the chops are cooked, remove them to a hot dish. Pour off the fat and swill the pan out with stock or wine or, if preferred, retain a little fat and use this to make a *roux* for a thickened gravy. See *Gravy*, page 246.

Grilled or fried tomatoes or mushrooms
Grilled or fried apple rings or apple sauce
Redcurrant jelly
Grilled halves of canned peaches
Grilled slices of pineapple

Serve any of these as garnishes for the chops.

PORK CHOPS WITH SAUCE ROBERT

Cooking Time 30–45 mins. *Quantities* for 4.

2 onions

Skin and chop finely.

1 oz. *butter* (25 g.)

Heat this in a small pan and fry the onions in it until they begin to brown.

¼ *pt. stock* (⅛ l.) 1 *tsp. chopped parsley*

Add to the onions and boil gently until the quantity is reduced by half.

Salt and pepper 1 *tsp. vinegar*
1 *tsp. dry mustard*

Mix the mustard to a paste with the vinegar and add it to the sauce, seasoning to taste with salt and pepper. Keep the sauce hot while cooking the chops.

4 pork chops

Grill these and serve them with the sauce poured over them.

PORK CHOPS IN CIDER SAUCE

Cooking Time 1 hr. to marinade and 20–25 mins. to cook.
Quantities for 4.

4 thick pork chops (spare rib or loin)

Use a small sharp knife and score the chops in two or three places each side.

2 Tbs. chopped green herbs   Oil   Salt and pepper

Mix the herbs with plenty of seasoning and enough oil to make a paste. Rub the mixture into the slits in the meat. Leave for an hour or more in a cold place. Put the chops on a grill rack and cook under a moderate heat for about 20 mins., turning once. Remove chops and pour off surplus fat. Put chops back in the bottom of the grill pan.

¾ pt. cider (1½ dl.)

Pour into the pan, heat gently, and mix and shake to incorporate all the juices in the pan.

1 Tbs. chopped gherkins   1 Tbs. chopped capers

Add to the sauce and serve the chops with the sauce poured over them.

Grilled apple rings, or pineapple slices, or mushrooms

Serve as garnishes if desired.

PORK AND APPLE PIE

Cooking Time 1½–2 hrs.
Temperature E.450° (220°C), G.8 for 10 mins. then 325° (160°C), G.4.
Quantities for a 2 pint pie dish with funnel (1 *l.*).

1¼ lb. fillet of pork (½ kg.)   1 tsp. salt
Pinch each of pepper and grated nutmeg

Cut the pork in thin slices and sprinkle it with the seasonings.

1 lb. apples (½ kg.)

Peel and slice the apples. Put them in the pie dish in layers with the pork.

    1 tsp. brown sugar   *¼ pt. white wine (150 ml.)*
                  1 oz. butter (25 g.)

Add sugar and wine to the pie dish and then the butter in small pieces dotted over the top.

        8 oz. ready-made puff pastry (250 g.)

Cover the pie in the usual way and bake until the meat is tender. Serve hot or cold.

CASSEROLE OF SPARE RIBS OF PORK

Cooking Time 1½ hrs.   *Temperature* E.400° (200°C), G.6.
Quantities for 4

          4 thick spare rib chops

Put the chops in a wide, shallow casserole and bake without the lid for about 30 mins. or until they are well browned.

    1 small onion   *½ oz. butter or oil (15 g.)*

Peel and chop the onion and fry it brown in the butter or oil, using a small pan.

1 stalk celery	*2 tsp. tomato paste*
1 Tbs. brown sugar	*1 Tbs. Worcester sauce*
2 tsp. dry mustard	*¼ pt. water (1½ dl.)*
1 tsp. salt	*½ tsp. paprika pepper*
1 Tbs. vinegar	*2 Tbs. lemon juice*

Wash and chop the celery. Mix sugar and seasonings with the tomato, sauces, and liquids and add this and the celery to the fried onion. Pour off any dripping surrounding the chops and pour the sauce over them. Cover with the lid and continue baking for about ¾ hr. or until the chops are quite tender and the vegetables cooked.

BOILED PICKLED OR SALT PORK

Cooking Time. Pieces under 1 lb. (½ kg.) need 45 mins.; 1–2 lb. (½–1 kg.) needs 1–1½ hrs.; over 3 lb. (1½ kg.) allow 30 mins. per lb. (½ kg.).
Pressure cooking allow 12 mins. per lb. (½ kg.).
Quantities 6–8 oz. per person (175–250 g.).

Soak small pieces in cold water for 1 hr., larger pieces soak for 4–5 hrs. or more. Put the meat in cold water to cover, bring slowly to the boil, and remove any scum.

1 onion	or	6 peppercorns
4–5 cloves		1 bay leaf

If the onion is used, skin it and stick the cloves into it. Put in the water or add the peppercorns and bay leaf. Cover, and simmer for the required time.

Vegetables such as carrots, turnips, potatoes, celery, or parsnips

Vegetables may be cooked with the meat for about the last hour. Prepare them in the usual way and cut them into large pieces. They will take longer than usual to cook because the water is simmering and not boiling.

Chopped parsley

When meat and vegetables are cooked, lift out the vegetables with a strainer. Remove the meat, cut off the rind, and slice the meat. Arrange on a platter with some of the vegetables as a garnish and a little of the cooking liquid to moisten. Sprinkle with chopped parsley.

Pressure Cooker Method. Allow ½ pt. water (¼ l.) for each 15 mins. of cooking time. Put meat on a trivet in the bottom of the pan with the fat side uppermost. Add 3 or 4 cloves and 1 Tbs. brown sugar and cook. Allow pressure to drop slowly before removing the meat.

MINCED PORK PATTIES

Cooking Time 50–60 mins. on top or in the oven.
Temperature E.375° (190°C), G.5. *Quantities for 4.*

1 lb. lean fillet pork (½ kg.)	1 shallot or small onion
3 oz. stale bread (3 slices or 75 g.)	

Cut pork and bread in rough pieces and skin the onion or shallot. Put these through the mincer twice to make smooth.

1 tsp. salt	¼ tsp. pepper	Milk

Pinch each of ground nutmeg, ginger, clove, and mace

Add to the pork with enough milk to moisten. Mix well and divide into 8 portions. Pat each into a flat cake about 1 in. (2 cm.) thick.

Lard or oil

Heat enough to cover the bottom of the pan or casserole which should be large enough to allow the patties to lie in a single layer. Fry patties until brown on both sides. Remove and keep hot.

1 onion   2 stalks celery   2 tomatoes

Skin the onion and chop finely. Wash and chop celery and tomatoes. Add to the pan and fry for a few minutes.

1 oz. flour (25 g.)

Add to the vegetables and mix and cook for a minute or two.

½ pt. stock (¼ l.)   Salt and pepper
2 Tbs. wine or wine vinegar

Add to the pan and stir until the sauce boils. Return the patties to the sauce, cover, and cook gently on top or in the oven for 45 mins.

COLD PORK

Is excellent for sandwiches of all kinds. When it is being served as a cold meat, serve with it either:

Potato salad   Sweet pickled fruit
Beetroot and chicory salad   Potato and apple salad
Pickles or chutney   Cole slaw

Also suitable for use in Shepherd's Pie or Hash.

SOUSE OF COLD PORK

Put slices of cold pork in a shallow dish. Sprinkle liberally with lemon juice, salt and pepper, cover and store several hours in the refrigerator. Serve with diced cucumber mixed with French dressing.

8 Ham and Bacon

HAM

Is the hind leg of a pig cut off and cured separately, very much more slowly than gammon or bacon. The cut end is usually rounded but may be squared off when the ham is known as 'short cut'. A well-cured ham develops a bluish-green mould on the cut end. The fat may be white or have a pinkish tinge, e.g. York ham. Hams are cured in a variety of ways but all methods include salting and smoking.

BOILED HAM OR GAMMON

Cooking Times (weights after soaking). 12 lb. (5 kg.) 3½ hrs.; 14 lb. (6 kg.) 3¾ hrs.; 16 lb. (7 kg.) 4 hrs.; 18 lb. (8 kg.) 4¼ hrs.; 20 lb. (9 kg.) 4½ hrs.

Quantities. Allow 4–6 oz. per portion (120–180 g.).

Soak the ham in cold water to cover for 24 hrs. (soak gammon over-night). Scrub off any 'bloom' or mould. Place the ham or gammon in a pan with cold water (use fresh water). Special large oval pans are made for cooking hams. Bring the water slowly to the boil, reduce the heat and simmer for the required time. Turn off the heat and leave the ham in the water for an hour.

To Serve Hot. Remove the skin, sprinkle the fat with golden crumbs or dried crusts crushed to make crumbs. Dress the knuckle with a paper ham frill.

To Bake. After removing the skin from the boiled ham, score the fat in a criss-cross fashion to form diamond-shaped cuts, stick a clove in each diamond, sprinkle the fat with brown sugar and cook until brown, 20–30 mins. in a hot oven, E.450° (230°C), G.8.

To Serve Cold. Put the cooked ham in a cold place for 24 hrs. Remove the skin, sprinkle the fat with crumbs as above, and put a paper ham frill on the end of the bone.

Ham is carved with a special long, thin carving knife known as a 'ham knife'.

Accompaniments for ham. With hot ham serve parsley sauce, pease pudding, and mustard, with boiled potatoes and vegetables. With cold ham serve salad, and sweet pickled fruit or apple or cranberry sauce or jelly.

HAM AND EGGS

Slices of ham are used in the same way as gammon rashers. See page 91.

HAM MOUSSE
Quantities for 4.

6 oz. minced cooked ham (175 g.) Pinch of dry mustard
½ pt. Béchamel sauce (¼ l.)

Mix these together.

1 *Tbs. gelatine* 4 *Tbs. stock*

Dissolve the gelatine in the stock, add it to the ham mixture, and leave to become cold.

4 *Tbs. whipping cream or chilled evaporated milk*

Whisk until stiff and fold into the other mixture.

1 *egg white*

Beat the egg white until stiff and fold it into the other mixture. Pour into a mould or *soufflé* dish and leave to set. Unmould.

Salad vegetables and rolls of hams

Use these to garnish the mousse.

BACON

Is the salted and cured meat from a special kind of pig bred for the purpose, and known as a bacon pig. Different countries breed different kinds of bacon pigs. The curing may be done by the use of dry salt (not very common today) or by the use of a brine solution (brining). It may then be smoked or unsmoked.

The latter is known as green bacon, doesn't keep as long as the smoked, and has a milder flavour. It is also usually cheaper.

Approximately half the bacon eaten in Britain is imported, mainly from Denmark, but also from Poland, Holland, and Eire.

CHOOSING BACON

There is such a wide variety of types and grades of bacon and no clear system of labelling that the best thing to do is to find a shop that keeps the kind of bacon you like and stick to it.

In general, cuts from the back leg (gammon) provide the choicest meat; the front leg and shoulder (hock, butt, fore slipper, collar) are saltier and coarser. The middle of the animal provides most of the rashers (back and streaky). It is not possible to tell the degree of saltiness by the look of the bacon which is another reason for buying it from the same source, especially if the shop assistants know your preference.

Smoked bacon has a dark rind, green or unsmoked a pale rind. Some brands are stamped on the rind, e.g. Danish and Polish.

After cutting, bacon dries quickly and becomes hard, so buy your bacon from a shop that has a quick turn-over and do not buy it if it looks dark and dry.

Bacon sold in transparent sealed packets is a better buy than bacon cut and exposed to warm dry air. Freshly cut bacon has a deep pink or good bright red colour and looks freshly cut. The fat should be white and firm. Poor-quality bacon fat may have yellow or green stains and be soft and oily.

BACON CUTS AND THEIR USE

GAMMON

Is the hind leg of a bacon pig, cut off the side of bacon and shows the square-cut surface at the top (a ham is rounded at this end). It may be boiled whole and used in the same way as ham but is more frequently cut into four smaller pieces as follows:

GAMMON SLIPPER

Is a small lean joint, almost triangular in shape, weighs approximately 1¼ lb. (¾ kg) and is good for boiling.

GAMMON HOCK

Is the foot end of the gammon, weighs approximately 4½ lb. (2 kg) and is suitable for baking and very good cold. Is perhaps most satisfactory when boned and rolled.

84

MIDDLE GAMMON

Is an even-shaped bit out of the middle of the leg and is the best bit for boiling and baking, approximate weight 5 lb. (2½ kg.). Gammon rashers for grilling are cut from it. It usually costs more than the other cuts.

CORNER GAMMON

Is another triangular bit from the top of the leg, weighing approximately 4 lb. (2 kg.). It is suitable for boiling and rashers are also cut from it.

FOREHOCK

Is the front leg and is sometimes sold whole as a picnic ham or picnic shoulder but is more often cut into three smaller joints as follows:

SMALL HOCK

Which is the foot end of the shoulder, approximate weight 3 lb. (1½ kg.). Suitable for boning and rolling, then boiling or to cut up for casserole cooking. It is a very economical joint.

FORE SLIPPER

Is the next bit of meat above the small hock and weighs approximately 1½ lb. (¾ kg.). It is fairly fatty but is suitable for boiling, or for baking if wrapped in aluminium foil.

THE BUTT

Is the shoulder blade bit and is very lean and good for boiling or baking if wrapped in aluminium foil. Approximate weight, 3¾ lb. (2 kg.).

STREAKY BACON

Is usually cut into rashers but sometimes sold in pieces for boiling. Prime streaky has less fat than the others. They all have alternating strips of lean and fat but more fat in proportion to meat than in other rashers.

COLLAR

Comes from behind the neck of the animal. This may be sold as one joint for boiling and is economical, weighing approximately 8 lb. (4 kg.). It is more often either cut into rashers or into two pieces,

85

Prime collar and End of collar, the former being the better bit. Both bits of collar are suitable for boiling or baking, the end collar usually being skinned and pressed after cooking.

LONG BACK

Comes from just above the gammon, usually sold as rashers and about as dear as gammon. Next to it, going up the animal, is the *Oyster*, fatter than the long back and sold as small rashers.

SHORT BACK

Comes next, sold as rashers.

BACK AND RIBS

Also sold as rashers or for boiling.

TOP BACK

Is just behind the collar and is sold for boiling or braising or as thick rashers.

FLANK

Is the belly and very fatty, useful for flavouring other dishes and for larding.

BACON RASHERS

When bacon is cut on a slicer the grocer can obtain any of 1 to 25 thicknesses, which are used as follows:

- 1–3 for very thin rashers suitable for rolling and grilling or baking. Rashers are too thin for frying or grilling flat.
- 4–7 covers the usual rashers with 5 and 6 being the most common.
- 8–10 gives thick rashers.
- 11–14 usually only for thick gammon rashers for frying or grilling.
- 15 upwards for very thick steaks of gammon for baking or cooking in a casserole.

SALTY BACON

Large pieces need soaking in cold water overnight but if there isn't time to do this, soak for as long as possible and then throw away the first lot of water in which it is brought to the boil, and start again with fresh cold water.

For rashers, soak ½ hr. or so in warm water, drain and dry before frying or grilling.

BATH CHAPS

Are the boned and cured (salted) cheek of a pig. Most frequently sold cooked and ready for slicing to fry or serve cold with salad. They are a fairly fatty meat. If raw, they are boiled in the same way as bacon or ham.

FRIED BACON AND EGGS

Remove the rinds from the rashers and place them in a cold pan, overlapping, with the fat sides touching the bottom of the pan. Cook slowly, for 6–8 mins., turning occasionally and, if crisp bacon is liked, keep pouring the fat off. (Easier though to get crisp bacon by grilling.) Frying bacon too quickly makes it frizzle and curl up. Remove the cooked bacon to a hot dish.

Crack the eggs separately into a cup and slide into the hot fat, turn down the heat, and cook gently, 2–3 mins., until they are set. Cooking too fast makes the whites tough and unappetising. Lift the eggs out of the pan with a slice and serve with the bacon. If fried bread is wanted too you may need to add some more fat. Increase the heat, put in the bread, turn to coat each side, and then fry quickly until brown. Bread soaks up a great deal of fat and is consequently a high-Calorie food.

GRILLED BACON AND EGGS

Quicker than frying, less messy, and very good. Remove the rinds and place the bacon on the grill rack. Cook under a moderate heat (or some distance from the heat). Cook 2 mins. each side or until done as you like it. Remove and keep hot. Lift out the grill rack and crack an egg into a cup. Slide it into the drippings. If you are not doing enough eggs to fill the pan, tilt it to one side and start the cooking like this. As soon as the edges set you can right the pan to finish cooking. Lift the eggs out with a slice. Bread can be grilled, after dipping both sides in hot fat, but is not as satisfactory as fried bread.

BACON AND EGGS IN THE OVEN

A very good method to use if you have a lot to do and the frying pan is on the small side.

Trim the rinds from the rashers and roll the bacon up. Put in a greased fireproof dish. Crack the eggs separately into a cup and put them in the same dish. Chipolata sausages and tomatoes may also be added. Cook at E.375° (190°C), G.5 for about 30 mins. or until the eggs are set.

Alternatively, the bacon rashers may be put in unrolled and the eggs on top of them.

BAKED BACON RASHERS

Cooking Time 30 mins.   *Temperature* E.375° (190°C), G.5.
Quantities 1–2 rashers per person.

Remove the rinds, using kitchen scissors or a very sharp knife. Place rashers in a baking tin in over-lapping rows. Bake at the top of the oven.

Alternative method. Roll the rashers up, fasten with cocktail sticks or thread on metal skewers, and bake as before.

Tomatoes, chipolata sausages, kidneys, or mushrooms may be baked at the same time in the same dish.

BACON ROLLS

Used as a garnish for many savoury dishes or as part of grills such as a *kebab*. Streaky bacon is the best to use and have it cut thin. Trim off the rinds and roll the rashers up.

Secure them with cocktail sticks or thread them on metal skewers. Either grill them for about 6–8 mins. under a moderate heat, turning once; or bake about 30 mins. in a moderate oven E.375 (190°C), G.5, until the outside fat is crisp (preferably on a rack to let the fat run down into a tin below).

FRIED BACON AND PARSLEY SAUCE

Cooking Time about 20–30 mins.   *Quantities* for 4.

1½ lb. potatoes (¾ kg.)

Peel these and put them on to boil in salted water.

1½ Tbs. flour	
1 oz. butter or margarine (25 g.)	Salt and pepper
½ pt. creamy milk (¼ l.)	2 Tbs. chopped parsley

Make a sauce by the *roux* method, adding the parsley just before serving.

8 oz. bacon rashers (250 g.)

Trim off the rinds and fry the bacon. Serve the bacon with the potatoes and serve the sauce separately.

BAKED BACON RASHERS WITH CIDER

For this use thick rashers or steaks.

Cooking Time 30 mins. *Temperature* E.375° (190°C), G.5. *Quantities* for 4.

4 thick lean bacon rashers ¼ pt. dry cider (1½ dl.)

Remove the rinds from the rashers and put the bacon in a shallow fireproof dish. Pour the cider in and leave to stand in a cool place for 2 hrs., turning the rashers over at half-time.

Bake in a moderate oven and serve with the liquid as a sauce.

BOILED BACON OR PIECES OF GAMMON

Cuts to Use. Middle gammon, corner gammon, gammon hock, prime collar, prime streaky, back and ribs, long back, top streaky, top back and short back.

Cooking Time. Pieces under 1 lb. (½ kg.) 45 mins.; pieces of 1–2 lb. (½–1 kg.) allow 1–1½ hrs.; pieces of 3 lb. (1½ kg.) and over allow 30 mins. per lb. (½ kg.). Pressure cooking allow 12 mins. per lb. (½ kg.). *Quantities.* Allow 6–8 oz. per portion (175–250 g.).

Unless you know the bacon is very lightly salted, it is wise to soak small pieces in cold water to cover for about 1 hr., larger pieces 4–5 hrs. If very salty, soak overnight.

Put the bacon in cold water to cover and add an onion stuck with 4 or 5 cloves or add 6 peppercorns and a bay leaf. Bring slowly to the boil, put on the lid, and reduce the heat to simmering or 186° (85°C) for the required time.

Vegetables which are to be served with the meat may be cooked alongside it, *e.g.* carrots, turnips, swedes, celery, potatoes, onions. Cut them in fairly large pieces and allow about an hour for cooking as they take longer at a temperature below boiling, and the bacon should not boil.

Remove the rind and cut the bacon in slices. Serve on a large dish with the vegetables round it. Serve some of the cooking liquid as a sauce. Or make a parsley sauce or one using mixed herbs, chives, parsley, tarragon, etc.

Pressure Cooking. Use ½ pt. (¼ l.) of water for every 15 mins. cooking time. Place the meat on a trivet in the bottom of the cooker, with the fat side up, add 3 or 4 cloves and 1 Tbs. brown sugar. Cook at 15 lb.

pressure. Allow the pressure to drop slowly before removing the meat.

Vegetables to serve with Boiled Bacon. Those cooked with it, or serve green beans cooked separately, cabbage, or broad beans with a sauce made with some of the bacon stock.

Cold Boiled Bacon. Lift the meat out of the cooking liquid and cool as quickly as possible. Store in the refrigerator in a polythene bag. Before serving, remove the rind and sprinkle the fat with browned crumbs. Serve with potato salad, beetroot, other salad, or pickles. N.B. Very small joints of bacon are best cooked wrapped in aluminium foil. If you cook vegetables round it the stock will still have a good flavour to use for a sauce.

BOILED WHOLE GAMMON. See *Boiled Ham*, page 92.
Soak the gammon overnight before boiling.

BAKED BACON

Cuts to use. Gammon, forehock, prime collar. See *Cuts and their Uses.*
Cooking Time 45 mins. per lb. (½ kg) for small joints up to 6 lb. (3 kg.), 30 mins. for larger joints.
Temperature E.325° (160°C), G.3, until the last ½ hr. and then E.375° (190°C), G.5.
Quantities 4–6 oz. per person (125–195 g.).

METHOD 1
Wrap the bacon loosely in aluminium foil, place in a baking pan and cook slowly until the last half-hour then increase the temperature. Remove the foil so that the bacon can brown. During this last half-hour the meat may be basted with melted jelly, honey, syrup, treacle, cider, stout, or orange juice; or with a mixture of one of the first four, with one of the liquids. Use this as a sauce. Otherwise serve the bacon with a separate sauce such as mustard sauce or other sharp sauce.

METHOD 2
This is the better method to use if you have any reason to think the bacon is rather too salty for your taste. Soak it 2–3 hrs. in cold water, or overnight if it is very heavily salted. Boil the bacon for half the required cooking time, lift out, remove the rind, and score the fat in

diamond patterns with a sharp knife. Stick a clove in each diamond, pressing it into the fat. Put the meat in a baking pan and put a thin layer of treacle, syrup, honey, or brown sugar on top and pour ½ pt. (¼ l.) cider, stout, or orange juice round it. Bake slowly for the remainder of the time, basting frequently with the liquid. Serve some of this liquid as a sauce.

Vegetables to serve with baked bacon: boiled or mashed potatoes, peas, green beans, broad beans, spinach, red cabbage. Serve cold baked bacon with potato and/or green salad, or use it in sandwiches.

GRILLED GAMMON

Cooking Time 10–20 mins. depending on thickness (may be ¼–½ in. thick or ½–1 cm.).

Quantities. One rasher per person, or half a very thick one or a small thick one from corner gammon.

If the rashers seem salty, soak them in cold water for from ½–1 hr. Drain and dry well on absorbent kitchen paper. Remove rind with kitchen scissors and snip the fat at intervals of about 1 in. (2 cm.) to help it keep flat. Brush rashers with oil and pre-heat the grill. Place rashers on grill rack and cook until the fat looks clear and the meat is tender, turning frequently during cooking. It is better to cook with a moderate heat or, alternatively, place the pan farther from the heat than you would for quicker cooking. Otherwise the meat may become dry before it is done.

Tomatoes, mushrooms, and other accompaniments may be cooked at the same time. Brush them with oil too. Alternatively, cook them under the grill rack, giving them a few minutes longer after you have removed the rashers and the rack.

Vegetables to serve with grilled gammon: boiled potatoes; boiled rice and braised onions; spinach, peas, green beans, chicory, braised celery, grilled tomatoes, or mushrooms; grilled apple rings; grilled pineapple slices or grilled peaches.

BACON HOT POT

Cooking Time 3 hrs.   *Temperature* E.300° (150°C), G.2.
Quantities for 4.

6 oz. butter beans (175 g.)

1½ *lb. piece thick streaky bacon* (¾ *kg.*)

Soak the beans and bacon separately overnight in plenty of cold water, drain. Cut the bacon into 4 pieces and put bacon and beans in a casserole.

Peel and slice the onion. Wash and chop the celery. Add both to the casserole.

> 1 pt. stock (½ l.)   ¼ tsp. pepper
> ¼ tsp. mustard   2 Tbs. black treacle

Mix mustard, pepper, and treacle with some of the stock and add to the casserole, using more stock to cover the ingredients. Put on the lid and cook slowly for 2 hrs. Remove the lid and raise the pieces of bacon to the top. Cook another hour to brown the meat and concentrate the stock. Serve from the casserole.

This dish is complete on its own but, if preferred, serve some boiled potatoes with it. Better still, serve a salad afterwards.

EGG AND BACON PIE

Cooking Time 30-40 mins.   Temperature E.425° (220°C), G.6.
Quantities for 4.

> Short crust pastry using 6 oz. flour (175 g.)
> or use ½ lb. (250 g.) ready-made

Roll half the pastry to line an 8 in. (20 cm.) pie plate or flan ring. Roll the other half for a lid.

> 4 rashers bacon   Salt and pepper
> 4 eggs   1 Tbs. chopped parsley
> Few sliced mushrooms or tomatoes optional

Remove the rinds and cut the bacon in small pieces. Spread over the bottom pastry. Beat the eggs just to blend whites and yolks, add seasoning and parsley and pour into the pastry case. Add tomatoes and mushrooms, if used. Cover with the pastry lid, moistening the edges to make a seal. Trim the edges and decorate by pinching or by pressing with the prongs of a fork. Cut a small hole in the centre. Add a little water to the egg remains and use this to brush the top of the pie. Bake until the pastry is light brown top and bottom. Serve hot or cold.

9 Veal

Veal is the flesh of the calf or immature bovine, the best being not more than 4 months old. The best veal comes from calves of beef breeds rather than dairy cows. If the animal has been exclusively milk fed the veal is usually better than that from those allowed to graze. Milk-fed veal is very tender, grass-fed less so, but some people prefer the flavour of the latter. The flesh should be fine, and pale pink or off-white in colour. Any mottling or blue or brown tints indicate stale meat which should not be purchased as veal keeps badly and quickly develops 'off' flavours. There should not be any gristle but there is a lot of fine connective tissue with some cuts and this softens readily on cooking to give a very gelatinous stock. Veal bones and trimmings make excellent-setting stock. The ratio of flesh to bone is low and there is little fat and no 'marbling'.

VEAL CUTS AND THEIR USE

BREAST

This is the belly of the animal and contains a few gristly bones which are easily removed. It can be boned, stuffed, and rolled up to roast or boil, or cut in pieces and used for stews and casseroles. It is usually the cheapest cut of veal and a very good buy.

CHOPS

These may be loin chops or chump chops, which are cut from the lower end of the loin. They are suitable for grilling or frying, but the latter is the better method as they tend to be a bit dry for grilling.

CUTLETS

These come from the best end of neck, at the top of the loin. Suitable for frying, braising, and stewing. Allow 1 to 2 cutlets per portion. Fry in the same way as chops.

VEAL

ESCALOPES

These are very thin slices of veal and should be cut from the fillet which is either the top part of the leg or rump, or else the under part of the loin. The slices are beaten with a cutlet bat to make them very thin. They are usually fried in butter or oil and garnished in a variety of ways, or combined with a sauce.

FILLET

In England this is the boned top of the leg which is either stuffed and roasted or cut in thin slices to make *escalopes*. Continental fillet is either the under part of the loin or the rump.

HOCK

Is the lower part of the leg and is sold separately for stewing, pies, soups. It can be boned and stuffed and then braised or pot roasted.

KNUCKLE

This is the lower part of the shoulder and is often sold separately. It can be used for stewing and pies or for making stock or soup.

LEG

This is the hind leg and is usually roasted, sometimes boned and stuffed.

LOIN

This consists of a row of chops, loin chops. Chump chops are cut from the bottom end and are bigger than the loin chops with a bone in the middle. See *Chops*. Loin can be roasted on the bone or boned and stuffed.

NECK

This comes from the top of the loin and consists of cutlets which are sometimes used separately (see *Cutlets*), or the piece may be braised or stewed.

SHOULDER

This is a bony awkward joint. The butcher often bones it and sells the meat as stewing or pie veal or he may bone and roll it and sell it as 'oyster' which makes a cheaper joint than leg of veal for roasting. It may be stuffed before rolling. A small shoulder is suitable for roasting on the bone.

ROAST VEAL

For methods, see *Roasting*, page 13.

Cooking Time and Temperatures

Moderate-Temperature Roasting E.375–400° (190–200°C), G.5–6. Pieces with bone allow 20 mins. per lb. ($\frac{1}{2}$ kg.). Boned and rolled joints allow 30 mins. per lb.

Slow Roasting E.325° (160°C), G.3. Pieces with bone allow 30 mins. per lb. ($\frac{1}{2}$ kg.). Boned and rolled joints allow 40 mins. per lb. Pieces under 3 lb. allow $1\frac{1}{2}$–2 hrs.

Using a Meat Thermometer. Internal temperature 180° (85°C). Times as above depending on the oven temperature.

Quantities. With bone allow $\frac{1}{3}$–$\frac{1}{4}$ lb. ($\frac{1}{4}$ kg.) per person; no bone allow 4–6 oz. per person (125–175 g.).

Place the meat in the roasting pan, preferably on a rack. Sprinkle meat with flour and cover with strips of fat bacon or bard it with a piece of fat.

Alternatively, put a piece of foil loosely over the meat and remove it for the last $\frac{1}{2}$ hr. to allow the meat to brown. If the veal is completely wrapped in foil it will take longer to cook, unless a higher temperature is used, e.g. E.450° (230°C), G.8. When the meat is cooked, make the gravy in the pan or swill the pan out with stock and make the gravy in a saucepan. Veal should be thoroughly cooked as it is unpalatable and indigestible when underdone.

Accompaniments. Veal forcemeat balls (see *Stuffings*), boiled or grilled bacon or boiled salt pork, roast or mashed potatoes, a green vegetable.

ROAST STUFFED VEAL

Use the times for boned and rolled joints.

Joints boned and stuffed are leg, breast, loin, and shoulder. Breast of veal is boned, spread with stuffing, and rolled up, or, after boning cut a pocket in the meat, stuff, and sew up. Loin is stuffed by separating the meat from the bone sufficiently to make a pocket for the stuffing. Then sew up.

For stuffings use either veal forcemeat or lemon stuffing. See *Stuffings*, pages 258–60.

FRIED VEAL CHOPS

Cooking Time 20 mins.   *Quantities* 1 chop per person.

Fry in a mixture of half butter and half lard or olive oil. Brown them quickly each side and then reduce the heat, cover the pan, and finish cooking slowly. They take at least 20 mins. to cook through. Swill the pan out with a little stock, lemon juice, wine, or cider and pour it over the chops. Garnish with chopped parsley and a little finely chopped onion.

VEAL CUTLETS WITH CIDER

Cooking Time 20–25 mins.   *Quantities* for 4.

2 oz. butter or oil (50 g.)   4 veal cutlets

Heat the fat and fry the cutlets for about 10 mins. or until they are brown.

2 medium-sized onions

Skin and chop and add to the fat in the pan. Fry until they are pale brown.

2 Tbs. flour

Add to the pan, stir, and cook for 1–2 mins.

¼ pt. dry cider (1½ dl.)   ¼ pt. water (1½ dl.)

Gradually stir into the pan and stir until it thickens. Boil for a few minutes and season to taste. Return the cutlets for about 3 mins.

Chopped parsley

Serve sprinkled with the parsley.

ITALIAN VEAL STEW

Cooking Time ¾ hr.   *Quantities* for 4.

4 veal chops   4 Tbs. olive oil

Heat the oil in a sauté pan or shallow saucepan and fry the chops until brown on both sides.

1 stalk celery, chopped   1 medium carrot, chopped
1 medium onion, chopped

Add to the pan, lower the heat, cover with a lid or with foil and cook slowly until the vegetables are tender, about 10 mins.

1 Tbs. tomato paste   ¼ pt. dry sherry (150 ml.)

Salt and pepper

Add to the pan and continue cooking until the meat is tender, about 20 mins., adding water if necessary during the cooking.

Chopped parsley   Mashed potatoes

Sprinkle liberally with parsley and serve with the potatoes.

VEAL ESCALOPES

Cooking Time 3–4 mins.

Quantities 1 escalope per portion (about 3–4 oz. or 95–125 g.).

Escalopes with Lemon. Fry them in butter. Remove from the pan and keep hot. Add a very little hot water to the pan and boil hard for a minute or two. For every 4 escalopes add the juice of ½ lemon and pour the juice over the escalopes. Serve with potatoes and lettuce salad.

Wiener Schnitzel. Coat the escalopes with egg and breadcrumbs and fry for 3–4 mins. in oil. Drain on kitchen paper and serve at once, garnished with anchovy fillets and wedges of lemon.

VEAL PARMESAN

Cooking Time 10–15 mins.   Quantities for 4.

4 escalopes of veal   Small piece of finely chopped garlic

1 oz. butter (25 g.)   or use garlic salt

Heat the butter in a frying pan and add the garlic and then the veal.

2 Tbs. grated Parmesan cheese   2 tsp. paprika pepper

Salt and pepper

Sprinkle this on the meat and fry it gently until brown on both sides. Lift out and keep hot. Swill out the pan with a little stock, lemon juice or white wine and pour the liquid over the meat. Serve with

Spaghetti or noodles and a green salad.

VEAL GOULASH

Cooking Times 2–3 hrs.   Temperature E.300° (150°C), G.3.

Quantities for 4.

4 oz. fat salt pork (125 g.)   1 lb. boned shoulder of veal (½ kg.)

Cut the salt pork in small cubes and the veal in larger cubes. Heat the pork in a frying pan until the fat begins to run and then fry until it turns brown.

1 large onion

Skin and chop. Remove the pork from the pan, add the veal and onion, and cook until brown. Put the meat in a casserole. Discard the pork.

    ¾ pt. stock (5 dl.)   1 tsp. salt
    1½ Tbs. flour   1 tsp. paprika pepper

Put the stock in the frying pan and stir well to dissolve the brown bits. Blend the flour and seasonings with a little cold water and stir into the stock. Stir until it boils and pour it over the meat.

    4 small potatoes   4 small carrots
    4 small onions   1 bay leaf

Peel and slice the potatoes thickly. Skin the onions, scrape or peel the carrots, and cut them in strips. Add vegetables and bay leaf to meat, cover, and cook gently until the meat is tender, the longer the better.

Variation. More paprika pepper may be used if a hot goulash is preferred.

CASSEROLE OF VEAL WITH CREAM AND GRAPEFRUIT JUICE

Cooking Time 1½ hrs.   *Temperature* E.350° (180°C), G.4.
Quantities for 4.

    1 lb. boneless veal (½ kg.) or 1½ lb. neck of veal (¾ kg.)
    2–3 small onions   1 oz. butter (25 g.)
    2 Tbs. olive oil

Cut the meat in small pieces. Skin and chop the onions. Heat the butter and oil in a frying pan or casserole. Toss the veal and onions in this until the fat is absorbed but the meat is not browned. If necessary transfer to the casserole.

    Salt and pepper   ¼ pt. white wine (150 ml.)
    4 Tbs. double cream

Add to the veal. Cover and cook gently until the meat is tender.

    Juice of half a small grapefruit

Add to the casserole just before serving. Serve with
Rice or noodles.

VEAL OLIVES OR BIRDS

Cooking Time 1¼ hrs. on top or in the oven.
Temperature E.325° (160°C), G.3. *Quantities for* 4.

1 *lb. fillet or leg of veal cut in very thin slices* (¼ *kg.*)
Veal forcemeat, see page 260

The veal should be cut as thinly as possible and in pieces about
4 × 3 in. (10 × 8 cm.). Spread a little forcemeat on each and roll up
tightly. Fasten with a wooden cocktail stick or tie with coarse white
cotton.

1 *Tbs. chopped onion*   1½ *oz. butter or oil* (45 *g.*)

Heat the butter or oil and fry the olives until brown all over, adding
the onion towards the end of cooking. Place meat in a casserole.

3 *Tbs. flour*   ¾ *pt. stock* (5 *dl.*)

Add flour to pan and mix well, stirring and cooking until crumbly.
Remove from the heat and gradually add the stock. Return to the
heat and stir until it boils.

1 *Tbs. chopped parsley*   ¼ *tsp. pepper*
1 *tsp. salt*

Add parsley and seasonings to the pan and pour over the olives.
Cover and cook slowly until tender. Remove the string or sticks from
the olives and serve with the sauce poured over them.

Variation. Roll each olive in a rasher of bacon before tying it up.

BRAISED VEAL

Cooking Time 3 hrs.   *Temperature* E.350° (180°C), G.4.
Quantities for 4.

8 *carrots*   1 *rasher bacon*
6 *small onions or shallots*

Scrape or peel the carrots and slice them. Skin the onions. Remove
rind and chop bacon.

3 *lb. best end of neck of veal or scrag end or middle neck* (1½ *kg.*)
2 *oz. butter or olive oil* (50 *g.*)

Heat the butter or oil in a casserole or saucepan and fry the meat

99

in it until well browned. Remove the meat and pour off excess fat. If the cooking is to be done in this pan put the vegetables in the bottom with the bacon, otherwise put them in the casserole.

1 tsp. salt ¼ tsp. pepper Stock to moisten
A bouquet garni or a sprig of rosemary

Add seasoning to the vegetables and enough stock to come half way up the vegetables. Put the meat on top, cover, and simmer until the meat is tender. This may be done on top or in the oven. Add a little more stock during cooking if it begins to dry up. Lift out the meat and carve it into portions. Arrange it on a serving dish with the vegetables as a garnish. If liked, thicken the sauce with a little roux or serve as it is. Alternatively, put vegetables and stock in the electric blender to make a thickened sauce. Reheat and pour over the meat.

Chopped parsley

Serve hot sprinkled with chopped parsley.

BOILED BREAST OF VEAL

Cooking Time 1½–2 hrs. or 20 mins. pressure cooking.
Quantities. Allow 8 oz. per person (250 g.).

1 breast of veal or a piece of one

Ask the butcher not to chop the breast in pieces but to bone it for you. Keep the bones.

Veal forcemeat. See Stuffings, page 260.

Put the meat on a board, skin side down, and spread the forcemeat over it, but keeping about 1 in. (2½ cm.) in from the edges. Roll it up and tie securely with fine string, putting the string round in several places to make sure it keeps a good shape.

A bouquet garni

Put enough water in a pan just to cover the meat, bring it to the boil, add the meat, bones and bouquet and simmer until tender when pierced with a metal skewer. For the pressure cooker use ⅔ pt. water (5 dl.).

To serve hot. Remove the strings and slice the meat like a Swiss roll. Use some of the stock to make a sauce to go with it, e.g. parsley or tomato.

To serve cold. Leave the string on and, while the meat is still hot, put it between two plates with a weight on top and put in a cold place to cool quickly. When cool enough, put it in the refrigerator. Slice when cold and serve with salad, *e.g.* tomato or orange salad.

VEAL BLANQUETTE

Cooking Time 2 hrs. or 30 mins. pressure cooking.
Quantities for 4.

1½ *lb. breast or shoulder of veal weighed without bone* (¾ *kg.*)

Cut the meat in small pieces as for a stew.

> 1 onion   1 stick celery
> 1 carrot   1 clove

Skin the onion and stick the clove in it. Scrape or peel and chop the carrot. Wash and chop the celery.

> ½ *Tbs. salt   Pinch mixed herbs*

Put all in a stew pan or in the pressure cooker, adding 1 pt. (½ l.) of water to the pan and ½ pt. (¼ l.) for the pressure cooker. Bring to the boil and simmer for 1 hr. or pressure cook for 20 mins. Strain and put the meat aside to use later.

> ¾ *oz. butter* (25 *g.*)   ¼ *pt. veal stock* (¼ *l.*)
> 1½ *Tbs. flour*

Melt the butter in a pan and add the flour. Stir and cook until crumbly. Remove from the heat and gradually add the stock. Return to the heat and stir until it boils.

> 2 *oz. button mushrooms* (50 *g.*)   *Pinch of pepper*
> 6 *small onions or shallots*

Wash and slice the mushrooms. Peel the onions. Add to the sauce. Boil gently for 45 mins. or until the onions are tender. Add pepper to taste.

> 1 *egg yolk*   1½ *Tbs. cream*
> *Juice of* ½ *lemon*

Mix these together and stir into the sauce, heating without boiling again. Add the meat and allow to become hot but not to boil.

> 2 *Tbs. chopped parsley*
> *Grilled bacon rolls and lemon wedges* (*optional*)

Serve the dish sprinkled with chopped parsley, and the garnish of bacon and lemon if desired.

VEAL HOCK or *Osso Buco*

Cooking Time 1½–2 hrs. or 20 mins. pressure cooking.
Quantities for 4.

| 2 veal hocks | 2 onions |
| 1 large carrot | Flour |

Ask the butcher to saw the hocks into 3 in. (8 cm.) pieces. Skin and chop the onions. Scrape or peel and chop the carrots. Coat the pieces of hock in flour.

Heat the fat in a deep stew pan or casserole and fry meat and vegetables in it until they are brown.

| 2 oz. butter or olive oil (50 g. or 4 Tbs.) |

¼ pt. red wine (1½ dl.)	1 pt. stock (½ l.) approx.
2 Tbs. tomato paste	1 tsp. salt
Bouquet garni	¼ tsp. pepper

Add to the meat using enough stock to come half way up the meat in the pressure cooker and just cover the meat in the pan or casserole. Simmer until the meat is tender. This may be done in the oven. Remove the *bouquet garni*.

A little grated lemon rind   Chopped parsley

Serve the meat and sauce sprinkled with lemon and parsley. Serve with

Boiled potatoes or boiled rice.

SAUTÉ VEAL WITH RICE

Cooking Time ¾–¾ hr.   *Quantities* for 4–6.

1½ lb. fillet or leg of veal (¾ kg.), cut in ¼ in. (6 mm.) slices
Seasoned flour

Cut the veal in pieces for serving and coat it in the seasoned flour.

| 2 oz. fat or oil (50 g. or 4 Tbs.) |

Heat this in a frying pan or casserole and fry the veal until brown on both sides. Add about ¼ pt. (1½ dl.) water, cover the pan, and simmer for 20–30 mins. or until the meat is tender. While it is cooking prepare the rice as follows:

Boil the rice.

| 8 oz. rice (250 g.) |

| 1 small onion | 1 small red sweet pepper |
| 1 small green sweet pepper | 1 tomato |
| 1 stick celery |

Skin the onion and mince or chop it finely. Wash the other vegetables and chop them finely.

Heat this in a frying pan and fry the onion, green pepper, and celery in it until tender. Add the rice and stir until heated. Add the red pepper and tomato. Arrange the rice down one side of the serving dish and the veal down the other.

1½ oz. fat or oil (45 g.)

VEAL GALANTINE

Cooking Time 2–3 hrs.
Quantities for 12 or more portions.

3 eggs

Hard-boil and slice them.

3 lb. breast of veal in one piece (1½ kg.)

Bone the meat and keep the bones.

8 oz. gammon or lean bacon (250 g.)
1 lb. pork sausage meat (½ kg.)

Remove the rind and chop the bacon. Mix it with the sausage meat. Put the veal on a board, skin side down. Spread half the sausage over the top, add the sliced eggs, and then the rest of the sausage. Roll the meat up and wrap firmly in a piece of foil, making the joins secure.

½ tsp. salt   ½ bay leaf
Sprig of parsley   Sprig of thyme

Put the veal bones in a pan with these flavourings, and cold water to cover. Bring to the boil and simmer for a few minutes. Add the galantine and simmer for 2–3 hrs. or until tender. Lift it out of the stock, remove the foil, and press the meat between two plates with a weight on top. Put to cool quickly and as soon as cold enough store it in the refrigerator.

2 Tbs. gelatine   1½ pt. stock (1 l.)

Dissolve the gelatine in the stock and boil hard until it is reduced to about ½ pt. (¼ l.).

Gravy browning

Colour with the browning and leave to cool. When it is beginning to set, brush it thickly over the galantine. Leave for the coating to set. To serve, slice the galantine thinly and serve with salad.

103

VEAL MOULD (Jellied Veal)

Cooking Time 1–1½ hrs, or 20 mins. pressure cooking.
Quantities for 6–8.

1½ lb. boneless veal (¾ kg.) from neck, shoulder, or hock	
Bacon or ham bone	1 onion
1 carrot	Bouquet garni
1 turnip	2 tsp. salt
1½ pt. water (1 l.)	
¼ Tbs. gelatine	Pepper

Wash the meat and peel the vegetables. Put all the ingredients in a pan and add any veal bones as well. (For pressure cooking use only 1 pt. (½ l.) water.) Bring to the boil and simmer until the meat is tender. Strain, and cut the meat into small pieces.

Heat ¾ pt. (½ l.) of the stock and dissolve the gelatine in it. Add the meat and season to taste, adding more salt if needed. Pour into a mould and leave to set. Unmould and cut in slices like a brawn. Use the rest of the stock for soup or sauce.

TERRINE OF VEAL

Cooking Time 2 hrs.   Temperature E.325° (160°C), G.3.
Quantities for 6.

1 lb. boneless veal, any cut (½ kg.)	2 oz. liver, calf's or lamb's (50 g.)
8 oz. belly of pork (250 g.)	1 shallot or small onion

Keep about 4 oz. (125 g.) thinly sliced veal and mince the rest with the other meats and the onion, mincing twice to make it fine.

1 Tbs. chopped parsley	1 tsp. salt
¼ tsp. mixed spice	Pinch of pepper

Add to the meat and mix well.

8 oz. streaky bacon (250 g.), thinly sliced   1 bay leaf

Remove the rinds from the bacon. Wash the bay leaf and put it in the bottom of a 6 in. (15 cm.) cake tin or straight-sided ovenproof dish. Line the dish with some of the bacon rashers, put in a layer of the minced meat and then a layer of veal slices, then bacon rashers. Repeat these layers until all ingredients are used up, finishing with a layer of bacon. Cover with a lid or a piece of foil pressed well down over the top. Bake the terrine slowly until it feels tender when pierced in the middle. Remove the lid, put a plate a little smaller than the dish on top of the meat and put a weight on top. Put in a cold place and when cool enough into the refrigerator. To serve, turn out of the mould and slice. Leave the layer of fat on top of the terrine until it is to be served.

VEAL *FRICASSÉE*. See Chicken *Fricassée*, page 143, substituting cooked veal for chicken.

CREAMED VEAL. See Creamed Chicken, page 142, substituting veal for chicken.

VEAL AND HAM PIE

Cooking Time 2 hrs.
Temperature E.450° (230°C), G.8, then E.325° (160°C), G.3 for the rest of the time.
Quantities for 4–6.

6 oz. *flour made into short crust or flaky pastry* (175 g.)
or use 8–12 oz. *ready-made pastry* (250–375 g.)
1 *hard-boiled egg* 1½ *lb. boneless veal* (¾ *kg.*) 6 *oz. bacon* (175 g.)

Slice the egg and cut the veal in small pieces. Remove rind and cut bacon in small pieces.

1 *tsp. chopped parsley*   1 *tsp. grated lemon rind*
1 *tsp. salt*   ¼ *tsp. pepper*

Put the meat, egg, and seasonings in layers in a pie dish, having it well filled.

About 4 *Tbs. stock or water*

Add stock or water to come half way up the meat. Roll the pastry and cover the pie. Cut a hole in the centre and brush the pastry with

Beaten egg mixed with a little water or milk

Bake in a hot oven for about 10 mins. and then more slowly to cook the meat. If the pastry is browning too much, cover it with a piece of foil or greaseproof paper.

If the pie is to be eaten cold make some stock from veal bones and fill the cooked pie with stock, using a small plastic funnel in the centre hole.

Variation. Small balls of veal forcemeat (see page 260) can be added for extra flavouring.

10 Sausages

These are made from minced or finely chopped meat with some fat and seasonings. The mixture is put into skins and tied at intervals to give individual sausages. Edible skins are made from the intestines of animals but some of the ready-cooked sausages which are eaten cold have synthetic skins which must be removed.

The variety of sausages made is enormous and many are imported into Britain, especially from Germany and Italy. The majority of these are cooked sausages to be served as cold meats.

English sausages usually contain less meat than imported ones and instead have bread and cereal as a filler. In poor-quality sausages this can be as high as 70 per cent whereas a good sausage is all meat. The majority are flavoured with 'sausage seasoning' which is a blend of spices and herbs made to a definite formula. Occasionally a sausage-maker departs from this formula and makes sausages with an indivi-dual flavour.

Raw English sausages are either made with pork or beef. When sold without skins they are called 'skinless sausages', or 'sausage meat' if not shaped like a sausage.

Unless otherwise stated English sausages are the ones used in the following recipes.

BLACK PUDDING

Made from blood (pig's, sheep's, or ox), mixed with a cereal (some-times oatmeal), onions, suet, and seasoning, filled into skins and cooked. When served they only need to be boiled for 10–15 mins. to make them hot or they can be grilled. The best accompaniment is creamy mashed potatoes or potato *purée*. Although they contain blood the iron in the blood is not readily available for absorption so they cannot be looked on as iron-rich foods.

CHIPOLATA

The name of a small, thin, highly flavoured sausage, used mainly for garnishing and for cocktail snacks. They may be cooked in any of the ways used for sausages but take less time, about half that of larger sausages.

FRANKFURTERS OR FRANKFORT SAUSAGES

A smoked sausage usually sold cooked or canned and eaten cold or reheated.

The latter are an important ingredient of 'Hot Dogs'. Frankfurters are usually all meat with no bread filling. To heat them, place in a pan and cover with boiling water. Put the lid on and leave to stand for 6–10 mins. They may then be served or further heated by splitting in half and grilling. Grill skin side down until they are brown.

LIVER SAUSAGE

Sold by butchers, grocers, and delicatessen shops. It is already cooked and is eaten like other cooked meats. The quality of liver sausage varies and so does the price. Continental liver sausage is usually better quality than the local product which is often over-full of bread and seasoning.

MORTADELLA

A large pork sausage originating in Italy. It is sold cooked, and is chiefly used as an *hors-d'œuvre* or as part of a cold meat platter.

SALAMI

A special type of pork sausage which originated in Italy but is now made in many different countries. The sausage is sold ready for eating, is sliced thinly, the skin removed, and served for *hors-d'œuvre* or in salads and sandwiches.

SAVELOYS

Smoked English sausages made with pork and sold ready-cooked. They are usually served hot after being boiled gently for about 10 mins.

STRASSBURG SAUSAGES

These are German smoked sausages sometimes sold in delicatessens in Britain. They are cooked like Frankfurter sausages and served with *sauerkraut*.

107

TOULOUSE SAUSAGES

These are sometimes sold in Britain, especially in shops dealing in French food. They are the size of an ordinary English sausage but the meat is chopped up small instead of being minced. They are cooked like ordinary sausages but are very much better.

FRIED SAUSAGES

Cooking Time 30 mins.

Heat a little fat in the frying pan and cook the sausages very slowly until they are well browned. If cooked too fast they will tend to burst and will be over-cooked outside before the middles are done properly.

GRILLED SAUSAGES

Cooking Time 15–20 mins.

Grill fairly slowly under a moderate heat, turning them frequently until they are well browned and cooked right through. Cut one open to be sure. Grilled bacon rolls and apple rings can be cooked at the same time.

BAKED SAUSAGES

Cooking Time 30 mins.   *Temperature* E.425° (220°C), G.7. Put the sausages in a single row in a shallow baking tin and bake until well browned. This is one of the best ways of cooking sausages as it is rare for them to burst and they get a thorough cooking. Baked tomatoes, mushrooms, and other foods can be cooked at the same time.

SMOTHERED SAUSAGES

Cooking Time 5–10 mins. grilling, followed by ½ hr. baking. *Temperature* E.400° (200°C), G.6.   *Quantities* for 3 –4.

1 lb. pork sausages (½ kg.)

Make the grill very hot and brown the sausages quickly all over. They do not need to cook through.

Bacon rashers, as many as there are sausages

Remove the rinds and wrap a rasher of bacon round each sausage. Pack them side by side in a single layer in a casserole just big enough to hold them.

1 or 2 large cooking apples

Peel, core, and slice into rings. Put in an overlapping layer on top of the sausages.

$\frac{1}{4}$ *pt. of stock* (1$\frac{1}{2}$ *dl.*)

Pour in the stock, cover, and bake until the apples and bacon are cooked. Serve in the casserole.

SMOKED SAUSAGES WITH PAPRIKA POTATOES

Cooking Time 40–50 mins. *Quantities for 4.*

1 oz. fat (25 g.) 4 oz. chopped onion (125 g.)

Heat the fat and fry the onion in it until it begins to brown.

1 oz. flour (3 Tbs. or 25 g.) 1 tsp. paprika pepper

Add flour and pepper and mix well.

1 Tbs. wine vinegar $\frac{1}{2}$ pt. stock ($\frac{1}{4}$ l.)
2 tsp. salt

Add to the pan and stir until it boils.

1$\frac{1}{2}$ lb. potatoes ($\frac{3}{4}$ kg.)

Peel and cut in pieces about half the size of an egg. Add them to the sauce. Cover the pan and boil gently until the potatoes are tender, stirring occasionally.

1$\frac{1}{2}$ lb. Frankfurter or other smoked sausages ($\frac{3}{4}$ kg.)

Boil the sausages separately for 10 mins. to heat them, or put them on top of the potatoes to heat through. Serve potatoes with sausages arranged on top.

NORFOLK PORK SAUSAGES

Cooking Time 25–30 mins. *Quantities for 3–4.*

1 small onion or shallot $\frac{3}{4}$ pt. milk (5 dl.)

Skin and chop the onion finely. Heat all but 2 Tbs of the milk in a large stew-pan. Add the onion and bring to the boil.

1 lb. sausages ($\frac{1}{2}$ kg.)

Separate the sausages and prick them well. Drop them into the boiling milk and simmer for about 20 mins. Lift out and keep hot.

1 Tbs cornflour 1 tsp. dry mustard

Mix these to a smooth paste with the 2 Tbs. of milk and add the

SAUSAGES

hot milk, stirring quickly until smooth. Return to the pan and stir until it boils. Boil for 5 mins.

Salt and pepper Chopped parsley

Season to taste, return the sausages, and heat for a minute. Serve with the chopped parsley sprinkled over the sausages.

SAUSAGE GALANTINE

Cooking Time 1½ hrs. or 20 mins. pressure cooking.
Quantities for 4–6.

> 2 oz. lean bacon (2 rashers) 2 tsp. chopped parsley
> 1 egg 4 Tbs. dried breadcrumbs or cereal crumbs

Remove rind and chop bacon. Beat the egg. Wash and chop the parsley. Prepare the crumbs.

> 1 lb. pork sausage meat (½ kg.) 1 tsp. Worcester sauce
> Pinch of dried herbs 1 tsp. dry mustard
> 1 Tbs. chutney Stock to moisten

Put all the ingredients in a basin, mixing the mustard smooth with a little stock before adding it. Use the beaten egg and more stock to mix to a soft consistency. Grease a 1 pt. (½ l.) pudding basin or a 1 lb. (½ kg.) loaf tin. Pack the mixture into it and cover with a lid of foil. Steam or pressure cook, allowing the pressure to drop slowly after cooking. Leave the galantine to cool in the mould and store in the refrigerator. Slice and serve as any cold meat.

SAUSAGE TOAD-IN-THE-HOLE. See Yorkshire Pudding, page 33–4.

SAUSAGE ROLLS

Cooking Time 25–30 mins. *Temperature* E.425° (220°C), G.7.
Quantities for 8 rolls.

> 4 oz. flour made into short crust or flaky pastry (125 g.)
> or use 6–8 oz. ready-made (175–250 g.)

Roll the pastry into an even oblong about ¼ in. thick. Cut into 8 rectangles about 3 in. × 4 in. (8 × 10 cm.).

> 8 oz. sausage meat (250 g.)

Divide into 8 pieces and roll into small sausage shapes using a little flour. Place one on each piece of pastry. Moisten the edges with

110

water, fold over pressing the edges together. Slash the edges with a small knife to make layers and cut 3 diagonal slits in the top of each roll.

Beaten egg mixed with a little cold water

Brush the tops with egg and bake until the pastry is well browned. They need thorough cooking to bake the sausage right through. Serve hot or cold.

11 Offal

BRAINS

The kinds most frequently used are ox, calf's, sheep's, and pig's brains, the last three being often cooked with the head in such dishes as *Calf's Head Vinaigrette*, or Pork Brawn. They can also be used by themselves to make a variety of dishes. Brains do not keep well and should be used while they are very fresh.

Brains are usually sold in 'sets', one set being a complete brain. They are also sometimes sold by the lb., 1 lb. ($\frac{1}{2}$ kg.) being enough for 4 portions.

One set of calf's or ox brains give 1–1$\frac{1}{2}$ portions depending on the animal. The brain does not increase much in size as an animal grows but it does become more close in texture.

One pig's or sheep's brain gives $\frac{3}{4}$–1 portion.

PREPARATION OF BRAINS

For all varieties the preparation is the same. They need soaking in plenty of cold water for several hours or until all traces of blood have gone. Change the water several times during soaking. Then remove the skin and any membranes.

HEART

Heart consists of very close compact muscle and has a very high nutritive value.

The size of the heart varies with the size of the animal, ox being the largest. This is a very large heart with thick strong muscles, inclined to be tough. It needs slow moist cooking to make it tender, and stewing and braising are the best methods. It may be sliced or chopped and mixed with other meats or cooked on its own either in pieces, or stuffed and braised whole. It needs strong flavourings such as onions and herbs. One heart weighs about 4 lb. (2 kg.) and is a very economical buy. It is sold whole, or sliced by the lb. Allow 6–8 oz. per portion (175–250 g.).

Sheep's hearts are much smaller and more quickly cooked. Allow one per portion. They are usually stuffed and then roasted or braised for about 1½ hrs.

The hearts of poultry and game form part of the giblets and are used for making stock or soup, but may also be cooked, chopped, and added to stuffing.

KIDNEY

BULLOCK, BEEF, OR OX KIDNEY

A large many-lobed kidney which is usually the cheapest one available. It tends to have a strong flavour and is usually eaten with beef steak in stews, pies, and puddings. They are very large and are usually cut up and sold by the pound. The fat round beef kidneys makes the best suet.

CALF'S KIDNEY

This is also a many-lobed kidney but smaller than ox kidney. It is sometimes used to make a dish on its own or combined with steak in the same way as ox kidney.

LAMB'S OR SHEEP'S KIDNEY

These are small bean-shaped kidneys and are considered the best for grilling, frying, and kidney dishes in general. They are usually sold still encased in their layer of suet, but if not make sure they are firm and fresh-looking and not dry on the outside. Softness and dryness indicate a stale kidney which will be difficult to handle and have a strong flavour. They are cooked whole, halved, or chopped.

PIG'S KIDNEY

The same shape as lamb's but larger and flatter and tends to have a stronger flavour. They are cooked in the same way as lamb's kidney.

LIVER

One of the most important organs in any animal. It is concerned with the metabolism of nutrients, acts as a store for iron, certain vitamins and glycogen, and is important as part of the digestive system because bile is made in it and secreted into the small intestine to aid the digestion of fats.

113

The livers of most domestic birds and animals and some game are eaten as human food and the livers of certain fish such as cod and halibut form an important source of vitamins A and D.

BULLOCK OR OX LIVER

This is the largest and coarsest liver used. It can have a very strong flavour or be practically tasteless. It is usually the cheapest liver and is excellent when stewed, alone or with steak, or if used in minced dishes.

CALF'S LIVER

Usually considered the best liver and is the most expensive. Suitable for frying or grilling and for making liver terrine.

SHEEP'S OR LAMB'S LIVER

Is usually cheaper than calf's liver and has a stronger flavour. Can be cooked by any method and is usually tender unless over-cooked.

PIG'S LIVER

This has a stronger flavour than lamb's liver and is usually cheaper. For those who dislike the strong flavour, use it in galantines, loaves, and stews.

CHICKEN LIVERS

These are sold by the pound in some poulterers and delicatessens. Used for making pilaff, risotto, omelets, and terrines or pâtés.

OTHER LIVERS

Are usually cooked with the giblets to make stock or added to a stuffing used in the preparation of the bird.

PREPARATION OF LIVER

Wash liver thoroughly in warm water and cut out any tubes and bits of fat. Remove the skin. Drain and dry thoroughly on paper kitchen towels. Use a very sharp knife for chopping or slicing.

SWEETBREADS

These are glandular meats and may be either the pancreas or the thymus gland. The latter is only found in young animals. Sweetbreads must be fresh and should be used up as soon as purchased. Frozen sweetbreads are imported and sold by the lb. and are very good if

114

used as soon as defrosted, 1 lb. is enough for 3–4 portions. Bullock or ox sweetbreads are the cheapest but need longer and slower cooking than other kinds.

Calf's sweetbreads are more tender but also expensive. Allow 1 pair per portion.

Lamb's sweetbreads are more plentiful but are still fairly expensive. They are the most tender and delicately flavoured. Allow 1 pair per portion. Most of the frozen sweetbreads are sheep's.

TONGUE

The tongues usually cooked as a separate dish are ox or bullock's tongues and sheep's tongues. The latter are also sometimes left in the head and boiled with it to make a brawn as is pig's tongue and calf's tongue. When calf's head is cooked for a main hot meat dish the tongue is cooked with it. See *Calf's Head Vinaigrette*. Cooked ox tongue is one of the popular cold meats sold by the pound and ox, calf, and lamb tongues are available canned and ready for slicing and serving. Chill before opening otherwise they are difficult to slice.

TRIPE

This is the lining of the stomach of beef or ox. It varies in appearance because the animal has four parts to its stomach and three of these are used for making tripe. Some of the names used for tripe are: honeycomb, blanket, monk's head, seam, and book.

Tripe is cleaned by liming and then is usually partly cooked before it is sold and it may need very little cooking before it is ready to serve, but this varies from place to place.

BRAINS WITH BLACK BUTTER SAUCE

Cooking Time 15–30 mins. depending on the kind of brains.
Quantities for 4.

1 *lb. brains* ($\frac{1}{2}$ *kg.*)

Put the brains in a basin with plenty of cold water and soak several hours or until all blood is removed, change the water once or twice. Remove skin and any fibres. Wash again. Put them in a pan with cold water to cover and add

2 *Tbs. vinegar*   4 *peppercorns*
1 *tsp. salt*   4 *cloves*
            Bouquet garni

115

Bring slowly to the boil and simmer for 15 mins. for sheep's and pig's, 20 mins. for calf's, 30 mins. for ox. Strain, cut in portions, arrange on a hot dish, and keep hot.

4 oz. butter (125 g.)   1 Tbs. wine vinegar

2 tsp. chopped parsley

Heat the butter in a small saucepan until it turns nut brown, add the parsley and cook for a minute, add the vinegar and pour at once over the brains. Serve at once.

Accompaniments. Boiled or mashed potatoes.

BOILED BRAINS

Boil the brains as in the previous recipe and serve them with a sauce such as Parsley, Tomato, *Béchamel.* They may be served in a border of mashed potatoes with accompanying vegetables.

FRIED BRAINS

Boil the brains for half the normal time. Drain well and cut in thickish slices. Dip in beaten egg and then in breadcrumbs or coat with batter and fry until golden brown. Serve with parsley or tomato sauce.

OXTAIL STEW

Cooking Time 2–3 hrs. or 20 mins. pressure cooking.
Quantities for 4–6.

1 ox tail

Ask the butcher to joint the ox tail. Remove any outside fat, wash the meat and dry well.

1 onion   1 carrot   1 stick celery   1 small turnip

Skin and slice the onion, peel or scrape and slice the carrot, peel and slice the turnip, wash and chop the celery.

1 oz. flour (25 g.)   ¼ tsp. pepper   2 tsp. salt

Mix these and coat the pieces of tail by shaking all together in a paper bag.

2 oz. fat or oil (50 g. or 4 Tbs.)

Heat in a pan or casserole and fry the meat until it is well browned.

Add the vegetables towards the end of frying. Sprinkle in any flour left from the coating and mix well.

> 1 pt. stock (½ l.) or use half stock and half stout or red wine
> Bouquet garni

Add to the meat, mix well, bring to the boil, and simmer on top or in the oven until the meat is tender.

PIG'S FEET OR TROTTERS

Cooking Time 2 hrs. or 40 mins. pressure cooking, plus 3–4 mins.
Quantities for 2–4.

> 4 trotters

Ask the butcher to split these in half lengthwise. Wash them well. Put in a pan.

> 2 onions   Strip of lemon rind
> Pinch of ground mace or nutmeg

Skin and slice the onion and put it and the flavourings in the pan.

> 1 pt. white stock (½ l.) or ¾ pt. in a pressure cooker (5 dl.)   Salt

Add to the pan, using salt sparingly. Bring to the boil and simmer for 2 hrs. or pressure cook 40 mins. Remove the trotters and keep them hot.

> 1½ Tbs. flour

Blend this smooth with a little cold water and stir into the stock. Stir until it boils and boil for 5 mins.

> Salt and pepper   Chopped parsley

Season the sauce to taste, pour it over the trotters, and garnish with chopped parsley. Serve as a supper dish with bread and butter or with potatoes and vegetables.

PORK BRAWN

Cooking Time 5 hrs. or 1 hr. pressure cooking.
Quantities for 4–6.

> ½ pig's head

Wash and then soak in warm water for about 15 mins. Drain and rinse. Put in a large pan with cold water to cover. (1 pt. (½ l.) pressure cooking.)

> 1 onion   12 peppercorns   2 carrots
> 2 tsp. salt   Bouquet garni

Add to the pan, bring to the boil, cover and simmer for 5 hrs. (or pressure cook 1 hr.). Cook until the meat easily leaves the bones. Remove from the pan and cut the meat into small pieces or narrow strips.

1 Tbs. chopped parsley   Grated nutmeg
Salt and pepper   Cayenne pepper

Season the meat highly and put in a basin or mould. Strain the cooking liquid and put in a basin or mould. Strain the cooking liquid and add enough to the brawn to just cover the meat. Cool quickly and store in the refrigerator. When set, unmould, and cut in slices.

CALF'S HEAD VINAIGRETTE

Cooking Time. Blanching 20 mins. Cooking 2 hrs. or 40 mins. pressure cooking.

Quantities for 6 or more.

½ calf's head

Remove the brains and wash the head thoroughly. Put the brains in a bowl of cold water to soak for an hour, changing the water several times. Remove the membrane with your fingers. Rinse the brains and tie in a piece of muslin.

Put the head in cold water and bring to the boil, boil for 20 mins., and then plunge into cold water.

½ lemon

Rub the head all over with the cut lemon to help keep it a good colour during cooking.

1 oz. flour (3 Tbs. or 25 g.)

Mix the flour to a cream with cold water and then add more water to have enough to cover the head.

2 onions   2 Tbs. vinegar
2 carrots   6 peppercorns
Bouquet garni

Peel or skin the vegetables and put in the pan with the flavourings, and the water. Bring to the boil and add the head. Cover and simmer until the meat easily leaves the bone. Add the brains tied in muslin, 30 mins. before the end of cooking.

¼ tsp. salt   4 Tbs. olive oil
Pinch of pepper   1 tsp. each of finely chopped
½ tsp. made mustard   gherkins, shallots, and parsley
2 Tbs. vinegar

Combine all these to make the vinaigrette sauce. Serve separately from the meat. Slice the meat, skin and slice the tongue, and slice the brains. Arrange on a serving dish and garnish with parsley. (If preferred, the brains can be mashed and added to the sauce.)

Variation. If you have no pan big enough for the head it can be boned and rolled before cooking.

CALF'S HEART or Love in Disguise

Cooking Time 1½ hrs. *Temperature* E.375° (190°C), G.5.
Quantities for 4.

2 hearts or enough for 4 portions

Prepare the heart by cutting off all flaps, gristle, and tubes and cut the membrane which divides the heart in two, making one cavity for stuffing. Soak several hours in cold water, drain, and dry on paper towels.

Veal forcemeat (double the recipe on page 260)

Make the stuffing and put it in the heart. Sew up the opening with a needle and coarse white cotton.

4 or 5 rashers of fat bacon *Fat for baking*

Remove rinds and wrap the heart in the rashers, tying them on or fastening with cocktail sticks. Put in a baking tin with a little fat and cook in a moderate oven for 1½ hrs.

1 oz. *vermicelli* (25 g.)

Break in small pieces and cook in boiling salted water. Drain.

1 oz. *fresh breadcrumbs* (⅓ c. or 25 g.) 1 egg yolk

Mix breadcrumbs with the cold vermicelli. When the heart is cooked, brush it with the egg yolk mixed with a little cold water, and roll it in the vermicelli.

Put back in the tin and bake until the crumbs are brown.

Bacon rolls *Baked tomatoes*

Serve the heart on a hot dish garnished with bacon rolls and tomatoes. Make gravy in the pan.

119

ROAST OX OR BULLOCK HEART

Cooking Time. Boiling for 2 hrs., or pressure cooking ½ hr. and then roasting 1 hr.

Temperature for roasting E.400° (200°C), G.6.

Quantities for 5–6.

1 heart

Hearts are usually sold prepared for cooking but if not, cut off all the gristle and cut out the membrane which divides the heart into two chambers. Use kitchen scissors for this. Soak for several hours in cold water, drain, and dry on paper towels.

4 oz. sage and onion stuffing or veal forcemeat
(home-made or packet variety) (125 g.)
Pieces of fat bacon   Dripping

Stuff the heart cavity with the forcemeat and sew up the opening with a needle and coarse white cotton. Wrap the heart in a piece of aluminium foil. Boil for 2 hrs. in water to cover or for ½ hr. in a pressure cooker with 1 pt. water. Drain and remove the foil. Place in a roasting pan with the top covered with pieces of fat bacon and add some dripping. Roast for 1 hr. basting frequently. Lift out and slice for serving. Make gravy in the roasting pan.

BEEF HEART IN WINE SAUCE

Reheat slices of roast heart in the following sauce:

½ pt. thickened gravy (¼ l.)   1 Tbs. red currant jelly
¼ pt. port, claret, or ale (1½ dl.)

Combine the ingredients and heat until the jelly melts. Add the slices of meat and bring to the boil. Serve with pieces of thin crisp toast and a green salad. The quantities of sauce are sufficient for 2–4 portions, depending on how much meat there is to use.

KIDNEY RAGOUT

Cooking Time 20 mins.   *Quantities* for 4.

6 lamb's or 4 calf's kidneys

Skin, slice and remove the hard central core of the lamb's kidney. If calf's are used, skin them and cut in slices, rejecting the central core. Sprinkle with salt and pepper.

1 oz. fat (25 g.)

Heat the fat and fry the kidneys in it for 5 mins., turning once. Remove and keep hot.

½ Tbs. finely chopped onion   1 oz. flour (3 Tbs. or 25 g.)

Add the onion to the fat and fry until brown. Add flour, mix well, and cook for a few minutes.

¾ pt. stock (5 dl.)

Stir gradually and bring to the boil.

2 oz. mushrooms (50 g.)   Salt and pepper

Wash and slice and add to the sauce. Return the kidneys and cook for a few minutes longer. Season to taste. Serve in a border of Mashed potatoes.

FRIED KIDNEYS

Fry the split kidneys as in the previous recipe or alternatively cut them in ¼ in. (6 mm.) slices and fry for 3–4 mins.

GRILLED KIDNEYS (lamb's or pig's)

Cooking Time 5–10 mins.

They may be left whole and with some of the layer of suet still covering them. Grill gently first one side and then the other until the fat has melted and beads of blood begin to appear on the surface.

Alternatively, remove the suet, skin the kidneys, and cut out the hard central core.

Grill them whole, or cut in halves almost through and opened out like a book. Grill each side until beads of blood begin to appear on the surface. Serve with grilled bacon or as part of a mixed grill.

GRILLED KIDNEYS EN BROCHETTE

Skin lamb's kidneys and remove the hard core. Slice in ¼ in. slices and thread on skewers alternately with pieces of bacon and small mushrooms. Grill until beads of blood begin to show on the surface and the bacon and mushrooms are cooked. Serve with fried potatoes and watercress.

DEVILLED KIDNEYS

Cooking Time 1 hr.   Quantities for 3–4.

6 sheep's kidneys

121

Remove fat and skin and cut out the core with a pair of kitchen scissors or sharp knife. Wash in warm water and dry in paper towels. Cut in half but not quite through and open out like a book.

1 onion 1 small carrot

Peel and chop onion, scrape or peel and chop carrot.

1 oz. fat, dripping, or oil (2 Tbs. or 25 g.)

Heat this in a small pan and fry the vegetables in it until they begin to brown.

1 oz. flour (3 Tbs. or 25 g.)

Add this to the pan and stir and cook until it browns, about 15 mins. Remove from the heat.

½ pt. stock (¼ l.)

Gradually add to the pan and stir until it boils.

Small piece of bay leaf Sprig of parsley

Add to the sauce and simmer for ½ hr. Add water if it tends to become too thick. Strain and reheat.

1 Tbs. made mustard	*1 Tbs. Worcester sauce*	
1 tsp. curry powder	*1 tsp. anchovy sauce*	

Mix the dry ingredients to a smooth paste with the sauces and add to the other sauce in the pan. Season with salt and pepper. Keep hot.

1 oz. fat, dripping, or oil (25 g.)

Fry the kidneys in this until small beads of blood begin to appear on top, turn, and cook the other side Put on a serving dish and pour the sauce over them. Serve with one of the following:

Fingers of toast, mashed potatoes, boiled rice, macaroni, spaghetti. Alternatively, use as a filling for omelets.

FRIED LIVER

Cooking Time 5–10 mins.

Quantities. Allow 4 oz. per person (125 g.).

Calf's, lamb's, sheep's, and pig's livers are all suitable. It is usually sold sliced, about ½ in. (1¼ cm.) thick but is better about half this thickness. To prepare it for cooking see *Preparation,* page 114.

Coat the slices in seasoned flour. Use butter, oil, or better still a mixture of the two. Heat just enough to coat the bottom of the pan. Fry the liver until it is brown on both sides, turning once during cooking. Some people like it still pink inside, others like it cooked through. When it reaches this stage, small beads of blood begin to ooze out to the surface. If it is cooked beyond this stage it will become hard and tough.

Remove the liver to a hot dish and swill out the pan with a little stock, boiling, while stirring with a wooden spoon, to dissolve all the sediment stuck to the pan. If necessary boil rapidly to reduce to the amount desired, season to taste, and pour over the liver.

FRIED LIVER AND BACON

Proceed as for fried liver above but cook 1–2 rashers per person before frying the liver in the same pan. If fat bacon is used some of the fat will help in frying the liver and will add flavour. Keep the bacon hot while the liver is being fried.

GRILLED LIVER

Cooking Time 5–10 mins.

Quantities. Allow 4 oz. per person (125 g.).

To prepare the liver, see *Preparation*, page 114. Use calf's, sheep's, lamb's, or pig's liver. It should be cut in about ½ in. (1½ cm.) thick slices. Brush the pieces with oil, place them in the bottom of the grill pan and cook until the liver is brown. If you want it to be still pink in the centre, cook it under a fiercer heat than if it is required well done. In the latter case, small beads of blood oozing to the surface indicate that it is done. Do not cook beyond this stage or the liver will be hard and dry.

Alternatively, the liver may be threaded on skewers and grilled. See *Kebabs*.

It can also be grilled satisfactorily without any additional fat. If bacon and other items are being cooked with the liver, put them round it and the bacon on top at the beginning of the cooking to baste the liver.

Yet another way is to brush the liver with French dressing before grilling.

123

LIVER GALANTINE

Cooking Time 1½ hrs. or 20-25 mins. pressure cooking.

Quantities for 8.

1 lb. liver (½ kg. any kind) 2 oz. fat bacon (50 g.)

Prepare the liver. See *Preparation*, page 114. Remove bacon rinds. Mince the two meats twice.

1 egg	1 tsp. salt (less if bacon salty)
2 Tbs. chopped parsley	Pinch of dried herbs
1 Tbs. chutney	1 tsp. Worcester sauce
¼ tsp. pepper	1 Tbs. stock or wine
1 oz. dried breadcrumbs or cereal crumbs or rolled oats	
(4 Tbs. or 25 g.)	

Beat the egg and mix all the ingredients with the meat, mixing until well blended and fairly moist. Press the mixture into a greased basin or other mould 1½ pt. size (1 l.). Cover with foil and steam. Leave in the dish to cool as rapidly as possible.

Turn out of the mould and cover with crumbs. Slice and serve like cold meat.

Dried breadcrumbs or cereal crumbs

LIVER KEBABS

Cooking Time 10-15 mins. after ½ hr. marinating.

Quantities for 4.

1 lb. liver (½ kg. calf's, sheep's, lamb's, or pig's in one piece)

Prepare it (see *Preparation*, page 114) then cut into pieces approximately 1½ in. cubes (4 cm.).

2 medium-sized onions	8 oz. mushrooms (250 g.)
8 medium-sized tomatoes	Fresh bay leaves

Peel and quarter the onions, wash tomatoes and cut in quarters. Wash the mushrooms and if they are large, cut them in halves. Wash the bay leaves. Take 8 long thin skewers or *brochettes* and thread the ingredients on them in the following order: bay leaf, liver, mushroom, tomato, onion; repeating these until all are used. Put in the bottom of the grill pan (not a tin one).

Oil, vinegar, salt, and pepper

Brush the ingredients with oil and sprinkle with vinegar and seasonings. Leave to marinate for ½ hr. Grill for 8–10 mins. Remove to a hot dish.

Chopped parsley   Juice of 1 lemon

Add a little water or stock to the grill pan to make gravy. Boil hard on top of the stove to reduce the gravy and dissolve the sediment. If the pan is not suitable for this, pour the stock and sediment into a small pan.

Add parsley and lemon juice and pour over the meat. Serve with

Boiled rice or a rice dish.

CALF'S LIVER VENEZIANA
Cooking Time 5–8 mins.   Quantities for 2–3.

8 oz. liver (250 g.)

Have the liver sliced very thinly and then cut the slices into 1 in. (2¼ cm.) squares.

2 medium onions   *Olive oil*

Peel the onions and slice them very finely. Brown them in a little hot oil. Add the liver and cook for two minutes, stirring all the time.

Salt and pepper   2 tsp. chopped parsley
3 leaves fresh sage or a pinch of dried

Chop the fresh sage finely and add it to the liver with the other seasonings. Cook for about half a minute and then serve at once.

Accompaniments. Sauté potatoes and/or a green salad.

LIVER WITH YOGHURT SAUCE
Cooking Time 5–10 mins.   Quantities for 4–5.

1 lb. thinly sliced liver (½ kg.)   1 Tbs. oil

Heat the oil and brown the liver quickly. Remove and keep hot. Drain off any oil left in the pan.

8–10 oz. yoghurt (250 ml.)   *Salt and pepper*
1 Tbs. chopped herbs   Pinch of paprika pepper

Add to the pan and stir and heat until the sediment in the pan is dissolved. Add a little water if necessary. Return the liver and cook to make sure it is hot and done to taste. Serve with the sauce.

Accompaniments. Boiled or mashed potatoes, followed by a mixed salad.

LIVER LOAF

Cooking Time ¾ hr. *Temperature* E.400° (200°C), G.6.
Quantities for 6.

8 oz. liver (250 g. any kind)   2 oz. onion (1 small)
½ oz. fat (15 g.)

Buy the liver in one piece and prepare it. See *Preparation*, page 114.
Peel and chop the onion. Heat the fat and brown the liver and onion
in it quickly.

2 oz. bacon (2 rashers)

Remove bacon rinds and mince liver, bacon, and onions.

4 oz. sausage meat (125 g.)	1 egg beaten,
2 oz. fresh breadcrumbs (1 c. or 150 g.)	1 Tbs. lemon juice
1 tsp. Worcester sauce	1 tsp. celery salt
Approx. ¼ pt. water (1½ dl.)	Pinch of pepper

Mix all the ingredients together using enough water to make a
smooth, soft consistency. Press the mixture into a greased loaf tin
and cover with aluminium foil. Bake. Turn out of the tin and mask
with

Tomato sauce or brown sauce

Cut in slices and serve with vegetables. Alternatively, omit the
sauce and leave the loaf to become cold. Slice and use like cold meat.

LIVER TERRINE

Cooking Time 1½–2 hrs.   *Temperature* E.350° (180°C), G.4.
Quantities for 4–6.

8 oz. liver (¼ kg. calf's or lamb's)   8 oz. lean raw pork (¼ kg.)

Prepare the liver (see *Preparation*, page 114); mince liver and pork
together and mix well.

½ tsp. salt	Pinch of ground cloves
¼ tsp. pepper	Pinch of ground mace

Add the seasonings to the meat and work in well. Divide the
mixture into two parts.

About 8 oz. wafer-thin slices of fat or streaky bacon (¼ kg.)
(both mild cure) or fat salt pork   1 bay leaf

Line a 1 pt. (½ l.) size earthenware oven dish with some of the fat
bacon or pork. Put in the two lots of liver mixture with a layer of

the bacon or pork in the middle and another on top. Put the bay leaf on top. Cover with a lid of foil twisted over the edge to seal well and put a heavy lid on top of this. Stand the dish in a tin with hot water coming half way up the sides. Cook slowly. Remove dish from water and allow to cool. Serve in the dish or turn out. Cut in slices and serve as *hors-d'œuvre* with crisp toast or use as a sandwich filling.

LIVER PILAF

Cooking Time ½ hr.   *Quantities* for 4–6.

   2 *oz. butter* (50 g.)   1 *pt. chicken or veal stock* (½ *l.*)

Put in a large pan and bring to the boil.

   8 *oz. long grain rice* (250 g.)

Add the rice, stir, and cook very slowly. This can be done in a slow oven, E.350° (180°C), G.4. Cook until the rice is quite tender, 20–30 mins., and the stock all absorbed.

Salt and pepper

Season rice to taste. Dish in a mound on a hot plate or pack into a border mould or into individual moulds. Keep hot.

   8–12 *oz. liver* (250–375 g.)   *Salt and pepper*
      1–2 *oz. butter* (25–50 g.)

Prepare the liver (see *Preparation*, page 114); cut it into small cubes. Heat the butter and fry the liver in it until lightly browned. Season with salt and pepper.

Pile this on top of the rice and surround with cooked vegetables such as

Young green peas or baked or grilled tomatoes.

LIVER RISOTTO

Cooking Time 25–30 mins.   *Quantities* for 4–6.

   4 *oz. fat* (125 g.)   6 *oz. onion* (175 g.)

Use a deep thick frying pan or a *sauté* pan. Heat the fat in it and fry the peeled and chopped onion until it begins to brown.

   12 *oz. long grain rice* (375 g.)

Add rice to the pan and cook for a further 3 mins., stirring all the time.

   2 *pt. hot stock* (1 *l.*)

127

Add a quarter of the stock and stir until it boils. Continue boiling gently, adding more of the stock, until all is used, and the rice tender, about 15–20 mins.

Remove the rinds from the bacon and chop it. Prepare the liver (see *Preparation*, page 114) and cut it into small pieces. Heat the butter and fry the bacon. Finally add the liver and cook it very quickly until brown, but not tough. Add to the cooked rice.

> 1 oz. butter (25 g.) 2 oz. bacon (2 rashers)
>
> 8 oz. liver (lamb's or calf's) (250 g.)

> *Salt and pepper* 4 oz. grated cheese (1 c. or 125 g.)
>
> 4 oz. canned or cooked sweet red peppers (125 g.)

Slice the red pepper and add it to the rice. Season to taste. Serve hot with the cheese handed separately.

STUFFED OX LIVER

Cooking Time 1 hr. *Temperature* E.375° (190°C), G.5.
Quantities for 4.

> 1 lb. ox liver (½ kg.) (thinly sliced)

Prepare the liver (see *Preparation*, page 114); arrange in shallow dish.

> 4–5 rashers of bacon *A little stock*

> *Veal forcemeat or other stuffing* (see pages 258–60)

Remove the bacon rinds, chop 1 rasher finely and mix with the stuffing. Spread this on top of the liver and cover with the remaining rashers. Add enough stock to moisten the bottom of the baking dish. Cook until the liver is tender and the bacon cooked. Serve hot.

BRAISED SWEETBREADS

Cooking Time 1–1¼ hrs. *Temperature* E.350° (180°C), G.4.
Quantities for 3–4.

> 1 lb. sweetbreads (½ kg.)

Soak them in cold water for at least an hour. Drain and put in a pan with cold water to cover and a few drops of lemon juice. Bring slowly to the boil and simmer 5 mins. for sheep's and 10 mins. for calf's. Plunge them into a bowl of cold water and remove any gristle and skin.

> *Mixed vegetables*

Prepare and chop enough vegetables to make a 1 in. (2 cm.) thick layer in the bottom of a wide shallow casserole large enough to take the sweetbreads in a single layer. Season the vegetables with salt and pepper and place the sweetbreads on top.

Stock

Add enough barely to cover the vegetables. Cover with a lid. Simmer for 45 mins. on top or in the oven. Lift out the sweetbreads and surround with the strained vegetables.

Cornflour or made roux   Chopped parsley

Blend a little cornflour with cold water and use it to thicken the stock, or stir in enough ready-prepared *roux*. Pour the sauce over the sweetbreads and vegetables and sprinkle with plenty of parsley.

CREAMED SWEETBREADS

Cooking Time 1–1¼ hrs.   *Quantities* for 3–4.

1 lb. sweetbreads (½ kg.)

Prepare and blanch the sweetbreads as in the previous recipe. Then put them in 1 pt. (½ l.) of boiling water and simmer until they are tender, about 45–60 mins. Remove from the water and keep them hot.

2 oz. butter or margarine (50 g.)   ½ pt. milk (¼ l.)
2 oz. flour (50 g.)   ½ pt. stock from the sweetbreads (¼ l.)

Melt the fat and add the flour, stirring and cooking until crumbly. Remove from the heat and gradually stir in the stock and milk. Return to the heat and stir until it boils. Boil for 5 mins.

Salt and pepper   Lemon juice   Chopped parsley

Season the sauce to taste with salt and pepper and lemon juice. Return the sweetbreads to the sauce to make hot. Serve sprinkled with chopped parsley, and

Small fingers of toast or fried bread
Fried button mushrooms.

TONGUE WITH CHEESE SAUCE

Cooking Time 20 mins.   *Quantities* for 4.

1 pt. White or Béchamel sauce (½ l.)   1 tsp. made mustard
1 Tbs. chopped chives   2 oz. grated cheese (½ c. or 50 g.)

129

OFFAL

Put the sauce in the top of a double boiler and add the chives, mustard, and cheese. Leave to get hot.

Add to the sauce and leave to become hot.

8 oz. sliced cooked or canned tongue (250 g.)

Boil the spinach (see page 213), drain thoroughly, and arrange in a layer in the bottom of a shallow baking dish. Pour the tongue and sauce over the spinach.

1½ lb. spinach (¾ kg.)

Sprinkle on top of the sauce and brown under the grill. Serve at once.

1 oz. grated cheese (¼ c. or 25 g.)

BOILED OX TONGUE

Cooking Time 2½–3 hrs.

Quantities. Allow 4 oz. per portion (125 g.). One tongue will weigh 4 lb. more or less (2 kg.).

1 ox tongue

Usually the tongue will be sold after some days in a pickling solution, but whether fresh or pickled, it needs to be soaked in cold water to cover overnight. Keep it in a cool place.

2 bay leaves	6 peppercorns
1 onion	1 piece of turnip
1 carrot	2 stalks of celery

Skin the onion, scrape or peel the carrot, peel the turnip, wash the celery. Put the tongue in a large pan, cover with cold water, bring to the boil, and simmer for 5 mins. Drain away the water, add fresh cold water to cover and then the vegetables and flavourings. Bring to the boil and simmer until tender. Remove any scum as it rises to the top. When it is cooked plunge the tongue into cold water, remove the skin and any bones and pieces of gristle at the root end. Serve in one of the following ways:

PRESSED TONGUE

Coil the tongue up tightly in a straight-sided basin or cake tin to make a tight fit. Add a little of the stock to fill the crevices. Put a flat plate or slightly smaller tin on top and a heavy weight on that. Leave until

130

cold, and store in the refrigerator. Turn out of the mould and slice horizontally.

HOT TONGUE

Slice the tongue thinly, from tip towards root, and serve it in a sauce such as tomato, parsley, *espagnole*.

Serve potatoes and vegetables with it.

GLAZED TONGUE

Put the tongue on a board or large flat dish and arrange it straight as it is when in the mouth. Leave to become cold. Brush with aspic jelly which is on the point of setting. Garnish with salad vegetables. Slice thinly as for hot tongue.

SHEEP'S TONGUE, boiled

Cooking Time 2¼ hrs.   *Quantities for 4.*

1 large onion   4 tongues
2 tsp. salt   Bouquet garni
1 pt. water (½ l.)

Peel the onion and slice it thinly. Put in a pan with the other ingredients. Boil gently for 1½ hrs., or until the tongues are tender. Remove the tongues from the stock, cool them a little, and then peel off the skin and remove any small bones at the base of the tongues.

½ oz. margarine (15 g.)   ½ oz. lard (15 g.)

Melt the fats in a pan.

1 oz. flour (3 Tbs. or 25 g.)

Stir in the flour and cook and stir until crumbly. Strain the stock and add 1 pt. (½ l.) to this *roux*, stirring until it boils.

4 small onions or shallots

Skin the onions or shallots and add to the sauce together with the tongues and simmer for 30 mins., or until the onions are tender.

Chopped parsley

Serve the tongues sprinkled with chopped parsley.

131

SHEEP'S TONGUE AND TOMATO MOULD

Cooking Time 1½–2 hrs., ¾ hr. pressure cooking. *Quantities for 4.*

4 tongues, fresh or salted

If the tongues are salted, soak them in cold water for 12 hrs.: if fresh, soak them for an hour or two.

1 small onion   1 bay leaf

Skin the onion and put it in a pan with the bay leaf, the tongues, and cold water to cover. Bring to the boil and simmer until the tongues are tender. Lift out the tongues, cool enough to handle, and then skin them. Trim the roots, removing small bones and any gristly bits. Cut the tongues into small pieces as for a brawn.

¼ pt. canned tomato juice (¼ L)   1 small onion

1 bay leaf

Simmer these together for 5 mins., strain.

1 Tbs. gelatine   ¼ pt. hot water (1½ dl.)

Stir until the gelatine dissolves. Add to the tomato mixture.

Salt and pepper   Grated nutmeg

Season to taste, add the tongue, pour into a mould, and leave to set. Unmould, slice, and serve with

Salad

TRIPE *AU GRATIN*

Cooking Time 1¼ hrs.   *Quantities for 4.*

1 lb. tripe (½ kg.)

Cut the tripe into fingers and cover with cold water. Bring to the boil and boil for 2 mins. Strain.

1 large onion   ½ lemon   1 tsp. salt

Skin the onion and put it in a pan with the tripe, salt, and cold water just to cover. Add a squeeze of lemon juice. Bring to the boil, cover, and simmer for 1 hr.

1 oz. butter (25 g.)   ½ pt. milk (1½ dl.)

1 oz. flour (3 Tbs. or 25 g.)   ¼ pt. tripe stock (1½ dl.)

Melt the butter and stir in the flour, cooking and stirring until crumbly. Remove from the heat and stir in the milk and stock.

Return to the heat and stir until it boils, cooking for a few minutes.

Salt and pepper

Season the sauce to taste and add the tripe and the onion, chopped. Pour into a hot baking dish.

½ oz. butter (15 g.)   1½ oz. breadcrumbs (½ c. or 45 g)
1½ oz. grated cheese (4 Tbs.)

Melt the butter in a small pan and add the crumbs. Stir to coat well and then add the cheese. Sprinkle on top of the tripe and under the grill.

TRIPE CASSEROLE

Cooking Time 2–3 hrs.   *Temperature* E.300° (150°C), G.3.
Quantities for 4.

1 oz. lard or oil (25 g.)
1 oz. flour (3 Tbs. or 25 g.)   ¾ pt. stock (5 dl.)

Heat the fat or oil in a casserole or stewpan, add the flour, and cook and stir until it turns yellow. Remove from the heat and stir in the stock. Return to the heat and stir until it boils.

1 onion   2 small turnips   2 carrots   2 sticks celery
½ tsp. mixed dried herbs   Pinch of cayenne pepper
1 lb. tripe cut in small pieces (½ kg.)   2 tsp. salt
¼ tsp. each of ground ginger, nutmeg, and cloves

Prepare and slice the vegetables. Add to the pan together with the flavourings and the tripe. Cover and cook gently in the oven, the longer the better.

1 tsp. chopped fresh marjoram   2 Tbs. grated cheese

Serve the tripe with these sprinkled on top.

TRIPE AND ONIONS

Cooking Time 1 hr. or 12–15 mins. pressure cooking.
Quantities for 4.

1 lb. tripe (½ kg.)   1 pt. milk (½ l.)   4 onions

Wash the tripe and cut it in small pieces. Skin and slice the onions. Put tripe and onions into a pan with the milk and simmer for 1 hr. or until tender. If the pressure cooker is used, cook the tripe and onions in ¼ pt. water (¼ l.) for 12–15 mins. Reduce the pressure with

133

cold water. Strain the tripe, keeping the milk used for cooking, or the stock.

1 oz. butter (25 g.)   1 oz. flour (3 Tbs. or 25 g.)

Melt the butter and stir in the flour. Stir and cook until crumbly. Remove from the heat and gradually stir in the milk or the stock. Bring to the boil and boil for a few minutes adding more milk if needed for thinning.

Salt and pepper   Chopped parsley
Pinch of ground mace

Season to taste and add the tripe. Reheat and serve, sprinkled with chopped parsley.

SCALLOPED TRIPE

Cooking Time 1½ hrs. or less.   Temperature E.375° (190°C), G.5.
Quantities for 4.

1 lb. tripe (½ kg.)

Simmer the tripe in cold water to cover until it is tender. Drain and cut in thin strips.

4 Tbs. oil   4 Tbs. vinegar

Mix together and soak the tripe in it for 1 hr.

1 onion   1 oz. butter (25 g.)

Skin and chop the onion finely. Heat the butter and fry the onion for a few minutes.

8 oz. mushrooms (250 g.)

Wash and slice and add to the onions. Cook gently for 10 mins.

1 oz. flour (3 Tbs. or 25 g.)   1 pt. sieved canned tomatoes (½ l.)

Stir the flour into the mushrooms and then add the tomato. Stir until it boils and thickens. Drain the tripe and put half of it in a greased baking dish, add a third of the sauce, all the mushrooms and onions, more sauce.

2 oz. breadcrumbs (1 c. or 50 g.)

Sprinkle half the crumbs on top, add the rest of the tripe and the sauce, and top with crumbs.

1 oz. butter (25 g.)

Dot the top with the butter and bake for 20 mins. in a moderate oven.

12 Poultry

CHICKEN

In modern usage the name is applied to all domestic fowls prepared for the table. This includes very small young birds of about 1 lb. (½ kg.) weight, known as 'spring chickens', 'poussins', or 'broilers'; small roasters of 2–4 lb. weight (1–2 kg.), the 2 lb. ones being suitable for frying; large roasters up to 8 lb. (4 kg.); capons of 6–8 lb. (3–4 kg.); and boilers or 'poules' of 3½–7 lb. (1½–3½ kg.).

The modern broiler and small roaster is a young bird, 9–10 weeks old, and does not have the same flavour as the older bird. It is, however, suitable for many dishes, especially those with plenty of added flavourings.

A capon is a cock bird which has been castrated when young, to make it grow large, fat and succulent. Boiling fowls include old hens and cocks.

In most shops chicken is fairly reliably labelled according to its type and the choice depends on the method of cooking to be followed.

QUANTITIES TO ALLOW

A 1 lb. (½ kg.) chicken split down the middle gives two portions.
A 2 lb. (1 kg.) chicken divides into four portions.
Larger chickens, allow ½ lb. (¼ kg.) per portion.

PREPARING CHICKEN FOR COOKING

Most chicken sold in shops today is ready prepared or else the butcher is ready to prepare it for you.

If you have to clean and prepare the chicken yourself it is not diffi-cult, only messy. If it still has the feathers on, put the chicken in a bucket, and pour a kettle of boiling water over it. This will make the feathers easier to pull out. Be careful not to tear the skin, and remove

135

the pin feathers with the aid of a pointed knife. Singe off the hairs by holding the chicken over a gas flame, lighted taper, or spill of lighted paper.

Cut off the head. Pull back the skin over the neck, and sever the neck from the body, leaving the flap of skin attached to the body. Keep the neck to cook with the other giblets for stock. Put your fingers inside the neck end and remove the crop and wind pipe and loosen the top entrails by working round inside the top of the body with your finger.

Turn the bird on its back. Lift up the skin above the vent and make a wide cut in it. Hold the bird firmly with the left hand, pressing it down on the table, and insert your right hand in the slit you have cut and work round the inside walls of the body loosening the entrails. Feel for the hard gizzard, grasp it, pull out gently and everything else except the lungs and kidneys will come out too. Then cut out the vent so that you can remove the entrails from the body. Feel along the back of the inside for the small spongy lungs and the kidneys and remove them too. Sort out the liver, gizzard, and heart and keep them. Wash the bird inside and out in cold running water and leave to drain.

Cut off the feet and add them to the giblets. Break the legs at the next joint up, to expose the tendons. Lever up the exposed tendons with a skewer and pull them out.

If the bird is to be stuffed, this is done from the neck end and then the flap of skin from the neck is folded over the opening and secured at the back. Any surplus stuffing can go in the body.

To truss, fold the wings backwards and inwards over the neck skin and tie or skewer them. Draw the thighs close to the body and cross the legs over the vent. Tie them in position.

FROZEN CHICKEN

Leave it in the wrapper until it is completely thawed which will take 6–8 hrs. at room temperature (60°F or 15°C); or thaw for 24 hrs. in the refrigerator or cold larder. Chicken joints need about 3 hrs. at room temperature or 6 hrs. in the refrigerator.

Before cooking whole chicken be sure to remove the packet of giblets from the inside and also a rubber band some suppliers use instead of string for trussing. Wipe the chicken inside and out with a clean damp cloth.

JOINTING A CHICKEN

A small chicken may simply be divided into two portions by cutting through the middle of the breast bone and back bone so that each piece has a wing and a leg. Larger ones are cut into quarters by cutting the halves through between the wing and the thigh so that there are two pieces with wing attached and two with thighs. Larger birds still, can have the legs and wings removed and the legs cut into two portions through the knee joints. The body is cut in half through the rib cage and the breast cut across in half diagonally to give two pieces. When cutting through chicken bones use a sharp cook's knife and tap it sharply with a mallet or heavy weight. The back may be cooked with the rest for flavouring, or use it for stock.

CHICKEN GIBLETS

These are the neck, feet, heart, liver, and gizzard. The small young chickens which are sold ready prepared usually have the giblets in a paper wrapping inside the carcase (feet usually not included), and they are ready for cooking.

To prepare giblets proceed as follows. The gizzard is cut through and the thick wrinkled skin peeled off and discarded. Wash the remaining bit thoroughly. The heart is cut open lengthwise and washed. Remove the gall bladder from the liver, together with any discoloured bit of the liver. Scald the feet in boiling water for a minute or two and then peel off the skin. Wash the neck. The best way of using the liver is either in the stuffing or cut in small pieces and rolled up in a half rasher of bacon to be grilled or baked with the chicken and used as a garnish. Chicken livers are also used for omelets and for other liver dishes. The gizzard and heart may be cooked and used in the stuffing, or boil them with the feet and neck and a few vegetables to make chicken stock for a sauce or soup. They should be cooked for 1–2 hrs. or 20 mins. pressure cooking.

CARVING CHICKEN

First remove the legs at the joint nearest the body. The simplest way is to hold the end of the leg in one hand and pull the leg slightly away from the body while severing the joint with a knife or poultry scissors. If desired, the leg may be cut into two portions at the knee joint.

Next, remove the wing together with a small piece of the breast. Then the wish-bone, by slicing down across the breast at the neck end.

The breast is carved in slices cutting from the bottom upwards. It is usual to give a slice of breast to each person along with a portion of leg or wing.

ROAST CHICKEN

For preparations see above.

Suitable stuffings are: Veal Forcemeat, Lemon Stuffing, or Oatmeal Stuffing. See page 258–60.

The bird can of course be cooked without stuffing. Put a knob of butter inside it and an onion or some herbs, e.g. a sprig of rosemary. Check the weight of the bird and calculate on the prepared weight.

For birds up to 3½ lb. (1½ kg) in weight allow 20 mins. per lb. (½ kg) plus 20 mins.

Temperature E.375° (180°C), G.5.

For larger birds allow 25 mins. per lb. (½ kg).

Temperature E.325–350° (160–180°C), G.3.

Brush the bird with oil or softened butter and put it on a trivet in the roasting pan. To keep the breast moist it needs the protection either of barding with bacon fat or of a piece of aluminium foil loosely over the top. Remove both of these for the last 20 mins. of cooking to allow the breast to brown. Some chopped vegetables can be put in the roasting pan to help flavour the gravy.

After dishing up the chicken, make gravy in the pan using chicken stock made from giblets.

Accompaniments. Bread sauce, grilled bacon rolls (or back them separately or beside the chicken), chipolata sausages; sliced boiled ham; gravy; stuffing. For vegetables serve mashed, roast, or fried potatoes. For other vegetables: cauliflower, carrots, peas or green beans, onions, celery; or serve watercress or a lettuce salad.

SPIT ROASTED CHICKEN

2½–3 lb. (1–1½ kg) for 1 hour.

POT ROASTED CHICKEN

Cooking Time 1–1¼ hrs.   *Temperature* E.325° (160°C), G.3.
Quantities for 4.

A 2½–3 *lb. chicken* (1–1½ kg)   1 tsp. salt
2 oz. butter (50 g.)   ¼ tsp. pepper

The chicken should be cleaned and trussed. Take a saucepan or suitable casserole to hold the chicken. Heat the butter in it and fry the chicken until it is brown on all sides. Sprinkle with salt and pepper, cover, and bake slowly until the chicken is tender. Have the chicken lying on its side and turn it once or twice during cooking. Carve the chicken, arrange it on the serving dish, and pour the juices over it.

Watercress

Garnish with this.

FRIED CHICKEN—Shallow frying
Cooking Time 20–25 mins.   *Quantities for 4.*

> 4 *portions of frying chicken*   2 *tsp. salt.*
> 1 *oz. flour* (3 *Tbs. or* 25 *g.*)   ¼ *tsp. pepper*
>
> *Oil or cooking fat*

Mix the flour and seasonings and put in a paper bag. Shake the pieces of chicken in this until they are well coated with flour, using more if needed.

Use a frying pan large enough to let the pieces of chicken lie flat. Heat enough oil or fat in it to come to a depth of about ¼ in. (6 mm.). Fry the chicken, turning until brown all over. Then reduce the heat and continue cooking for another 15–20 mins. Drain well.

Raw quartered tomatoes   Watercress or lettuce

Serve the chicken garnished with tomato and watercress, or lettuce.

GRILLED CHICKEN

Pieces of broiler chicken or *poussin* are used. Half a chicken makes one portion though quarters of larger ones may be used. Season the pieces with salt and pepper and brush with melted butter or oil. Grill under a medium heat for about 20 mins., turning frequently and basting with more butter or oil. Serve with salad or vegetables. See also *Barbecue Chicken.*

BARBECUE CHICKEN
Cooking Time 25–30 mins.   *Quantities for 4.*

> 4 *portions of young chicken*

Wash the chicken and dry well. Place on the grill, skin side down. Place on a moderate heat, brushing occasionally with the rest of the liquid. Turn once during cooking.

Mix together and brush the chicken with it. Grill under a moderate heat, brushing occasionally with the rest of the liquid. Turn once during cooking.

Garnish with tomato quarters and bunches of watercress. Serve at once.

> 1 tsp. dry mustard   1½ oz. melted butter or
> 2 tsp. Worcester sauce   margarine (3 Tbs. or 45 g.)
>   2 Tbs. vinegar

Tomatoes and watercress to garnish

BOILED CHICKEN OR FOWL

Usually reserved for old birds which are too tough for other methods of cooking.

> 1 boiling fowl   A piece of lemon
>   Bacon fat or pork fat (optional)
>
> 1 onion   A bouquet garni
>   1 carrot

The fowl should be cleaned and trussed. Rub it over with a piece of cut lemon to help keep the flesh white. To help flavour the flesh and prevent drying out the chicken may be barded with fat. Place it in a pan just large enough to hold it comfortably.

Peel the vegetables and cut them into pieces. Add them to the pan together with enough water to cover the bird. Add the *bouquet garni* and bring the water to the boil. Immediately reduce the heat to simmering and cook gently until the thigh of the bird feels tender when pierced with a fork. This will take anything from 1½–2 hrs. or longer depending on the size and age of the bird; or ½–¾ hr. in a pressure cooker with ½ pt. (¼ l.) water.

Lift the cooked bird out of the liquid, remove the barding fat, and serve the bird with its breast masked with a sauce.

White or *Béchamel* sauce made with some of the cooking liquid or an egg sauce or parsley sauce.

Mushrooms or cooked vegetables are also used for garnishing if desired. Boiled rice is often served with boiled chicken or serve boiled macaroni or noodles, the last two being dressed with butter after they have been cooked.

CHICKEN CASSEROLE

Cooking Time 45 mins. for a broiler, 2½–3 hrs. for a boiling fowl.
Temperature E.350° (180°C), G.4 for the broiler; E.300–325° (150–160°C), G.1–2 for the boiling fowl.
Quantities for 4.

4 chicken joints	2 tsp. salt
1 oz. flour (3 Tbs.)	¼ tsp. pepper

Mix the flour and seasoning and put it in a paper bag with the chicken. Shake together until the chicken is well coated.

2 oz. oil or fat (4 Tbs. or 50 g.)

Heat the fat or oil and fry the chicken until brown all over. Then put the chicken in a casserole.

12 small onions   2 sticks celery, chopped
2–3 carrots, sliced   2 Tbs. tomato paste in ½ pt. water (¼ l.)

Add these to the casserole, cover, and cook gently until the chicken is tender.

8 oz. rice (250 g.)   1 tsp. salt
1 pt. water (½ l.)

About 20 mins. before the chicken is to be served, bring the rice, salt, and water to the boil in a casserole, transfer to the oven, and cook until all the water is absorbed and the rice is tender. Fluff it up lightly with a fork and serve with the chicken. If no suitable casserole is available for the rice, cook it on top of the stove over a very gentle heat.

BRAISED CHICKEN

Cooking Time 1 hr.   *Temperature* E.325° (160°C), G.3.
Quantities for 4–6.

1 chicken (3 lb. or 1½ kg.)   2 oz. butter (50 g.)
Salt and pepper

Season the chicken inside and out with salt and pepper. Heat the butter in a fireproof casserole large enough to take the chicken. If none is available do this part of the cooking in a saucepan. Cook the chicken in the hot butter, turning it until it is brown all over.

4 oz. chopped bacon (125 g.)   8 small onions or 2 medium
1 lb. other vegetables (½ kg.) (potatoes, celery, carrots, peas)

141

Peel the onions and, if medium ones are used, cut them in small pieces. Prepare the other vegetables chosen and cut them in small pieces. Add all these to the pan, cover, and cook gently until the chicken is tender. This may be done in the saucepan on top of the stove or in a casserole in the oven. Serve the chicken with the vegetables as a garnish and the liquid as a sauce.

CREAMED CHICKEN

Quantities for 4–6.

> 1 lb. *diced cooked chicken (2 c. or ½ kg.)*
> 1 pt. *Béchamel sauce (½ l.), see page 245*
> 4 oz. *chopped mushrooms fried in butter (125 g.)*
> *Celery salt and pepper to taste*

Heat these together to boiling point and make sure the mixture is well seasoned. Use it as a filling for potato borders or nests or for a flan case or a patty filling. If for the latter, about half the recipe will be enough for 4.

SPANISH CHICKEN

Cooking Time about 1 hr.   *Quantities for 4.*

> 4 *portions of chicken*   4 *Tbs. olive oil*
> *Salt and pepper*   1 *clove crushed garlic*

Season the chicken with salt and pepper. Heat the oil and garlic in a shallow saucepan or deep *sauté* pan. When it is brown, remove the garlic. Put in the chicken and fry it, turning it often.

> 8 oz. *lean gammon cut in strips (250 g.)*
> 4 *fresh or canned red peppers, chopped*
> 1 *medium onion, chopped finely*

When the chicken begins to brown add these ingredients, cover the pan, and simmer until the chicken is tender. Serve plain with rice or *pasta* or with a vegetable.

STEAMED CHICKEN

This is a better way than boiling, unless you happen to want a lot of stock for any purpose. Either a whole chicken or pieces may be steamed.

Put it in the top of a steamer with boiling water below and keep this boiling vigorously during cooking. Potatoes or noodles may be cooked in the lower pan and use some of the liquid to make a sauce to serve with the chicken. A suitable sauce is *Béchamel*, Egg, or Lemon.

Cooking Time ½ hr. for pieces of chicken and 1–3 hrs. for a whole bird depending on size and age.

To see if it is tender, pierce the thickest part of the thigh with a sharp fork or skewer.

CHICKEN *FRICASSÉE*
Cooking Time about 20 mins.   *Quantities for 4.*

¾ oz. butter or margarine (1½ Tbs.)
2¼ Tbs. flour   ½ pt. stock or milk (¼ l.)
Pinch of ground nutmeg   Salt and pepper to taste

Melt the fat in a small saucepan and add the flour, stirring and cooking until it looks crumbly. Remove from the heat and stir in the liquid. Return to the heat and stir until it boils. Cook for 5 mins. Season.

¾ lb. cooked chicken, diced (375 g.)

Add the chicken to the sauce and bring to the boil.

2 egg yolks

Add these to the mixture just before serving and heat for a minute or two without allowing the sauce to boil.

Juice of ½ lemon 1 Tbs. chopped parsley

Add to the sauce.

3 or 4 rolls of grilled or fried bacon

Use these to garnish the *fricassée*. Serve with mashed potatoes and spinach, peas, or carrots.

CHICKEN PAPRIKA
Cooking Time 1 hr.   *Quantities for 4.*

1 oz. oil or lard (2 Tbs. or 25 g.) 1 large onion, sliced

Heat the fat in a saucepan or suitable casserole. Fry the onion in it for a few minutes.

4 portions of chicken 1 tsp. paprika pepper

143

Add these to the pan and continue to fry for a few minutes.

1 tsp. salt

2 tomatoes or 2 tsp. tomato paste in a little water

Add to the chicken, cover, and cook very slowly for 1–2 hrs. or until the chicken is tender. Add extra water only if necessary to prevent burning.

2 Tbs. sour cream or yoghurt 1 Tbs. chopped parsley

Just before serving, stir in the cream or yoghurt. Serve sprinkled with chopped parsley. If desired this may be cooked in a casserole in the oven, E.300° (150°C), G.1–2.

BAKED CHICKEN WITH PINEAPPLE

Cooking Time 1 hr.   *Temperature* E.325° (160°C), G.3.
Quantities for 4.

4 portions of young chicken

¼ tsp. dried rosemary   ¼ tsp. pepper

1 tsp. salt

Wash the chicken and dry it thoroughly on paper towels or a clean cloth.

Mix these together and rub them into the chicken. Arrange the chicken skin side up in a shallow baking dish.

6 shallots or small onions

Slice these finely and strew them round the chicken.

¼ pt. canned pineapple juice, unsweetened (1¼ dl.)
¼ tsp. ground ginger ¼ tsp. paprika pepper

Combine these and pour the mixture over the chicken. Bake uncovered for an hour or until the chicken is tender.

CHICKEN À LA MARENGO

Cooking Time 1–2 hrs.   *Quantities for* 4.

4 portions of chicken 2 Tbs. olive oil

Heat the oil and fry the chicken in it quickly until brown all over. Remove the chicken.

1 Tbs. flour 4 Tbs. white wine
4 Tbs. stock

Add the flour to the oil and mix and cook for a few minutes.

Remove from the heat and add the stock, stirring until smooth. Then add the wine.

¼ clove garlic, chopped   ¼ tsp. pepper
Bouquet garni   1 Tbs. tomato paste
1 tsp. salt   4 oz. mushrooms, sliced (125 g.)

Add these to the sauce, return the chicken, cover, and simmer until the chicken is tender (¾–1½ hrs.). Remove the bouquet and serve the chicken with boiled potatoes and a vegetable such as spinach or green beans or serve with a lettuce salad.

CURRIED CHICKEN

Cooking Time 2 hrs.   *Quantities for 4.*

4 portions of chicken   1 oz. flour (3 Tbs. or 25 g.)
                        2 tsp. salt

Coat the chicken with the flour and salt.

2 medium-sized onions   1 tomato
2 small apples   Small bit of garlic

Skin and chop the onion and garlic, peel and chop the apple, chop the tomato.

1½ oz. dripping or oil (3 Tbs. or 45 g.)

Heat the fat and fry the chicken until it is brown, remove, and fry the vegetables.

2 Tbs. curry powder, more or less according to taste

Add the curry powder and any flour that was left from the coating. Mix and cook for a few mins.

½ pt. stock (¼ l.)   1 Tbs. desiccated coconut
Rind and juice of ½ lemon   2 Tbs. raisins or sultanas
                               1 tsp. brown sugar

Add the stock to the pan and stir and mix until smooth and boiling. Add the other ingredients and return the chicken. Cover and simmer on top or in the oven.
    Serve with   *Boiled rice and chutney.*

DUCK AND DUCKLING

The most famous kind of domestic duck is the variety known as Aylesbury, from the town where they were first reared in large numbers. They are larger than other varieties and have very white feathers. Wild ducks are usually smaller than domestic ones and they sometimes have a distinctive salty flavour. The Mallard variety is considered the best wild duck.

For most people duck is not an everyday article of diet and when it is served they prefer to roast it and eat it hot, or cold with salad. It can, however, be prepared in a wide variety of ways, using the same basic methods as with other meat and poultry. It can be braised, stewed, or casseroled (often with the bird left whole and trussed), curried, made into a terrine; either the whole duck or the carcase made into a soup; also suitable for pot roasting.

CHOOSING DUCK

Domestic ducks come fresh or deep-frozen, the latter generally being of a consistently good roasting quality. A fresh duck should have the head and feet on so that the purchaser can see its age. A duck of more than one year is too old for roasting. A young duck will have bright yellow feet and bill.

QUANTITIES TO ALLOW

The tendency today is for smaller ducks and more ducklings to be marketed and these will usually only provide 4–5 good portions (3–3½ lb. or 1½ kg. birds). For larger ones, reckon at least ¾ lb. (250 g.) trussed weight per person.

PREPARATION OF DUCKS. See *Chicken*, page 135.

CARVING DUCK AND DUCKLING. See *Chicken*, page 137.

ROAST DUCK OR DUCKLING

Cooking Time and Temperatures. Small duck or duckling: 1 hr. at E.350–375° (180–190°C), G.5–6; or 1¼–1½ hrs. at E.325° (160°C), G.3; or temperature on meat thermometer 185° (85°C). Large duck 15 mins. per lb. (½ kg.) at the higher temperature, 25 mins. per lb. at the lower temperature.

The bird may be stuffed with sage and onion stuffing, lemon butter stuffing, apple and prune stuffing, with a peeled onion and a sprig of sage, or with an unpeeled orange. Rub a little salt into the skin and place the bird in a baking pan without fat. Because of the fat in the bird neither the addition of fat nor basting is necessary. When the bird is done, lift out, and make gravy in the pan as with any roast meat. See page 246. Orange juice and/or wine are frequently added to the gravy.

Other Accompaniments. Duck with roast potatoes and green peas is a traditional dish, with or without apple sauce. Instead of apple sauce serve orange salad or a tart jelly. Serve boiled potatoes or other green vegetables as alternatives to the roast potatoes and peas.

ROASTING FROZEN DUCK

Cooking Time 30 mins. per lb. ($\frac{1}{2}$ kg.).
Temperature E.325° (160°C), G.3.

Thaw the duck and remove the parcel of giblets. Wipe the inside and rub a little salt into the skin. Put in a baking tin with 2 Tbs. water. There is no need to baste during cooking.

Thawing time: 24–36 hrs. in the refrigerator or cold larder; 6–8 hrs. at room temperature.

SPIT ROASTED DUCK

Small duck 40 mins. Large 25–30 mins. per lb. ($\frac{1}{2}$ kg.).

ROASTING WILD DUCK

Stuff with sliced apples and roast as for domestic duck. Serve with bread sauce and gravy, or roast unstuffed and serve with orange salad, watercress, and gravy. Serve roast potatoes or game chips.

GOOSE

Several varieties of domestic geese are used, some being small (about 6 lb. (3 kg.)) while others average about 10 lb. and can be as big as 20–24 lb. (9–11 kg.). In England the goose has always been a bird for special occasions, chiefly Michaelmas and Christmas, and it is usually stuffed and roasted. Stuffings used are Sage and Onion, or Apple and Prune, while for sauces use Apple or Gooseberry or Bread Sauce. They are cleaned and prepared in the same way as chicken. See *Chicken*, page 135.

ROAST GOOSE

Cooking Time see below. *Temperature* E.325° (160°C), G.3.
Quantities. Allow about $\frac{3}{4}$ lb. trussed weight per person (375 g.).

147

Stuff the bird and fasten up the openings securely. Put it in the baking pan and put a piece of foil lightly over the top, not pressed down. Bake for the required time, removing the foil for the last ½ hr. if the bird is not brown enough. Serve with brown gravy in addition to any other of the sauces.

Cooking Times for Geese

6 lb. bird (3 kg.)	1 hr. 40 mins.
12 lb. bird (5 kg.)	2 hrs. 20 mins.
18 lb. bird (8 kg.)	3 hrs. 10 mins.
24 lb. bird (11 kg.)	4 hrs.

COLD ROAST GOOSE

Cut in slices and serve with watercress salad.

FROZEN GOOSE

Thaw small ones as for duck: large ones as for turkey.

TURKEY

These are the largest of the domestic birds cultivated in Britain. They are found wild in parts of America but are said to have come originally from Turkey. They used to be eaten chiefly at Christmas time but more and smaller ones are now produced and available all the year round, often from the deep-freeze. A small turkey weighs 6–8 lb. (3–4 kg.) and a large one can be 20–25 lb. (9–11 kg.) and occasionally even bigger but these will not go into any but a very large oven. They are usually sold plucked and may be drawn as well, 'oven ready'. For most people, they are still only used on special occasions and are preferred roasted, usually stuffed. Left-over turkey is delicious cold with salad or as sandwich fillings, or cook it in one of the following ways.

CREAMED TURKEY. See *Creamed Chicken*, page 142.

DEVILLED TURKEY

Cooking Time about 10 mins. after 1 hr. or more standing. *Quantities* for 4.

The meat from 2 legs of turkey (cooked)

Divide the turkey into four pieces for serving, removing all the skin. Score the flesh deeply with a small sharp knife.

1 oz. butter (25 g.) *Pinch of cayenne pepper*
¼ *tsp. pepper* *Pinch of ground ginger*
¼ *tsp. curry powder*

Soften the butter slightly and work in the flavourings. Spread on to the turkey working it into the cuts. Leave to stand in a cold place for at least 1 hr. Grill until brown and crisp on the outside. Serve with

Cranberry sauce.

FRICASSÉE OF TURKEY. See *Chicken Fricassée*, page 143.

FROZEN TURKEY

Allow it to thaw completely and then roast by any of the methods below.

It is advisable to thaw them in the refrigerator or cold larder allowing 2 days for a small turkey and 3–4 days for a large one.

ROAST STUFFED TURKEY

Cooking Times and Temperatures. Cooking times are calculated either on the undrawn weight or on the drawn weight before stuffing. In fact, when a bird is stuffed it weighs approximately the same as it did before drawing and cleaning. Cooking times also vary with the temperature used and whether the bird is wrapped in foil or not. It is always wiser to allow plenty of time for the cooking. It does not matter if the bird is ready a bit too soon. It will keep warm without harm, and being early avoids any last-minute scramble in dishing up and making the gravy. To test if the bird is done, take the end of the leg in a paper towel and move it up and down. It should move easily at the joint. A meat thermometer can be used, inserted in the thick part of the inside of the thigh, where it should read 195° (90°C), or if inserted into the middle of the body stuffing it should read 180–185° (85°C).

Quantities. Undrawn weight allow approximately 1½ lb. (¾ kg.) per person; drawn weight allow approximately ¾ lb. per person (375 g.).

Preparation. See *Chicken Preparation*, page 135 for drawing and cleaning. Stuff the turkey just before roasting, allowing about ¼ lb.

(125 g.) stuffing per lb. of turkey. If the ingredients for the stuffing are prepared in advance, store any perishable items such as the giblets and sausage meat in the refrigerator and combine them just before stuffing the bird. Rinse the bird and pat it dry with paper towels. Use chestnut stuffing. See *Stuffings*, page 257. Stuff it first from the crop end to make a good plump shape and then cover the opening with the flap of skin and fasten the skin to the back with a small skewer. Spoon the stuffing into the body but do not pack tightly. Fasten up the opening with skewers and string and tie the legs to the tail to keep them close to the body. Brush the bird with oil or melted butter.

Roasting Method No. 1. *Temperature* E.325° (160°C), G.3.
Place the turkey in the roasting pan, preferably on a rack. Put a cap of foil over the breast but do not let it come down the side and do not press close to the breast as this interferes with heat transfer to the meat. At this low temperature it is pointless to wrap the whole bird in foil and would make it take much longer to cook. It will not become dry and there will be no splashing on to the oven walls as there is with higher temperatures. When the bird has cooked for about two-thirds of the required time, cut the string holding the legs together to allow the heat to penetrate to the inside of the thigh which is the part that takes longest to cook. If necessary, remove the foil for the last ½ hr. to allow the breast to brown. No basting is needed. Lift the bird on to the serving dish and put back in the oven to keep warm. Use the drippings to make gravy.

Times

lb.	*When weighed undrawn or after stuffing* *hrs.*	*When weighed drawn and before stuffing* *hrs.*
6–8 (3–4 kg.)	2½–3	3¼–3¾
8–10 (4–5 kg.)	3–3½	3¾–4¼
10–14 (5–6 kg.)	3½–4	4¼–4¾
14–18 (6–8 kg.)	4–4½	4¾–5¼
18–20 (8–9 kg.)	4½–5½	5¼–6¼
20–24 (9–11 kg.)	5½–6	6¼–7

Roasting Method No. 2 (foil wrapped).
Temperature E.450° (230°C), G.8.
This higher temperature reduces the cooking time especially for the

larger bird, and the foil wrapping keeps it from drying out and protects the oven from fat spashes. Use wide foil and place the stuffed turkey breast upwards in the centre of a piece of foil large enough to wrap it generously. If there are any sharp bone ends or skewers, wrap these first in a little foil. Bring one side of the foil up to the top and then the other to overlap for 2–3 in. (5–8 cm.). Make it fold neatly at crop and leg ends and bring the foil upwards at the ends high enough to prevent any juices from running out. Place in the roasting pan without a rack. About 30 mins. before the end of the estimated time, undo the wrapping, brush breast with oil, and let the breast brown. Use the juices in the foil for the gravy, adding stock from the giblets and thickening with a brown *roux*.

Times

lb.	*When weighed undrawn or after stuffing* *hrs.*	*When weighed drawn and before stuffing* *hrs.*
6–8 (3–4 kg.)	2–2¼	2½–3
8–10 (4–5 kg.)	2¼–2¾	3–3½
10–14 (5–6 kg.)	2¾–3	3½–3¾
14–18 (6–8 kg.)	3–3¼	3¾–4
18–20 (8–9 kg.)	3¼–3½	4–4¼
20–24 (9–11 kg.)	3½–3¾	4¼–4½

Roasting Method No. 3.

Temperature E.200–250° (95–120°C), G.½.

This is a convenient method for very large birds if you want to leave them unattended all day to be served at night. Prepare as for *Method* 1 but allow 2 hrs. or more longer than when cooking at 325° (160°C).

Spit Roasting—only suitable for small birds. Allow 20 mins. per lb. (½ kg.) stuffed weight.

Accompaniments. Potatoes, boiled, roast, or fried. Other vegetables: onion, Brussels sprouts, peas, or pumpkin. Garnishes: small sausages and grilled or fried bacon rolls. Sauces: brown gravy, cranberry sauce, bread sauce.

13 Game

Are wild animals and birds which are hunted for sport and which are covered by the Game Laws. This means the time of year during which they may be hunted is controlled and there is a 'closed season' during which it is illegal to hunt them. It is customary, however, to include under the heading of game, animals such as the rabbit, which is not included in the Game Laws.

In Britain the chief game birds are pheasant, grouse, partridge, pigeon, snipe, teal, wild duck, and the chief game animals, rabbit, hare, and deer (venison).

BLACKCOCK or Black Grouse—Female, Grey Hen

A game bird found in northern England, Scotland, and northern Europe. The male is a rich bluish-black with a lyre-shaped tail, while the female is only half the size and a brownish-grey colour. They are in season from 20th August to the 10th December, are usually well hung and the flesh is very delicate. They are cleaned and trussed like a chicken, and roasted in a moderate oven for $\frac{1}{2}$–$\frac{3}{4}$ hr. depending on the size ($3\frac{1}{2}$ lb. or ($1\frac{1}{2}$ kg) average). They tend to be dry birds, so should be basted with melted butter or else barded with fat bacon. Are usually served on buttered toast accompanied by gravy, bread sauce, and fried breadcrumbs.

Young ones may be split, skewered out flat and grilled for 25–30 mins., turning occasionally and brushing with melted butter. Serve with a brown sauce.

GROUSE

A game bird in season from 12th August to 10th December, after which it is too old for palatable roasting. It is a small bird weighing about $1\frac{1}{4}$ lb. (600 g.) and is sufficient for about 3 portions. It needs to be hung for 3–4 days but some people like it left until it is 'high'. It is plucked and trussed like chicken, then usually roasted, unstuffed

152

except for a piece of butter and some lemon juice. It may be roasted in a hot oven E.425° (220°C), G.6–7 for about 30 mins. or more slowly at E.325° (160°C), G.3 for 40–50 mins. In a hot oven, it may be cooked in a foil wrapping which is removed in time to allow the bird to brown.

Accompaniments are fried or grilled bacon or bacon rolls, game chips, watercress, and gravy made from the drippings in the pan. The liver is usually cooked separately, pounded to a paste, and spread on a piece of toast on which the bird is served.

Alternative method. Cover the breast of the bird with a piece of fat bacon, put the bird on a piece of toast and baste frequently during cooking. A few minutes before the end of cooking, remove the bacon, dredge the breast with flour, return to the oven to brown. Serve on the toast with giblet gravy, bread sauce, and fried breadcrumbs. Grouse are also good served cold.

GUINEA-FOWL

Available from January to June.

An African bird belonging to the same family as the pheasant. It has been naturalised and domesticated in many countries. Both the flesh and the eggs are eaten. It is cooked and served in the same way as chicken.

PARTRIDGE

In season from 1st September to 1st February.

A small game bird, one being usually only enough for 2 portions. Usually roasted with the breast covered with a piece of fat bacon or pork tied securely in place. They take about 30 mins. in a hot oven. Remove the piece of fat for the last 5 mins. to allow the breast to brown. Usually served with bread sauce.

PHEASANT

The common pheasant or *P. colchicus*, is the one usually eaten. The birds are bred for game purposes, the shooting season being from October to February.

The hen pheasant is considered better and is distinguished by a shorter tail and duller plumage than the male. Pheasants are hung for varying lengths of time before cooking to develop a good flavour.

153

Some people like them to be almost decomposing; not very pleasant for the cook. During the season pheasants are sold by some butchers and poulterers but they are always expensive for their size. One bird will serve 2–4 people depending on its size. They are very often sold in pairs (a brace) which serves 5–6 people.

Pheasant is cleaned and prepared like other poultry and can be cooked in similar ways. It is a luxury dish for most people and is preferred roasted or made into a game pie.

ROAST PHEASANT

Cooking Time. 40 mins.–1½ hrs., depending on oven temperature. See *Roasting*, page 13.

If the bird is stuffed it is necessary to allow a little longer than when not stuffed. A Walnut Stuffing is very good with it. See page 260.

The breast should be covered with a piece of fat pork or mild bacon, which is removed for the last 10 mins. to allow the skin to brown. The giblets should be roasted round the bird to provide a good gravy. Serve with bread sauce and brown gravy, and garnish with watercress.

PIGEONS

Two kinds are used, domestic pigeons and wood pigeons, the latter being the larger birds. Pigeons are sometimes available at butchers' and poulterers' shops. If the birds are young they can be roasted like a small chicken, but if older are best stewed, *e.g.* see *Jugged Hare*, using 2–3 pigeons in place of the hare.

PLOVER

Allow 1 bird per portion

A game bird which lives in marshes near the sea. Usually roasted as other game birds. In season from 1st September to 31st January.

QUAIL or *Coturnix*

Allow 1–2 birds per portion.

A small migratory game bird found in many parts of the world. It is usually roasted, after first being wrapped in vine leaves. Available in the summer.

SNIPE or *Gallinago*

Allow 1 bird per portion.

Migratory birds, similar to woodcock but much smaller. They live in marshes and have a long straight bill with which they dig for food. Snipe is usually roasted in a hot oven and served on toast with either a thin gravy or with melted butter and lemon. Some insist on having it roasted undrawn and under-done.

Cooking Time. 15–20 mins. (latter for well-done) E.450° (230°C), G.8. In season from 12th August to 31st January.

SWAN

Not often eaten today, but it used to be a popular food, usually roasted. It is said to be rather oily and strong in flavour.

TEAL

A wild water-fowl found in many parts of the world and used for food in the winter months. They are usually roasted. See *Duck*. Lemon juice is usually added to the gravy. They are also split open and grilled if they are young. Allow 1 per portion.

In season from 1st September to 31st January.

WIDGEON or *Mareca penelope*

A species of wild duck which come to Britain in the winter. In season from 1st September to 31st January. Cook as wild duck. See *Duck*. Roasting time in a hot oven: 15 mins. underdone; 20–25 mins. well done. A bird serves two.

WOODCOCK or *Scolopax rusticula*

A favourite game bird in Britain and a migratory one. It is small, giving only 1–2 portions per bird. Usually roasted for about 20–25 mins. in a hot oven and served on a piece of fried bread with any of the accompaniments served with poultry. In season from 1st October to 31st January.

HARE

Usually classed as game because it is hunted for food. Young hares are called 'leverets', males are 'bucks', and females 'does'. Leverets and youngish does are usually tender but old hares are very tough. They belong to the rodent family, are shy, run very swiftly, and make their nests above ground and not in burrows like the rabbit. They breed several times a year.

A hare needs to be well hung before cooking, up to a week for an old one and 3–4 days for a young one. Young ones are roasted, stewed or jugged. Old ones are best made into soup or stewed for a very long time.

A young hare has soft ears that are easily torn, the claws are not easily seen below the fur but are very sharp, the paws slender, and the coat smooth.

In season from September to February.

PREPARATION OF HARES FOR COOKING

The butcher will usually do this for you, but it is useful to know how to do it for yourself.

Cut off the legs at the first joint. Slit the skin all along the belly and loosen it from the body. Pull the skin off the hind legs and then pull it towards the head and off the front legs.

Slit the belly and draw out the entrails, keeping the liver and heart to use for stock.

Wash the hare thoroughly and cut off the head, remove eyes, split the head in half, and use it for stock.

If the hare is to be stuffed the legs are tied close to the body. If it is to be jointed, cut off the hind legs close to the body, and cut the body into 3 or 4 pieces cutting through the backbone. The piece with the fore legs should be cut in half lengthwise.

ROAST HARE

Cooking Time 1½–2 hrs.   *Temperature* E.325° (160°C), G.3.
Quantities for 6–8.

1 young hare   Rashers of bacon   Light ale or cider
Veal forcemeat or sage and onion stuffing. See above.

Prepare the hare. See above. Wash and dry the inside with paper towels. Line the cavity with slices of fat bacon and put in the stuffing. Sew up the opening with needle and coarse white cotton. Put in the roasting pan with a little beer or cider and cook gently, basting from time to time. Serve the liquid in place of gravy, thickening with cornflour or potato flour if desired. Serve with

Red currant jelly, boiled carrots, boiled or roast onions and any green vegetable.

JUGGED HARE

Cooking Time 3–4 hrs. *Temperature* E.300 (150°C), G.2.
Quantities for 6–8.

1 hare

Skin the hare (see *Preparation*), and cut it into joints.

1 oz. dripping or oil (25 g. or 2 Tbs.)

Heat the fat or oil and fry the pieces of meat in it until they are brown all over. Put them in a casserole, or, if the frying has been done in the casserole, lift the pieces out and return later.

2 onions, sliced	3 whole allspice
Bouquet garni	½ tsp. pepper
6 cloves	2 tsp. salt
1 tsp. grated lemon rind	

Prepare the flavourings and put them with the hare.

1 oz. butter or margarine (25 g.)
1 oz. flour (3 Tbs. or 25 g.)
¼ pt. vinegar (1½ dl.)
½ pt. red wine, cider, or beer (¼ l.)

Melt the butter or margarine in the pan in which the frying was done, add the flour and stir and cook for a few mintues. Add the liquid gradually and stir until it boils. Pour this over the hare or return hare and seasonings to the sauce. Cover and cook very slowly for 3–4 hrs. or until tender.

Veal forcemeat balls. See Stuffings, page 260

Shape the forcemeat into small balls and fry them until they are well browned. Serve with the hare. Also serve with it

Red currant jelly, a green vegetable, boiled potatoes.

RABBIT

Before myxamatosis destroyed a large part of the population of wild rabbits, these were a common food in both town and country. Today much of the rabbit sold is from tame animals and has a softer whiter flesh than the wild ones. It is frequently sold cut up into portions, and much of it is imported. For those who dislike the fairly strong flavour of rabbit, soaking it for ½ hr. in salted water and then blanching for 1 min. in boiling water is a help in removing some of the flavour. Then cook as directed in the recipe. Directions for skinning

157

and preparing rabbits are the same as for hares. See *Hares* (*Preparation of*, page 156).

BOILED RABBIT

This method of preparation is chiefly used as a preliminary to other cooking, e.g. creamed rabbit or when it is to be used cold in salads or moulds.

Cooking Time 40–60 mins. or 20–25 mins. pressure cooking.
Quantities 1 rabbit serves 4–5.

1 rabbit   1 onion   6 cloves   6 peppercorns   1 carrot

A small piece of salt pork or bacon trimmings

Skin the onion and stick the cloves in it. Scrape the carrot. Use a pan just large enough to hold the rabbit, and just enough water to cover ($\frac{1}{2}$ pt. or $\frac{1}{4}$ l. pressure cooking). Bring the water to the boil and add rabbit and flavourings. Cover and simmer until the meat is tender. Use the cooking liquid for sauces and soups.

RABBIT MOULD OR BRAWN

Cooking Time 40–60 mins. or $\frac{1}{4}$ hr. pressure cooking.
Quantities for 4–6.

1 rabbit	*A bouquet garni*
A few bacon trimmings	1 onion
1 carrot	2 tsp. salt
1 small turnip	Pinch pepper

1 Tbs. gelatine

Prepare the rabbit and vegetables and put all in a pan with water just to cover ($\frac{1}{2}$ pt. or $\frac{1}{4}$ l. pressure cooker). Bring to the boil and simmer until the meat is tender (or pressure cook). Strain the liquid.

Dissolve this in $\frac{1}{2}$ pt. or $\frac{1}{4}$ l. of the hot stock and cool until it is just beginning to set. Remove the rabbit from the bones and cut the meat in small cubes. Add it to the jelly and pour into a mould. Unmould, slice, and serve with salad.

CREAMED RABBIT

Cooking Time 20 mins.   *Quantities* for 4–6.

1 medium-sized onion   2 rashers bacon

3 stalks celery   1 oz. fat (25 g.)

Skin and chop the onion. Wash and chop the celery. Remove the rinds and chop the bacon. Heat the fat and fry these in it for a few minutes without browning.

1 oz. flour (3 Tbs. or 25 g.)   ¾ pt. rabbit stock (4 dl.)

Add the flour to the vegetables and mix well, cook for a minute or two. Add the stock and stir until it boils. Boil for at least 10 mins.

1 boiled rabbit

Remove the meat from the bones and cut it into cubes.

Salt and pepper   1 Tbs. lemon juice

Season the sauce well and add the lemon juice and the meat and heat for 10 mins.

2 Tbs. chopped parsley

Serve sprinkled with chopped parsley. This is suitable for serving in a border of potatoes or as a filling for patties or *vol-au-vent*.

RABBIT PIE

Cooking Time 1½–2 hrs.
Temperature E.450° (230°C), G.8 for 10 mins. then E.350° (180°C), G.4.
Quantities for 4–6.

Flaky pastry using 8 oz. flour (250 g.) or use
12 oz. ready-made pastry (375 g.)   1 rabbit

Make pastry and put in a cool place.

Divide the rabbit into joints and boil the trimmings for stock, preferably in a pressure cooker.

12 oz. bacon or pickled pork (375 g.)
Veal forcemeat balls (see Stuffings), page 260

Remove any rind and cut the bacon or pork into dice. Make the forcemeat balls. Pack the rabbit, bacon or pork, and the balls in layers in a 1½–2 pt. size pie dish (1 l.).

Salt and pepper   Stock

Season well with salt and pepper and add enough stock to three-quarters fill the dish. Cover with the pastry and bake in a hot oven to set the pastry and then slowly until the meat is tender. If necessary, cover the pastry with a piece of foil or greaseproof paper if it is brown enough before the meat is done. Serve hot or cold.

ROAST STUFFED RABBIT

See *Hare*, page 156, but use the shorter cooking time.

SMOTHERED RABBIT

Cooking Time 2½ hrs. *Temperature* E.325° (160°C), G.3.
Quantities for 4–6.

Prepare the rabbit by blanching it for 1 min. Then cut it in joints, or buy ready-jointed rabbit.

1 *rabbit*

Skin and slice thinly. Put the onions in a deep casserole with the rabbit on top.

2 *lb. onions* (1 *kg.*)

Add to the rabbit with barely enough cold water to cover. Bring to the boil, cover, and cook slowly in the oven or on top until the rabbit is tender and the onions cooked to a soft consistency.

2 *oz. butter* (50 *g.*)   2 *oz. flour* (6 *Tbs. or* 50 *g.*)

Melt the butter and add the flour, mixing to make a *roux*, cook until crumbly. Add this gradually to the casserole, stirring until the liquid thickens. Taste for seasoning.

Chopped parsley

Sprinkle with plenty of parsley and serve.

RABBIT CURRY. See *Curried Chicken*, page 145

Use 1 rabbit or 4 pieces.

JUGGED RABBIT. See *Jugged Hare*, page 157

Use 2 small rabbits or 6–8 pieces instead of 1 hare.

SQUIRREL

These are cooked in the same way as a young rabbit and the flesh is light in colour and in flavour something between a chicken and rabbit.

VENISON

The flesh of deer of all kinds, but chiefly the stag or red deer, roebuck, and fallow deer. It is in season from October to December. The leg and loin are considered the prime cuts and together make the 'haunch' which is a very large joint. It is usually roasted, though venison steaks and cutlets are grilled, and the meat from the shoulder sometimes stewed.

GRILLED VENISON CUTLETS

Cooking Time 20–25 mins. *Quantities*. Allow 1 per person.

Cutlets from the neck are used, cut 1 in. (2½ cm.) thick. Season with salt and pepper and turn every 2 mins. during grilling. Serve with a knob of butter, stewed mushrooms, and baked potatoes.

GRILLED VENISON STEAKS

Cooking Time 20–25 mins. *Quantities*. Allow 1 per person.

Steaks are cut 1 in. thick (2½ cm.) from the top of the leg or the loin. Turn every 2 mins. during cooking. Heat a baking dish and put in it 1 oz. butter for each lb. (25 g. for each ½ kg.) of meat, 1 Tbs. melted red currant jelly, 1 Tbs. warm stock, and salt and pepper. Add the cooked steak and turn it to coat well. Serve at once.

JUGGED VENISON. See *Jugged Hare*, page 157.

Substitute 2 lb. (1 kg.) venison shoulder meat for the hare.

ROAST VENISON

Cooking Times and Temperatures. See *Veal*, page 95.

Cuts. Leg, loin, and shoulder.

The meat can be foil wrapped to keep it moist, or baste it frequently with equal quantities of butter, red currant jelly, and water. Serve with brown gravy and red currant jelly.

A 6 lb. (3 kg.) haunch needs 3–4 hrs. roasting.

14 Vegetables

CHOOSING VEGETABLES

In general, vegetables brought straight from the garden to the kitchen have the best flavour and the highest nutritive value. When buying fresh vegetables from a shop choose those that look fresh, free from wilted, decayed or discoloured parts. Quick frozen vegetables are a better buy than stale 'fresh' vegetables. Tips on buying and using them are included with the individual vegetables listed in this section in alphabetical order.

GENERAL COOKING METHODS

BOILING VEGETABLES

For detailed directions see the individual vegetables.

The essential in boiling all vegetables is to cook them as quickly as possible in the minimum amount of water. This preserves the flavour and nutritive value and keeps them a natural colour. Any cooking liquid there may be at the end should be added to sauces or soups. Most vegetables are more palatable if they are either tossed in a little butter or served with a sauce. See *Vegetable Sauce*. Quick boiling is achieved by having the water boiling before the vegetables are put in, by cutting the vegetables in small pieces, and by cooking with the lid on the pan. Gentle boiling cooks as fast as a rapid boil and there is less danger of the pan boiling dry. Vegetables should be served as soon as cooked.

VEGETABLES STEWED IN FAT

Suitable for most, except potatoes, beetroot, or asparagus.

Cooking Time about 10–20 mins.   *Quantities for 4.*

1 lb. vegetables (½ kg.)   *Salt and pepper*
Butter, lard, dripping, or oil

Prepare the vegetables according to kind and cut them in slices or large dice. Heat enough fat to cover the bottom of the pan, add vegetables and salt, cover, and cook gently until they are tender. Shake the pan or stir the vegetables occasionally.

Chopped parsley

Serve with any liquid in the pan and with chopped parsley. Green vegetables should not be allowed to brown but root vegetables take on a very good flavour if lightly browned.

ROAST VEGETABLES

Suitable for potatoes, carrots, parsnips, marrows, pumpkin, turnip, onions, artichokes, and swedes.

Peel the vegetables and leave whole or cut in pieces to make them cook more quickly. Place in the hot fat round a roasting joint or heat a little fat or oil in a separate tin and roll the vegetables in it. Bake in a moderate to hot oven, turning occasionally. They will take 40 mins. to 1 hr. depending on kind and size. See individual vegetables.

VEGETABLES *AU GRATIN*

Cooking Time ½ hr.   *Temperature* E.450° (230°C), G.8.
Quantities for 4.

> 1–1½ *lb. any vegetables* (½–¾ *kg.*)   *Buttered crumbs*
> ½ *pt. cheese sauce* (¼ *l*), page 248

Boil the vegetables and use any liquid to add to the sauce. Put vegetables and sauce in layers in a baking dish and finish with a layer of crumbs. Brown and heat through in a hot oven. If sauce and vegetables are already hot it is sufficient to brown the top under the grill.

VEGETABLES IN A CASSEROLE

Suitable for carrots, celery, chicory, onions, parsnips, pumpkin, swedes, tomatoes, turnip, and vegetable marrow.

Cooking Time ½–1 hr.
Temperature E.325–375° (160–190°C), G.3–5.   *Quantities* for 4.

> 1 *lb. vegetables* (½ *kg.*)   *Pinch of pepper*
> ½ *oz. butter or other fat* (15 *g.*)   1–2 *Tbs. water*
> ½ *tsp. salt*

Prepare the vegetables in the usual way and cut large ones in pieces. Put in a casserole with the other ingredients, cover, and cook until tender. If the vegetables are first brought to the boil on top of the stove the cooking time will be shortened considerably.

Chopped parsley

Sprinkle generously on the vegetables just before serving.

VEGETABLE *JARDINIÈRE*

Cooking Time 1–1½ hrs.   *Quantities for* 4–5.

8 oz. lean salt pork or bacon (¼ kg.)
¼ oz. butter or margarine (1 Tbs. or 15 g.)

Remove skin or rind and cut the meat into dice. Heat the fat in a stew pan and fry the meat until it begins to brown.

1 lb. young carrots (½ kg.)   ¾ Tbs. flour
5 small onions

Scrape the carrots and slice them. Skin the onions. Add to the pan and sprinkle in the flour, continue to fry for 5 mins. Add water to cover, put on the lid, and cook slowly for ½ hr.

2 lb. green peas in the pod (1 kg.)   ¼ tsp. pepper
1 lb. new potatoes (½ kg.)   Bouquet garni
1 tsp. salt

Shell the peas and scrape the potatoes, cutting large ones in pieces. Add these to the pan with the seasonings and continue cooking until all the vegetables are tender. Remove the *bouquet* and serve at once. The cooking can be done in a casserole in a moderate oven but will take longer unless the vegetables are first brought to the boil on top.

ALPHABETICAL LIST OF VEGETABLES

ARTICHOKE, JERUSALEM or *HELIANTHUS TUBEROSUS*
Is a native of North America and belongs to the sunflower family, the tuber being the part eaten. They look like very knobbly potatoes; the small ones are extremely difficult to peel, and they must be peeled because the skins are very thick and fibrous.

They have a very distinctive flavour and texture which some people find objectionable.

164

BOILED JERUSALEM ARTICHOKES

Cooking Time 20-30 mins.

Quantities. Allow ½ lb. per person (¼ kg.).

Prepare the artichokes by scrubbing and peeling, cutting off the very small knobs to make them a more even shape. As you peel them put them into a bowl of cold water containing 1 Tbs. vinegar to each qt. (1.). This helps to keep them a good colour. Leave them in the water for ½ hr.

Put them in boiling salted water to cover, and boil until they are tender when tested with a fork.

They may also be boiled in milk and some of the milk used for a sauce to serve with them and the rest for a soup.

ARTICHOKES WITH CHEESE

Cooking Time ½-¾ hr.
Temperature E.450° (230°C), G.8 for 10 mins. only, or use the grill.
Quantities for 4.

2 lb. artichokes (1 kg.)   2 onions

¼ pt. milk (1½ dl.)   *Grated cheese*
Salt and pepper

Peel the artichokes. Peel and slice the onions. Boil until tender.

Mash the vegetables with the milk, and season to taste. Put them in a greased oven-proof dish and cover the top with a generous layer of grated cheese. Heat in the oven for 10 mins. to melt the cheese, or cook under the grill. Serve hot.

ARTICHOKE CRISPS. See *Potato Crisps*, page 206.

ARTICHOKE GLOBE or *CYNARA SCOLYMUS*

Belongs to the thistle family and is a very decorative garden plant. The flower heads are eaten while in the bud stage. They consist of a mass of closely overlapping green leaves springing from a flat base called the bottom. This is not seen until all the leaves have been removed. At the base of the larger leaves is a small soft, fleshy bit which is the part eaten. The leaves are torn off one by one, the base of each being dipped in the accompanying sauce and then pulled off by the teeth. When all the other leaves have been eaten the small inner ones and the fluffy centre are discarded leaving the bottom

165

which is then attacked with a knife and fork. Artichoke bottoms are sold in tins and can be used in a variety of ways.

Artichokes must be fresh and the leaves should be green without any brown tips or any horny appearance or they will be too old and stale to eat.

They are in season in the summer. They should be used as soon as possible after cutting but, if to be kept a short while, stand them with the stems in water, like a flower head.

BOILED GLOBE ARTICHOKES

Cooking Time 15–45 mins. depending on size and age.

Quantities. Allow 1 per person.

Cut off the stalks and remove the outer row of tough leaves. Trim the tops of the other leaves to make a neat shape. Kitchen scissors are the best tool to use for this. Soak the artichokes for an hour in plenty of cold water to which has been added some salt and 1 Tbs. of vinegar. This is to draw out any insects lurking in the leaves. Drain upside down.

Cook them, stem end down, in a little boiling salted water until an outside leaf pulls out easily when tested. Avoid over-cooking or the flavour will be lost.

Drain upside down, squeezing gently to remove some of the water.

They may be served as they are with a Vinaigrette Sauce handed separately, or serve with Hollandaise Sauce.

Artichokes may have the small centre leaves and the choke removed and the centre filled with Hollandaise Sauce.

Cold artichokes are usually served with Vinaigrette Sauce.

ARTICHOKE BOTTOMS

Quantities. Allow 1 or more per person, depending on how they are being used.

They are usually served cold as part of an *hors-d'œuvre*, or fried in a little butter or oil and used to garnish a meat dish, or in a salad. If fresh artichokes are used, pull off all the leaves and remove the choke. Use cold cooked ones for this. Canned artichoke bottoms are a very good alternative and, if you are wanting a number of them, generally work out cheaper than the fresh. Drain from the liquid, drying well in paper towels if they are going to be fried. Cold artichoke bottoms are usually dressed with a little Vinaigrette Sauce or French Dressing.

ASPARAGUS or *ASPARAGUS OFFICINALIS*

Is a native of Europe and is in season from mid-April to mid-June. It loses flavour very quickly after cutting and should preferably be cooked the day it is cut. It is always an expensive vegetable, and stale asparagus is not worth buying. It is best to buy bundles with even-sized heads otherwise some will be undercooked and some over-cooked. If necessary, the bundle should be sorted out into sizes for cooking.

Canned asparagus has a very different flavour from fresh but is a very pleasant vegetable nevertheless, and useful for soups, salads, garnishes, and *hors-d'œuvre.*

Deep-frozen asparagus comes somewhere between the two for flavour but is still a very expensive vegetable. For salads and garnish-ing it is to be preferred to the canned as it keeps its shape more readily, and is a more attractive colour.

BOILED ASPARAGUS

Cooking Time 15–30 mins. depending on size.
Quantities. Allow 6–8 medium-sized pieces per person.

Wash the asparagus, scrubbing the white ends and scraping down-wards with a sharp vegetable knife. Place in bundles of about a dozen, or in portions, and tie with white string, keeping the heads level. Trim the ends to an even length. Use these for vegetable stock or cook them with the asparagus for the same purpose.

If you cook asparagus often, it is worth while buying an asparagus boiler which is tall enough to take the stalks standing upright. It is important to try and improvise something of this sort, otherwise it is very difficult to get the thick lower stalks cooked at the same time as the delicate heads.

Use the deepest pan you have and, for a lid, use an inverted basin, preferably heat-resistant glass, so you can see what is going on. Heat enough water in the pan to cover the thick ends of the asparagus. Add salt, and bring to the boil. Stand the bundles upright and put on the lid. Boil gently until the tips are tender. Do not over-cook or flavour will be lost and the heads will fall off as you lift the asparagus out of the pan.

Drain it in a colander and serve hot with Brown Butter Sauce or Hollandaise Sauce. Serve cold with French Dressing or Vinaigrette Sauce.

AUBERGINE or EGG PLANT (*SOLANUM MELONGENA*)

It is a native of India but grows in many other countries. It is in season in the summer and autumn. It has a shiny, deep purple skin which will be unwrinkled if the aubergine is fresh, the fruit should be firm to the touch, and should be kept in a cool dry place. They are not worth buying if they are stale.

They may be peeled or not but most people prefer the flavour without the skins.

Quantity. Allow half a large one or 1 small or medium per person.

BAKED STUFFED AUBERGINE

Cooking Time 20–30 mins. *Temperature* E.425° (220°C), G.7.
Quantities for 4.

2 *large aubergines*	2 *medium tomatoes*
1 *slice of onion*	*Browned breadcrumbs or crushed*
½ *oz. fat* (15 *g.*)	*cornflakes or wheat germ*
	Salt and pepper

Wash the aubergines and boil them for 5 mins. in salted water. Cut in half and scoop out the centres.

Chop the onion and fry it in the fat. Add the chopped tomato, the aubergine pulp, and seasoning to taste. Put the mixture in the aubergine shells and sprinkle the tops with the crumbs or alternative. Bake in a hot oven until heated through and brown on top.

Variations. Add some chopped mushrooms to the tomatoes and/or some minced lamb. In the latter case heat the mixture long enough to cook the meat.

FRIED AUBERGINES

Peel and cut in ½ in. (1 cm.) slices. Dip the slices in a frying batter or in egg and breadcrumbs. Fry in hot fat and serve plain or with a tomato sauce.

GRILLED AUBERGINES

Prepare as for frying and then put in the bottom of a greased grill pan and cook gently for 6–8 mins. or until tender. Turn once during cooking. Serve with grated cheese sprinkled over the tops.

Alternative method. Peel the aubergine and cut in $\frac{1}{2}$ in. (1 cm.) slices. Mix 1 Tbs. oil with $\frac{1}{4}$ tsp. salt and a pinch of pepper. Dip the slices in this and put them in the bottom of the grill pan. Grill 3 mins. each side, or until tender. Serve with fried eggs or tomato sauce.

STEWED AUBERGINE

Peel, slice, and stew gently in a good tomato sauce until they are tender, about 20 mins.

BAMBOO SHOOTS

These are the young tender shoots of the bamboo plant, more familiar in this country as the fully grown stems used for bamboo canes in gardening.

The young shoots are cooked and eaten as a vegetable and are also pickled. Both fresh and pickled ones are used in Asiatic cooking and may be purchased canned in this country.

BEANS

The name given to the seeds or pods of a wide variety of plants belonging to the *Leguminosae*, commonly called *legumes*. The seeds are often used dried and known as 'pulses'. In many countries they form a very important part of the diet and beans from all over the world are now imported into this country and can be purchased in grocers' shops, especially those catering for foreign residents.

BEAN SPROUTS

Dried beans are soaked in water and kept in the warm until they begin to sprout and send out small shoots. When these are a fair size they are detached from the beans and cooked. They are used in Asiatic cooking.

Although dried beans contain no vitamin C, the sprouts do, and this is one way of obtaining the vitamin when the usual fruit and vegetable sources are unobtainable. The beans most commonly used for this are *Mung* beans or *Soybeans*.

BLACK BEANS

Dried beans used a lot in Central America and Asia.

169

BLACK-EYED BEANS

Like a haricot bean with a black eye and used the same way.

BROAD BEANS or *Vicia Fada*

Fresh ones are in season from June to August. Frozen and canned ones are obtainable all the year round. Neither of these have the flavour of a fresh bean but they make a welcome change when the fresh are out of season. Frozen ones have the better appearance but canned ones usually have the better flavour and can be very palatable served with a parsley sauce using some of the liquid from the tin to make the sauce.

Fresh broad beans are best when they are very young. The beans in the pods are quite small so allow not less than $\frac{1}{2}$ lb. ($\frac{1}{4}$ kg.) per portion. Older beans have thick skins which are rather indigestible but if the beans are cooked and sieved they make an excellent *purée* when seasoned and beaten with a little butter. They are also very good served in the skins and eaten in the fingers, when the bean inside can easily be squeezed out and eaten. Children like doing this.

When buying broad beans, ask to feel one or two, because young ones can look as if they had beans in them and when you start shelling you find practically nothing there. Very young pods can be sliced and boiled so you need not waste the very immature ones. Old ones look as if the pod was too tight for them, the pods are not as green as when young and may even have brown patches on them.

BOILED BROAD BEANS

Cooking Time 10–40 mins., depending on the age.
Quantities allow 1–2 lb. per portion ($\frac{1}{2}$–1 kg.).

Shell the beans. Put about 1 in. (2 cm.) of water in the pan and add 1 tsp. salt per 4 portions. When the water is boiling add the beans and cook gently until they are tender when tested with a fork. Drain, keeping the liquid for a sauce or for stock. Toss the beans in a little melted butter or margarine and sprinkle with chopped parsley or a little chopped savory. Alternatively, serve with a white sauce made with some of the vegetable water and some milk. Add some chopped parsley or savory.

For a supper dish garnish the beans with rolls of fried or grilled bacon.

Serve cold for salads or *hors-d'œuvre*.

BUTTER BEANS

There are two kinds known by this name. One is a yellow-podded French bean and is cooked in the same way as French beans. Sometimes also called Waxpod.

The other butter bean is a large white dried bean, also sold canned. It is used as a vegetable, in meat casseroles and stews, and for salads and *hors-d'œuvre*. For cooking see *Boiling Dried Beans*, below.

DRIED BEANS

Those most commonly used in Britain are the haricot (small white), and the butter bean (large white). Others available in some districts are flageolets, lima beans, brown beans, black beans, black-eyed beans, red beans, mungo beans, or green gram.

BOILING DRIED BEANS

Cooking Time 2–3 hrs. or 25–30 mins. pressure cooking.
Quantities. Allow 2 oz. dry weight (50 g.) per person. 1 lb. dried beans (½ kg.) gives 2 lb. cooked (1 kg).

Unless they are very old stock, dried beans do not need soaking before cooking, and even then they should not be soaked for more than 1–1½ hrs. or they may begin to ferment.

To boil them, heat 1 pt. (½ l.) water for every 4 oz. (125 g.) beans to be cooked. When it is boiling drop in the beans, cover, and simmer gently until they are tender when tested with a fork. Drain, keeping any liquid for stock. Season to taste with salt and pepper and chopped green herbs. For extra flavour cook an onion with the beans, and stick some cloves into it; or add a few bacon rinds.

When using the pressure cooker, be sure it is not more than half filled with water and beans, only a third full is safer.

DRIED BEANS *À LA BRETONNE*

Boiled dried beans are drained and mixed with the following flavourings:

For each 1 lb. (½ kg.) of beans being cooked fry 2 medium-sized onions cut in slices. Fry in oil or dripping. When the onions are brown add the beans and mix well. Sprinkle with chopped parsley and serve hot.

FLAGEOLET

A bean grown a great deal in France. It is used fresh or dried and keeps a delicate green colour even when dried.

FRENCH BEANS (also called Kidney or Dwarf beans)

The young green pods are eaten, or the young beans from mature pods, or as dried beans. The young green pods are in season from June to October but it is very difficult to buy good-quality ones. They should be flat and not show any sign of the bean inside, otherwise they will be stringy and unpleasant to eat. They may also be bought frozen but the flavour seems to be lost to a very large extent. Canned ones are not very much like fresh ones in flavour but are useful when the fresh are out of season. These are best used in salads and for garnishing.

BOILED FRENCH BEANS

Cooking Time 15–20 mins.

Quantities. Allow 6–8 oz. per person (175–250 g.).

Wash the beans and cut off the tops and tails but do not slice them if you want a good flavour. Boil about 1 in. (2½ cm.) of salted water, add the beans, and 1 tsp. salt per lb. (½ kg.) of beans. Cover and boil rapidly until the beans are just tender. Drain well and toss in a little melted butter. Serve at once.

HARICOT BEANS

Here we most commonly eat the dried variety of haricot bean but in France they eat them fresh too. The dried beans are used as a vegetable, for baked beans, in soups, in casseroles and stews, and in salads or *hors-d'œuvre*.

For cooking see *Boiling Dried Beans*, page 171.

ITALIAN BEANS

Cooking Time 2 hrs. or 25–30 mins. pressure cooking.

Quantities for 4.

8 oz. haricot or butter beans (250 g.)

Boil the beans until tender and then drain well; or use 1 lb. drained canned beans (½ kg. drained weight).

4 Tbs. oil   2 Tbs. tomato paste
2 fresh sage leaves   Salt and pepper

Chop the sage leaves. Heat the oil and sage together and, when hot, add the beans and cook until the fat is absorbed. Add the tomato paste and mix well, seasoning to taste.

LIMA BEAN

A native of South America. The beans are eaten fresh (similar to broad beans), or dried (like butter beans). They are also sold frozen and canned.

MUNGO BEAN or GREEN GRAM

This is a small green bean which is used in Asia, either as a bean, as a flour, or for making bean sprouts.

RED BEANS

Are small beans of the haricot variety and are used fresh or dried. Sometimes called Kidney beans.

SCARLET RUNNER BEANS

In season from July to September but, as with French beans it is difficult to buy good-quality ones and many have to be discarded as too mature and stringy. Young ones should be flat and show no sign of the bean inside. They are also sold frozen, but sliced so finely that little flavour is left after cooking.

BOILING RUNNER BEANS

Cooking Time 15–20 mins.
Quantities. Allow 6–8 oz. per person (175–250 g.).

Wash the beans and cut off the tops and tails. The flavour is better if they are not sliced but instead cut across into two or three largish pieces. Bring 1 in. (2½ cm.) of water to the boil in a saucepan and add 1 tsp. salt for each lb. (½ kg.) of beans. When the water is boiling add the beans, cover and boil rapidly until they are just tender. Drain thoroughly and then toss in a little butter. Serve at once.

173

RUNNER BEANS *BÉARNAISE*

Cooking Time 15–20 mins.   *Quantities for* 4.

1 *lb. runner beans*   2 *tomatoes chopped*
1 *Tbs. fat*   *Salt and pepper to taste*
      1–2 *oz. chopped bacon* (25–30 g.)

Boil the beans as described above. Drain and keep hot. Fry the bacon and tomatoes in the fat for a few minutes. Add the beans and mix well. Season to taste and serve hot.

SOYBEAN

A small roundish yellow bean which is very important in many countries especially for the production of oil, for bean shoots, for making bean curd (like cottage cheese), for soya flour, and for milk substitutes. In addition a hot condiment, *Soy* sauce, is made from it.

The *soybean* has the highest nutritive value of all beans, being a source of good-quality protein and B vitamins, as well as carbohydrate and energy.

Soya flour is used in some manufactured foods in this country, for example, soups and cakes. It is also available for household use. Used in the proportion of 1 part of soya flour to 7 parts of ordinary flour it improves the texture of cakes and puddings as well as increasing their nutritive value.

It is an important food for strict vegetarians as it supplies protein which other people get from animal foods, and it is used for this in countries where animal foods are scarce and expensive.

BEETROOT or *Beta vulgaris*

There are many varieties of *Beta vulgaris*, including the ordinary culinary beetroot, sugar beet, mangels (used for animal feeding), and a variety *Cicla* which includes spinach beet, chard, and others like them whose leaves are the most important part (see *Spinach*). The ordinary red beetroot is in season all the year round and is most commonly sold cooked. Raw beetroot is often difficult to find but it is cheaper and is much nicer home-cooked. It is not troublesome to do especially if you have a pressure cooker. It may also be bought canned or pickled in vinegar.

Choose small to medium ones as large ones may be woody in the middle. If buying raw ones, make sure neither the skins nor the roots are damaged otherwise they will lose colour when cooked. When buying cooked ones avoid any which look sticky on the outside because these will probably be stale and have an unpleasant taste.

BOILING BEETROOT

Cooking Time ½–1 hr. or more depending on size and age. Pressure cooking 10–40 mins.

Quantities. Allow 6–8 oz. per person (175–250 g.).

Wash the beetroot thoroughly and carefully so as not to damage the skin or roots. The tops should be twisted or cut off leaving about 2 in. (5 cm.) still on. Boil enough water to cover them, adding 1 Tbs. salt to every 2 lb. (1 kg.) of vegetables.

Boil until tender but do not test with a fork as this makes them bleed. Instead pinch the skin and if it comes off quite easily the beet-root is cooked. Leave to become cold before removing skins, tops, and root.

In the pressure cooker use only ½ pt. water (¼ l.) and cook for 10–15 mins. for small ones of about 4 oz. (125 g.); use 1 pt. water (½ l.) and cook 20 mins. for medium ones of about 8 oz. (250 g.); use 1½ pt. water (¾ l.) and cook for 35–40 mins. for large ones of about 1 lb. (½ kg.).

BEETS—HARVARD

This is a method of cooking beetroot to serve as a hot vegetable, very good with meat, especially pork, rabbit, and veal.

Cooking Time 10 mins.   *Quantities for 4.*

1 lb. cooked beetroot (2 c. diced or ½ kg.)

1 oz. margarine (25 g.)   1 oz. flour (3 Tbs. or 25 g.)

3 Tbs. vinegar made up to ½ pt. (¼ l.) with water
1 Tbs. sugar   1 tsp. salt   Pinch of pepper

Skin the beetroot and cut in small cubes.

Melt margarine and stir in the flour, cook gently for a few minutes.

Gradually stir in the vinegar, stirring until it boils and cook gently for about 5 mins. Add the seasoning to taste and the prepared beet-root. Heat gently for 5 mins. and serve hot.

175

BROCCOLI

Belongs to the same family as the cauliflower but is much hardier. There are three kinds.

1. The ordinary one which looks like a cauliflower and is cooked in the same way. See *Cauliflower*, page 183. It is in season practically all the year round but is most plentiful from December to May.

2. Sprouting broccoli which is usually in season from late winter to spring. There are purple and white kinds. They grow as a tall plant like kale or Brussels sprouts and the small shooting sprouts are the part eaten. They have a small head which resembles a green or purple cauliflower. They are obtainable frozen and sometimes the fresh ones are on sale though frequently these are rather too mature to be palatable and much of the shoot is too tough and has to be discarded. Most of the leaves are usually removed too. The shoots are boiled like any green vegetable (see page 162), and served with melted butter.

3. The calabrese, in season in the spring. It has a central head like a small green cauliflower and is cooked like one. Later the plant sends out shoots like the sprouting broccoli.

BRUSSELS SPROUTS

They belong to the same family as the cabbage, *Brassica*. They are in season from autumn to spring, but are at their best in the winter. They are also available deep-frozen.

The best sprouts are the very small tight ones which unfortunately are rather hard to buy. They look best and have a lovely nutty taste. Most of the deep-frozen ones are of this variety. If possible choose sprouts which are approximately all the same size so that they cook in the same time. This you can do if you have your own garden. Do not buy blighted ones as they are very hard to wash and you may find the insides unusable, nor buy any that look wilted and have yellow leaves as these will undoubtedly be stale. Very loose sprouts are a bad buy as they often have bad centres and become mushy when cooked.

BRUSSELS SPROUTS *AU GRATIN*. See *Vegetables au Gratin*, page 163

BOILED BRUSSELS SPROUTS

Cooking Time about 15 mins.

Quantities. Allow 6–8 oz. per person (175–250 g.).

Prepare the sprouts by cutting off any damaged leaves and cutting a cross in the bottom of the stem to help speed up the cooking. Wash quickly in plenty of cold water. If they vary widely in size grade them into two lots. Heat about 1 in. (2½ cm.) of water in a saucepan and add 1 tsp. salt for each lb. (½ kg.) of vegetables. Bring to the boil and add the larger sprouts; when the water reboils gradually drop in the smaller ones. Put on the lid and boil rapidly until they are just tender. Do not overcook as this spoils flavour and colour. They are nicest if still slightly firm. Drain well, return to the pan, add a knob of butter, and toss until it is melted and coats the sprouts. Serve at once.

BRUSSELS SPROUTS LYONNAISE

Cooking Time 20 mins. *Quantities for 4.*

1½ lb. sprouts (¾ kg.)

Boil the sprouts as directed above. Drain well.

1 oz. butter or dripping (25 g.) 2 Tbs. chopped onion

Heat the fat and fry the onion in it until it begins to brown. Then add the sprouts for a minute longer and serve at once.

BUBBLE AND SQUEAK

This is a popular fry-up for left-overs, but even nicer if made from freshly cooked vegetables. It consists of a mixture of boiled cabbage and sliced or mashed boiled potatoes which is fried in a little shallow fat over a moderate heat until a brown crust forms underneath, then cut into portions and serve brown side up. Very tasty with a bit of fried or grilled bacon but not to be recommended as a source of vitamin C, because this has probably been all destroyed by the double cooking.

CABBAGE

Is native to Britain and belongs to the *Brassica* family.

Many varieties are cultivated, maturing at different times of the year so that some variety is in season all the year round. Some cabbages have round heads or hearts, some pointed, some are large varieties and some very small. The Savoy cabbage, which is in season in the winter, has a large heart and crinkly leaves. One variety of red cabbage matures in the summer and another in the autumn.

Cabbage keeps well and transports well so if you see one looking tired and wilted you may be sure it is either pretty stale or has been left lying in a warm place. In any case it is a bad buy. Cabbages with large white hearts are nutritionally not as good a buy as the smaller and greener ones, though for cabbage salad the large hearts of Savoy cabbages are usually more tender.

Do not buy cabbages that have been cut in half for display purposes because you do not know how long they have been like that and they will have lost considerable nutritive value.

BOILED CABBAGE

Quantities. Allow 6–8 oz. per person (175–250 g.).

Remove any very coarse or damaged outer leaves and cut off any stalk. Cut the cabbage in halves or quarters and remove the hard inside stalk.

Wash the cabbage thoroughly, drain, and cut in ½ in. (1 cm.) slices.

Boil 1 in. water (2½ cm.) with 1 level tsp. salt to each lb. (½ kg.) and, when it is boiling, add the cabbage. Cover with the lid and boil rapidly until the cabbage is just tender but not mushy, about 15 mins. Drain, return to the pan, add a knob of butter and toss to coat the cabbage. Serve as soon as possible.

CABBAGE AND BACON

Cooking Time ½ hr. *Quantities* for 4.

1½ lb. *cabbage* (¾ *kg.*) 4 *rashers bacon*

4 *leeks or small onions*

Remove the outer leaves and the thick stalk of the cabbage. Remove green part and roots from the leeks and cut them in half. Peel the onion if used. Wash all the vegetables thoroughly and then shred the cabbage in about ¼ in. (6 mm.) strips and chop the leeks or onions. Remove rinds and chop bacon.

Heat ½ pt. water (¼ l.) and when it boils add the vegetables and bacon, cover, and boil until the cabbage is just tender. Drain, saving the liquid, and keep hot.

1 *oz. fat* (25 *g.*) 1 *oz. flour* (3 *Tbs. or* 25 *g.*)

¼ *pt. cabbage liquid* (⅛ *l.*) *made up with milk if necessary*

Melt the fat in the same pan in which the cabbage was cooked. Stir in the flour and cook for a minute or two and then gradually add the liquid. Stir until it boils and boil for 5 mins.

Salt and pepper   1 tsp. meat or yeast extract

Season to taste and add the extract. Pour over the cabbage and serve at once.

CREAMED CABBAGE

Cooking Time 15 mins.   Quantities for 4.

1½ *lb. cabbage* (¾ *kg.*)   ¼ *pt. water* (1½ *dl.*)
2 *tsp. salt*

Remove tough outer leaves from the cabbage and the thick centre stalk. Wash and drain. Then shred it in ¼ in. (6 mm.) strips. Boil the water and salt, add the cabbage, cover, and boil for 5 mins.

½ *oz. margarine or dripping* (15 *g.*)

Add to the cabbage.

1 *oz. flour* (3 *Tbs. or 25 g.*)   1 *oz. grated cheese* (4 *Tbs. or 25 g.*)
¼ *pt. water* (1½ *dl.*)

Blend the flour and cheese to a smooth cream with the water. Add it to the cabbage, stir well, and bring to the boil. Cook for another 10 mins. Season and serve.

FRIED CABBAGE

Cooking Time 15 mins.   Quantities for 4.

1½ *lb. cabbage* (¾ *kg.*)   Pinch ground mace or nutmeg
1 *medium-sized onion*   ½ *tsp. salt*
1 *rasher bacon*   Fat or oil for cooking

Remove the tough outer leaves and the centre core of the cabbage. Wash and drain. Shred into ¼ in. (6 mm.) slices. Peel and chop the onion. Remove rind and chop bacon. Heat enough fat or oil to cover the bottom of a stew pan and when it is hot, but not smoking, add the other ingredients. Cover and cook gently until the cabbage is just tender. Serve at once.

CABBAGE WITH SAUSAGES

Cooking Time ½ hr.   Quantities for 4.

1½ *lb. cabbage* (¾ *kg.*)

179

Remove any tough outer leaves and the centre stalk, wash and shred into ¼ in. (6 mm.) slices. Put in about 1 in. (2½ cm.) boiling salted water and boil with the lid on for 15 mins.

Drain well.

Return the cabbage to the pan with these ingredients and stew very gently for 15 mins.

| 1 oz. dripping (25 g.) | Salt and pepper |
| Pinch of grated nutmeg | 2–3 Tbs. milk |

Grill the sausages. Add the butter to the cabbage and serve it with the sausages.

1 lb. sausages (½ kg.)   Small knob butter

RED CABBAGE

Cooking Time ¾–1 hr.   Quantities for 4.

1 lb. red cabbage (½ kg.)   1 large onion

1 large apple

Remove any discoloured outer leaves from the cabbage, cut it in half, and remove the centre stalk. Wash and drain well and cut in slices about ¼ in. thick (6 mm.).

Peel and slice the onion and apple.

1 oz. dripping (25 g.)	1 tsp. salt
2 Tbs. water	Pinch of pepper
2 Tbs. vinegar	1 Tbs. brown sugar

Melt the dripping in a saucepan and add all the other ingredients. Cover, bring to the boil, and boil gently until the cabbage is tender, stirring occasionally. If it seems in danger of boiling dry, add a little more water but the pan should be practically dry by the time cooking is finished. If more convenient, put the cabbage in a casserole and cook it in a slow oven as for a stew. This is very good served with roast pork or with sausages.

CAPSICUMS

A family name for a number of edible pods. They include pods which are eaten as a vegetable, such as sweet peppers, pods which are used for pickling, such as chillies, and pods from which red peppers such as cayenne and paprika peppers are made. See Sweet Peppers, page 214.

CARROT or *Daucus carota var. sativa.*

One of the root vegetables in season all the year round and in mild dry places can be left in the ground all winter. There are two main types, the long-rooted and the shorter or stump-rooted, also known as the horn type.

Choose ones which are a good even shape and a moderate size. Very small ones are a nuisance to prepare and very large ones are sometimes woody inside and inclined to be dry and tasteless. Avoid any which show signs of worm infection because you will find there is a great deal of wastage, often the whole carrot being useless.

Some of the best carrots are sold ready washed in polythene bags, and this is a good way of buying them for you can see clearly what you are getting and it is worth paying a little more not to be landed with a high proportion of useless carrots.

To obtain the best flavour very young ones only need to be washed thoroughly and have the tops removed, and are then cooked whole. Older ones need scraping and the really old need peeling thinly with a vegetable knife. Cut out any damaged parts, cut off the tops and trim the roots. For quick cooking, cut in slices across the carrot or cut lengthwise to give strips about ½ to 1 in. wide (1–2 cm.).

BOILED CARROTS

Cooking Time about 20 mins.
Quantities. Allow 6–8 oz. per peson (175–250 g.).

Prepare the carrots (see above), and cut large ones into slices or rings. Boil about 1 in. of water (2½ cm.) in a pan and add 1 tsp. salt to each lb. of carrots (½ kg.). When the water is boiling, add the carrots, cover the pan, and boil until they are tender but not soft. Drain, keeping the water for stock, return to the pan with a knob of butter or margarine, and shake to coat them well. Serve with chopped parsley sprinkled on top.

Alternatively, after draining they may be served with a white or *Béchamel* sauce with plenty of chopped parsley in it. Use the cooking liquid from the carrots as part of the liquid for the sauce.

CARROTS AND BRUSSELS SPROUTS

Boil equal quantities of sliced carrots and whole sprouts together in a little boiling salted water until both vegetables are just tender. Drain and toss in a little butter or margarine to coat the vegetables well.

181

CARROTS AND PEAS

Cooking Time ¾ hr.   *Quantities for 4.*

8 oz. young carrots, diced (250 g.)   1 Tbs. sugar
1 oz. butter or margarine (25 g.)   ¼ pt. water (1½ dl.)
1 tsp. salt

Put all the ingredients in a pan, cover and boil gently for 5 mins.

8 oz. fresh or frozen peas (250 g.)

Add the peas to the pan and continue cooking until both vegetables are tender. There should be hardly any water left. Serve at once.

CARROT PURÉE

Cooking Time ½ hr.   *Quantities for 4.*

1½ lb. carrots (¾ kg.)

Prepare the carrots and slice them, then boil in a little salted water until they are tender. Drain and rub through a sieve or reduce to a *purée* in an electric blender.

1 small onion   ½ oz. dripping (15 g.)
Salt and pepper

Peel the onion and chop it very finely. Fry it in the dripping until it begins to brown. Add the carrot *purée*, and heat well, stirring all the time. Season to taste and serve hot.

VICHY CARROTS

Cooking Time 15–20 mins.   *Quantities for 4.*

1 lb. young carrots (½ kg.)

Wash and, if necessary, scrape the carrots. Remove the tops and cut carrots in slices.

1 oz. butter (25 g.)   1 tsp. sugar
½ tsp. salt

Melt the butter in a saucepan or casserole and add the other ingredients with the carrots. Cover and cook until the carrots are just tender.

1 Tbs. chopped parsley

Sprinkle over the carrots and serve hot.

CAULIFLOWER

A highly-prized vegetable belonging to the *Brassica* family and in season most of the year. See also *Broccoli*.

Choose ones with a nice white head and with plenty of fresh green leaves. Stale and yellow-leaved cauliflower have a poor flavour and may even be flabby instead of crisp.

BOILED CAULIFLOWER

Cooking Time 15–20 mins.
Quantities 1 large head for 4 portions.

Remove the stalk and all except the inner young leaves. The stalk may be sliced and cooked with the rest. The cauliflower may be boiled in small pieces, in individual flowerets, or left whole. The latter way takes a little longer to cook and has a stronger flavour but many people prefer the appearance of a whole cauliflower.

Boil about ½ in. (1 cm.) of salted water in a pan, add the cauliflower, flower side up if it is whole. Cover and boil until just tender. Avoid over-cooking or it will have a very strong flavour and will fall to pieces when handled. Drain well and serve as desired. It may be served with a white or *Béchamel* sauce or with Hollandaise or Brown Butter sauce.

CAULIFLOWER *AU GRATIN*. See *Vegetables au Gratin*, page 163

CAULIFLOWER POLONAISE

Cooking Time 25 mins. *Quantities* for 4.

1 *large cauliflower* 1 *egg*

2 *Tbs. breadcrumbs* 2 *Tbs. grated cheese*

2 *Tbs. chopped parsley*

1 *oz. butter (25 g.)*

Wash the cauliflower and boil it in a little salted water. Hard-boil the egg. Drain the cauliflower and keep hot. Shell, and chop the egg.

Mix these with the egg and sprinkle it over the cauliflower.

Heat the butter in a small pan until it is sizzling hot and pour it over the cauliflower. Serve at once.

183

CAULIFLOWER WITH BACON SAUCE

Cooking Time about ½ hr.   *Quantities for 4.*

1 *large cauliflower*

Wash the cauliflower and cook it either whole or divided up into flowerets. Boil it in a little water. Drain and keep hot.

2 *oz. fat* (50 g.)   1 *Tbs. chopped onion*
2 *oz. chopped bacon* (50 g.)

Heat the fat and fry the onion and bacon in it until they begin to brown.

2 *oz. flour* (6 *Tbs. or* 50 g.)   *Salt and pepper*
1 *pt. stock* (½ *l.*)   4 *Tbs. chopped parsley*

Add the flour and stir and cook for a few minutes. Add the stock and stir until it boils. Boil for 5 mins. Season to taste, add the parsley, and pour over the cauliflower.

CAULIFLOWER LYONNAISE

Cooking Time about 20 mins.   *Quantities for 4.*

1 *large cauliflower*

Wash the cauliflower and divide into sprigs. Boil it in a little salted water until just tender. Drain and keep hot.

1 *oz. dripping* (25 g.)   1 *large onion, chopped*

Heat the dripping and fry the onion and cauliflower in it until they just begin to brown. Serve hot.

CAULIFLOWER MILANAISE

Cooking Time 20-30 mins.   *Quantities for 4.*

1 *large cauliflower*

Wash the cauliflower and divide it into sprigs. Boil in a little salted water until just tender. Drain well.

2 *oz. grated cheese* (½ *c. or* 50 g.)   2 *oz. butter or magarine* (50 g.)

Grease a shallow baking dish and sprinkle cheese over the bottom. Add the cauliflower, and sprinkle it with the rest of the cheese. Add half the butter cut into small pieces. Place in a hot oven or under the grill to melt and brown the cheese. Meanwhile heat the rest of the butter in a small pan until it turns light brown, pour it over the cauliflower and serve at once.

CELERY or *Apium graveolens*

A native British plant which has been cultivated for centuries and, by breeding, has been greatly improved. It used to be in season only in the autumn and winter but imported celery is now available all the year round, though it has not the flavour of the home grown variety. Celery is also available canned, and this is suitable for use as a vegetable, for a cream soup, a celery sauce or *au gratin*. A celery 'head' is a complete plant minus the roots and the coarse leaves. A celery 'stick' is one stalk from the head.

Make sure it is firm and crisp and that the leaves are fresh looking. Avoid over-large heads as the stalks often have soft pithy insides and are not much good for anything.

The small roots are always removed but the stump is left attached to the stalks. The green tops are usually cut off. Some people say they use them in soups but they tend to have an astringent 'bite' to them. The very young small leaves are different and make very good garnishes for a salad. The head is usually divided into stalks before washing, by breaking them off the root, leaving the root attached to the last 2–4 small centre stalks. Wash in plenty of cold water, scrubbing if necessary.

CELERY *AU GRATIN*

See *Vegetables au Gratin*, page 163, using 1–1½ lb. (½–¾ kg.) celery cut in 2–3 in. lengths (5–8 cm.).

BRAISED CELERY

Cooking Time 30 mins.   *Quantities* for 4.

1 large head of celery

1 carrot	2 rashers bacon
1 small turnip	Sprig parsley
1 onion	Piece of bay leaf
Salt and pepper	Stock

Separate the stalks and wash them well. Cut them in even lengths to fit in the saucepan.

Peel and slice the vegetables. Remove rind and chop bacon. Put vegetables and bacon in the bottom of the saucepan with flavourings and enough stock just to cover. Put in the celery, cover, and boil gently until tender.

1 Tbs. arrowroot to ½ pt. stock (¼ l.)

Lift the celery into a serving dish and remove the ties. Strain the stock and thicken it with the arrowroot blended to a paste with cold water. When it thickens, pour over the celery and serve.

CELERIAC or Turnip-rooted Celery or *Apium graveolens, var. rapaceum.*

Is a variety of celery having a large edible root. In season in the autumn and winter. It is washed, peeled, and cut in slices or chunks and cooked and served like celery. It is also very good in soups and grated raw in salads or *hors-d'œuvre.*

CHICORY or *Cichorium*

There are two kinds of *Cichorium* grown for food. *C. Endiva* is like a curly blanched lettuce and usually known in Britain as 'endive'. See *Endive.*

The other is *C. intybus*, called '*endive*' by the French and in Britain known as 'Belgian' or 'Brussels chicory'. Both root and leaves of this chicory are used for food. The root is grown for drying and grinding to make chicory which is mixed with coffee. This is regarded as an adulterant by many, others think white coffee is improved by the addition of a little chicory.

The chicory used as a vegetable consists of the leaves of the plant which have been bleached by being grown under about 5 in. of soil. It is in season from September to May and is a very useful winter vegetable.

Chicory should be crisp and white with pale yellow tips. If the tips are green it shows the chicory has been exposed to the light for some time and will most probably be very bitter.

Rinse the heads under cold water. Cut a thin slice from the base. For cooking chicory, with a pointed knife, remove a cone-shaped piece from the base. This is to allow the hot water to penetrate the thick end more easily and help the cooking.

BOILED CHICORY

The simplest way is to boil it for about 20 mins. in a little salted water to which a few drops of lemon juice have been added to make the chicory white. It can then be served just plain or chopped and re-heated in a little melted butter with a pinch of sugar added.

BRAISED CHICORY

Cooking Time 45 mins.   Quantities for 4.

1½ lb. chicory (¾ kg.)   Juice of ¼ lemon
2 oz. butter (50 g.)   1 tsp. salt
3 Tbs. water

Wash and prepare the chicory. Melt the butter in a saucepan or casserole and add the chicory and other ingredients. Cover and cook gently for about 45 mins. or until the chicory is tender. Serve with the cooking liquor.

CHICORY POLONAISE

Cooking Time ½ hr.   Quantities for 4.

1 lb. chicory (½ kg.)   2 Tbs. milk
½ oz. fat or oil (1 Tbs. or 15 g.)   4 Tbs. stock
½ tsp. salt
1 egg

Wash and prepare the chicory and put it in a pan with the other ingredients. Cover and boil for ½ hr.

Meanwhile hard-boil the egg and chop it finely. Serve the chicory with the egg sprinkled over it.

COLCANNON or KOLCANNON or KAILKENNY

Many versions of the recipe exist. Its origin is said to be either Scottish or Irish and the following is a typical recipe.

Cooking Time about 40 mins.   Quantities for 4.

1 lb. potatoes (½ kg.)   8 oz. young green cabbage (250 g.)

Peel the potatoes and boil until tender. Wash, shred, and boil the cabbage in a very little salted water. Drain cabbage and chop finely. Mash the potatoes. Mix the two together.

1 Tbs. finely chopped onion   Plenty of salt and pepper
1 Tbs. butter or cream

Add these to the vegetable mixture and beat well. Replace in the pan and make very hot.

4 bacon rashers

Remove rinds and cut rashers in half. Roll up each piece and fasten on a skewer. Grill until the outside is crisp and serve as a garnish.

187

CORN

A collective term used for the seeds of cereals such as wheat, rye, oats, barley, and maize. In cookery it usually means maize or sweet corn products such as corn-on-the-cob, cornflour, cornflakes, and canned corn.

CORN-ON-THE-COB

This is fresh green corn boiled and served either as a vegetable with meat or as a separate course.

Cooking Time 10–20 mins. or pressure cook 4 mins. *Quantities.* Allow 1 ear per person.

One piece of corn is known as a 'head' or 'ear' and consists of a stalk with the corn grains attached to it in closely packed rows, the grain being covered with thin strands known as 'silk' and the outside being a sheath of green leaves. The sheath and silk are removed before cooking.

Boil the ears in a small amount of salted water. (If they take more than 20 mins. to become tender it is an indication that the corn is too mature for serving in this way, pressure cook instead.) Drain and serve with plenty of melted butter. The corn may also be stripped off the cob and tossed in melted butter, seasoned, and served like any vegetable.

CREAMED CORN

Boil the corn as above and serve in a *Béchamel* sauce.

CORN AND TOMATOES

Cooking Time ¼ hr.   *Quantities for 4.*

    1 oz. butter or margarine (25 g.)   *A sprig of parsley*
    1 pt. chopped tomatoes (½ l.)   ¼ bay leaf, chopped
                1 small sprig thyme, chopped

Heat the fat in a saucepan and cook the tomatoes and herbs in it for 10 mins.

    1 pt. canned corn (½ l.)   Salt and pepper   1 tsp. sugar

Add the corn, sugar, and seasoning to taste. Cook for 20 mins. and serve hot as a vegetable.

COURGETTES or *Zucchini*

Baby marrows about 3–4 in. (8–10 cm.) long. They are usually cooked in butter in a covered pan for about 15 mins. Larger ones are sliced or slit lengthwise and cooked in the same way. See also *Vegetable Marrow*.

CUCUMBER or *Cucumis*

C. sativus is the ridge or field cucumber, *var anglicus* is the hot-house cucumber, *C. anguria* or Burr Gherkin is used for pickling. Ridge cucumbers are used for large gherkins. Cucumbers belong to the same family as melons and gourds. They are used as an ingredient in mixed pickles or pickled alone and some are preserved in a mild sour-sweet brine and sold in cans or sealed glass jars. This variety and the gherkins are often sold loose in delicatessens. Some people find them very indigestible and various methods of treating cucumbers are recommended to overcome this difficulty. Some say they should be sliced and salted for several hours before use in order to draw out the indigestible juices, others swear by the removal of the peel and seeds, while others say the peel must be left on. They are usually served raw in salads and sandwiches but, when cheap, are used as a vegetable in the same way as marrow.

CUCUMBER SAUTÉ (to serve as a garnish for meat and fish dishes)

Cooking Time about 5 mins.   *Quantities* for 4.

   1 *medium-sized cucumber*

Peel and cut in dice.

   1 *oz. butter* (25 g.)   Pinch of pepper
                          ½ *tsp. salt*

Heat the butter in a small pan, add cucumber and seasoning, cover, and simmer gently until the cucumber is tender.

STUFFED CUCUMBERS

Cooking Time 25–30 mins.   *Temperature* E.375° (190°C), G.5. *Quantities* for 4.

   2 *cucumbers*

Peel and cut in half lengthwise, removing the seeds to make a cavity for stuffing. Alternatively, the cucumber can be cut in pieces across and enough of the centre removed to make a cup.

   4 *Tbs. breadcrumbs*   2 *Tbs. cheese*
   4 *Tbs. chopped or minced ham*   *White stock*
                          Salt and pepper

Mix together using enough stock to moisten. Stuff the cucumbers and put them in a shallow baking dish with enough stock to moisten the bottom of the dish. Cover the dish and bake until the cucumber is tender.

Tomato or brown sauce

Serve with a little sauce poured over and more handed separately.

Variations. Other cooked meats can be used in place of the ham. A little chopped, fried, or grilled bacon mixed with other meats is an improvement.

FUNGI

A wide variety of plants which are either parasites on living plants and animals or else feed on dead organic matter.

Edible fungi are best known by the variety *Psalliota campestis* or field mushroom now very widely cultivated, especially for culinary purposes. See *Mushrooms*.

Many other edible fungi grow in Britain. As some fungi are poisonous anyone who wants to experiment with edible fungi is advised to study a specialist book on the subject, one which has reliable illustrations. It is also a good idea to visit a museum which has pictures of fungi to use as an aid in identification.

GHERKINS or *Cucumis*

These are of two kinds, the small prickly gherkins which are pickled and used for *hors-d'œuvre*, for serving with cocktails and for garnishing, *C. anguria* or 'burr gherkin'. The other is the large gherkin or ridge cucumber, *C. sativus*, which is usually made into a sour-sweet pickle frequently flavoured with dill.

GOURD or *Cucurbita*

A plant belonging to the same family as the marrow and pumpkin. There are edible kinds of gourds but those grown in Britain are usually small decorative ones of varying shapes and colours grown for ornament only and known as 'ornamental gourds'.

KALE

A green vegetable of which there are many varieties, all belonging to the *Brassica* family. It is in season from November to June, but is mainly eaten in the winter months. The leaves should be picked when the plant is young, otherwise the green parts need to be stripped from the coarse stalk. Young leaves are cooked whole and the coarser ones sliced. Cook in the same way as cabbage.

KOHL RABI or *Brassica Caulorapa*

The part eaten is a swollen shoot growing above ground and with numerous small leaves growing out of the top. They are easy to grow but need to be gathered while they are small, and used straight away as the flavour is not very lasting. They are peeled and prepared in the same way as turnips but they have a milder flavour. They are specially good boiled in a little water and served with a parsley sauce made with the cooking liquid. (Do not salt the water too much.) They are also eaten in salads, either raw and shredded, or cooked and diced or sliced.

LEEK or *Allium porrum*

One of the oldest of cultivated vegetables which belongs to the onion family, but has a distinctive flavour. Any seed catalogue shows that there are several varieties of leek available, two of the best known being the Giant Musselburg and the Lyon leek.

Leeks are in season for about nine months of the year (not usually about from June to August). During the cold weather they keep well left in the ground and are dug as required. They form an important flavouring ingredient in a wide variety of dishes such as soups, stews, casseroles, and as a vegetable on their own.

During the growing period, leeks are usually earthed up to keep them white, and soil becomes lodged between the top leaves. Careful washing is needed to make sure all this is removed. Begin by cutting off the green tops either entirely down to the white or leaving about 2 in. (5 cm.) of green, according to taste. Remove any coarse outer white leaves or any damaged parts. Cut off the roots, being sure to leave enough of the base to hold the white leaves in position.

Slit each leek about a third of the way down and wash them under running water, opening the top leaves back well to remove all dirt. Drain upside down.

Very small leeks are tied in bundles before cooking to make them easier to manage.

BOILED LEEKS

Cooking Time 10–20 mins. depending on size.
Quantities Allow at least ¼–⅓ lb. (250–375 g.) per person or 1–2 leeks. Prepare the leeks. See page 191. Use a pan large enough to let them lie flat. Heat about 1 in. (2½ cm.) water in the pan with 1 tsp. salt to 1 lb. (½ kg.) leeks.

When it is boiling, add the leeks, cover, and boil gently until they feel tender when pierced at the root ends. Drain them upside down in a colander to remove as much water as possible. Serve plain or with a sauce of melted butter or with a white sauce (using some vegetable water), *Béchamel*, cheese, caper, or tomato sauce.

LEEKS WITH CHEESE

Cooking Time 45 mins.   *Temperature* E.375° (190°C), G.5.
Quantities for **4.**

Prepare the leeks and boil until tender.

2 *lb. leeks* (1 *kg.*)

4 oz. grated cheese (1 *c. or* 125 *g.*)

Sprinkle a layer of cheese in a shallow baking dish. Drain the leeks and arrange them on the cheese. Cover with more of the cheese.

6 *Tbs. double cream*   *Salt and pepper*

Add cream, salt and pepper, and a final layer of cheese. Bake until golden brown and hot. Serve as a separate course or as a vegetable with chicken, veal, or fish.

LENTILS or *Lens esculenta*

Seeds of a small plant of which there are many varieties. It is grown widely in southern Europe, Egypt, and India. The plant has pods about ¾ in. long and ¼ in. broad (2 × 2½ cm.) containing two lens-shaped seeds. These are sold in the dry state.

BOILING LENTILS

Cooking Time about 15 mins. after soaking 1 hr.
Quantities Allow 2–4 oz. per person (50–125 g.).
If you want the lentils to keep their shape, soak them for an hour in cold water to cover and boil them for about 15 mins. in this water. They may be cooked without the soaking but will take longer to

cook and will go to a mush, suitable for a *purée* or soup. Add double their volume of cold water, a ham bone, or bacon rinds, an onion, a clove, and salt and pepper. When cooked, drain and toss in butter or margarine.

LENTIL CURRY

Cooking Time 1 hr.   *Quantities for 3-4.*

4 *oz. lentils* (125 g.)

Boil the lentils until tender, drain.

3 *oz. carrot* (75 g.)   2 *oz. butter or margarine* (50 g.)
1 *oz. onion* (25 g.)   1 *small green banana*
3 *oz. turnip* (75 g.)   1 *small apple*

Prepare the fruit and vegetables and cut into largish pieces. Heat the fat and cook them in it without browning.

1 *Tbs. curry powder or according to taste*

Add during the cooking of the vegetables. When the vegetables are tender, lift out and keep hot.

1 *small tomato*

Skin and cut up. Add lentils and tomato to the pan.

1 *oz. raisins* (25 g.)   1 *oz. coconut* (25 g.)

Add to the pan. Cook for a few minutes.

½ *pt. stock* (¼ *l.*)

Gradually add the stock during cooking, until it is all absorbed and continue cooking until the mixture is firm but not dry. Return the vegetables.

1 *Tbs. lemon juice*   1 *Tbs. chopped parsley*   *Salt*

Add to the pan. Season to taste. Serve with

Boiled rice.

LENTIL CUTLETS

Cooking Time 45-60 mins.   *Quantities for 4.*

1 *small onion*   1 *tsp. tomato ketchup*
½ *pt. water* (¼ *l.*)   *Pinch of ground mace*
Salt and pepper   1 *oz. margarine* (25 g.)
4 *oz. lentils* (125 g.) *soaked*

Skin and chop the onion and cook all together until the lentils are nearly tender.

Add and continue cooking for 10 mins. or until the mixture is fairly thick and the lentils tender. Spread the mixture out on a plate to cool. Divide into four and shape into cutlets or flat cakes.

2 Tbs. ground rice

Coat with beaten egg and then in crumbs.

Egg   Breadcrumbs

Frying oil

Fry until brown in deep or shallow oil. Serve hot.

MUSHROOMS

These are the most widely used of all edible fungi. They are also known as Field Mushrooms or *Psalliota campestris* or *Agaricus campestris*.

Mushrooms are an important cultivated crop with large quantities being grown indoors on beds of compost. They are sold as raw mushrooms, canned in a variety of preparations, and dried. They are also used for making canned and packet soups, and for mushroom ketchup. Dried ones are useful for flavouring soups and stews. Mushrooms vary in size from the very small button mushrooms which are pink and white, to the large fully-open mushrooms with a flat head and dark brown-black gills.

Cultivated mushrooms do not need peeling, simply wash and dry and cut the stalks off level with the sides of the mushrooms. These should not be wasted but chopped and used with the tops or in a separate dish or to make stock. Mushroom stalks are sometimes sold separately much more cheaply than whole mushrooms and are useful for flavouring purposes.

Mushrooms which have been gathered from the fields should be peeled in order to see if they have worms in them. If so, they should be discarded. A very large number of fully grown out-door mushrooms are infested and it is often a waste of time to gather any but the very small ones.

Button mushrooms are used for adding whole to a dish, for garnishing purposes, and for use in dishes where a light colour is required. Fully grown mushrooms darken the cooking liquid but have more flavour. Avoid over-cooking mushrooms as this causes loss of flavour.

BAKED MUSHROOMS

Cooking Time about 10 mins.   *Temperature* E.375° (190°C), G.5.
Quantities allow 1–2 oz. per portion (25–50 g.).

Wash the mushrooms and remove the stalks. Put them in a shallow baking dish which has been liberally greased with butter. Sprinkle with salt and pepper and cover with a lid. Bake until just tender and serve with any liquid that runs out.

MUSHROOMS WITH CREAM

Cooking Time 10–15 mins.   *Quantities* for 4.

½ *medium-sized onion*   2 *oz. butter* (50 g.)

1 *lb. mushrooms* (½ *kg.*)

½ *pt. double cream* (¼ *l.*)   *Salt and cayenne pepper*

Peel and chop the onion. Heat the butter and cook the onion in it without allowing it to brown.

Wash and chop the mushrooms and stalks coarsely. Add them to the onions and cook until they are almost tender.

Add the cream and cook very gently until it thickens. Season to taste and serve very hot. This is suitable for serving as a hot *hors-d'œuvre*, or as a vegetable course.

FRIED MUSHROOMS

Wash the mushrooms and remove the stalks. These may be sliced and fried with the tops. Dry thoroughly. Fry in a little butter or oil or in the fat from fried bacon. Cook until they are just tender. Fried mushrooms are very tasty but they soak up a lot of fat and are inclined to be indigestible. Keep the portions small. They are used as a garnish for meat dishes or to serve with bacon or as a snack meal served on fried bread or toast.

GRILLED MUSHROOMS

Wash and remove the stalks. Dry thoroughly. If they are to be cooked by themselves, put them gill sides up in the pan and put a knob of butter in each one. Grill gently until just tender. If they are being cooked with bacon, put them under the bacon so that the bacon fat bastes them; omit the butter.

They may also be grilled on skewers. See *Kebabs*, page 24.

195

NETTLES

These belong to the *Urtica* family. The two common ones are *U. dioica* (perennial), and *U. urens* (annual).

Country people still sometimes use young nettle tops as a spring vegetable, cooking them like spinach or spring cabbage. They have a curious dry, astringent effect in the mouth probably due to the presence of formic acid, the substance which is responsible for the rash produced by nettle stings.

Both wine and beer can be made from nettles.

OKRA or Gumbo, or Ladies' Fingers, or *Hibiscus esculentus*

This is a plant belonging to the mallow family. It is an annual growing to about 6 feet in height in warm countries. The immature green seed pods are eaten as a vegetable. They are sometimes on sale raw in shops in Britain but are also available canned. Fresh okra are boiled in a little salted water, drained, and dressed with melted butter or cream. They can also be stewed in a little butter with water to moisten. They contain useful amounts of vitamin C.

ONION or *Allium cepa*

A vegetable used chiefly for flavouring purposes but also as a dish on its own as well as for making sauces and soups. Soups are available in canned and dried form; and dried onion and onion salt for flavouring.

CHOPPED ONIONS

Chopping in the ordinary way with a cook's knife makes most people weep. There are special chopping gadgets on the market designed to keep the onions covered during chopping and so prevent the volatile and irritating vapours from reaching the eyes. Less troublesome than chopping is to slice the peeled onion almost through to the root end in thin layers and then to slice again at right angles. Finally slice horizontally when the onion will fall away into small dice, suitable for most recipes requiring chopped onion.

Onions can also be chopped in water in an electric blender or liquidiser.

ONIONS *AU GRATIN*. See *Vegetables au Gratin*, page 163

BAKED ONIONS. *Method 1*

Wrap the unpeeled onions in foil, singly, and stand them on a baking shelf. Cook in a moderate-hot oven until they are soft when squeezed, about 45–60 mins.

Method 2

Skin the onions and cook them in a little fat in a moderate or hot oven until they are tender. They may be baked round a joint of meat or cooked in a separate pan.

BOILED ONIONS

Cooking Time ¾–1½ hrs. depending on the size.
Quantities Allow 4–6 oz. per person (125–175 g.).

Remove the brown skins, put the onions in boiling salted water and boil gently until they are tender. Drain well and keep the water to make a sauce to serve with them (see *Vegetable Sauce*, page 253), or for stock for soups.

BOILED ONIONS. Pressure cooker method

Cooking Time 3–10 mins. depending on the size.
Quantities Allow 4–6 oz. per portion (125–175 g.).

Remove the brown skins and cut large onions in halves or pieces. Put ½ pt. (¼ l.) water in the cooker and put the onions on the rack or in the vegetable basket. Sprinkle them with salt and cook at 15 lb. pressure. Reduce pressure quickly. Serve as above.

FRIED ONIONS

Sliced onion may be shallow fried in a little hot fat. Cook them slowly, stirring occasionally until they are lightly browned and tender. Onion rings may also be fried in deep fat and are then crisp and useful for garnishing purposes. The onion rings are dipped in flour and then in milk and again in flour. Drop into hot oil and fry until brown and crisp.

See also *Fried Beef Steak and Onions*, page 35.

SUGARED OR GLAZED ONIONS

Cooking Time 45 mins.   *Quantities* for 3–4.
    1 lb. small onions or shallots (½ kg.)

197

Skin and leave whole. Boil in salted water until they are nearly tender. Drain well.

Heat the butter in a saucepan and fry the onions in it until they are brown all over.

2 oz. butter (50 g.)

1 oz. sugar (25 g.)

Sprinkle this over the onions, cover with a lid and cook gently for a few minutes or until the onions are quite tender. Serve hot with roast beef, lamb, or pork.

SPRING ONIONS

These are the thinnings from rows of ordinary onions. Both the white bulb and the green tops are edible. Cut off the roots, trim off any damaged leaves, and wash the onions well. Serve whole or sliced in salads, whole with cheese, or chopped in mashed potatoes, or use in place of onions in any dish.

TREE ONIONS or *Allium viviparum*

These have long stalks with clusters of small onions at the top. They can be used in the same way as ordinary onions and the green parts can be chopped and used like chives.

WELSH ONION or *Allium fistulosum*

These look like small leeks growing in clumps. They are used for flavouring in the same way as onions and the green parts can be chopped and used in place of chives for winter cooking when chives are not available. They may also be used in place of spring onions.

PARSNIP or *Pastinaca sativa*

A useful common root vegetable which does not require winter storage as it can be left in the ground and dug as required. It has a strong flavour and characteristic texture disliked by many people. But those who like them at all are usually very fond of parsnips.

To prepare them for cooking, scrub well, remove any small root-lets and the top bit where the leaves grew. Then peel, using a potato peeler. They gradually turn brown after peeling but not as quickly as potatoes. If peeled in advance keep them immersed in cold water.

BAKED OR ROAST PARSNIPS

Cooking Time E.½ hr. or more depending on size of pieces and temperature of oven.

Temperature E.350° (180°C), G.4 upwards.
Quantities Allow 6–8 oz. per person (175–250 g.).

Peel the parsnips and cut them in halves or quarters. Roll in hot fat and roast until they are tender and brown. Turn, if necessary, to make them brown all over. Parsnips contain some sugar and this caramelises on the outside to give a delicious flavour.

BOILED PARSNIPS

Cooking Time 15–30 mins. depending on size and age.
Quantities Allow 6–8 oz. per person (175–250 g.).

Peel the parsnips and cut them in pieces. Boil a little (about 1 in. or 2½ cm. in pan) salted water, add the vegetable, cover, and boil until they are tender. Drain well. Mash in the same way as potatoes and add a generous piece of butter or well-flavoured dripping and plenty of pepper. Beat until smooth.

PARSNIPS STEWED IN BUTTER OR DRIPPING

Cooking Time 15–20 mins.
Quantities Allow 6–8 oz. per person (175–250 g.).

Peel the parsnips and cut them in thick slices. Melt some butter or dripping to cover the bottom of a saucepan with a thin layer. Add the parsnips, sprinkle them with salt and pepper, cover, and stew slowly, shaking the pan occasionally. By the time they are tender they should be golden brown and most of the fat absorbed. Sprinkle with chopped parsley and serve hot.

PEA or *Pisum*

The garden pea belongs to the family of *Leguminosae. See Legumes.* There are many varieties grown and plant breeders are constantly improving on existing varieties. Fresh green peas are in season from late spring to early autumn.

Pods of young peas can be used to make stock and have a very good flavour. See *Vegetable Stock*, page 18. They can be used to make a pea soup, but the sieving needed is tedious unless you have an electrically-driven sieve.

CANNED PEAS

Several different types are available:

Processed Peas are mature dried peas which have been cooked and canned, usually with some green colouring added. It is the cheapest canned pea and one of the most popular.

Garden Peas are young green peas canned as soon as gathered. Some have mint added and some green colouring. Imported ones are usually mint and colouring-free.

Petits Pois are very small sweet imported peas, yellowish in colour but of excellent flavour.

Pea Soup and Pease Pudding are also sold in cans.

DRIED PEAS

There are two quite different varieties of these. The older type is a mature ripe pea which needs soaking and long cooking (2–3 hrs.) or cooking under pressure (¼ hr.). These peas are mainly used for canned processed peas and in dried and canned soups.

Modern dried peas are young green peas dried by new fast methods and require only about 15 mins. boiling, or according to directions on the packet.

Split peas are halved dried peas and may be yellow or green. They are used in soups and vegetarian cooking. They need soaking in boiling water overnight and then boiling for ½ hr. for the yellow ones and ¾–1 hr. for green ones.

FROZEN PEAS

Should be boiled while still frozen and can also be added frozen to casseroles, soups, and other recipes needing fresh green peas.

BOILED FRESH PEAS

Cooking Time 15–20 mins., depending on size and age.

Quantities Allow at least ½ lb (¼ kg.) unshelled per person according to the fullness of the pods. Shelled peas allow 3–4 oz. per person (75–125 g.).

Shell the peas, preferably just before using them and if they come from your own garden pick them as near the time they are to be used as possible.

Boil ½–1 in. (1–2 cm.) water in a pan with a little salt and sugar. When boiling, add the peas, cover, and boil gently until they are just tender. Drain, keeping any stock for gravy or soup, and toss the peas in a little butter or margarine.

Some people like to put a piece of mint with the peas during cooking, but this is a pity unless the peas are tasteless ones.

FRENCH METHOD OF COOKING PEAS

Cooking Time about ½ hr.   *Quantities for 4.*

4 or 5 outside leaves of a large lettuce

Wash and use them to line the bottom of the saucepan, either leave whole or shred them if the lettuce is a coarse one.

2 lb. well-filled pods (1 kg.) or 1 lb. frozen peas (½ kg.)
1 oz. butter or dripping (25 kg.)   Pinch of pepper
2 or 3 Tbs. water   2 rashers bacon   ½ tsp. salt
4 or 5 spring-onion bulbs or small onions

Shell peas. Remove the rind and chop the bacon. Skin the onions. Put all the ingredients in the saucepan, cover, and cook gently until the peas are just tender, adding more water if needed to prevent burning. Serve the peas with any liquid and the other ingredients.

SPANISH PEAS

Cooking Time ½ hr.   *Quantities for 4.*

1 Tbs. flour   2 Tbs. water
2 Tbs. tomato paste

Mix together.

2 lb. well-filled pods green peas (1 kg.) or 1 lb. frozen (½ kg.)
Shell the peas.

1 tsp. salt   2 Tbs. chopped parsley
Pinch of pepper   A speck of garlic
1 oz. lard or oil (25 g.)

Put in a pan with the peas and tomato mixture. Cover and cook over a gentle heat until the peas are tender.

2 oz. bacon (50 g.)   8 oz. chipolata sausages (¼ kg.)

Remove rinds and grill or fry the bacon and sausages. Cut in pieces. Add to the peas just before serving and make sure all are hot. Mix well and serve.

PEASE PUDDING

Cooking Time Dried peas about 2 hrs.; split peas $\frac{1}{2}$–$\frac{3}{4}$ hr. plus 1 hr. steaming in each case.
Quantities for 4.

8 oz. *dried or split peas* ($\frac{1}{4}$ kg.)

Wash the peas and tie them in a piece of muslin. Cooking time is reduced if they are soaked in cold or boiling water for 1 hr. or more before cooking but this is not essential. Use 2 pt. (1 l.) water for soaking and/or cooking.

1 *onion*   *Cloves*

Peel the onion and stick a few cloves in it. Put the bag of peas in the water with the onion and boil gently until tender. Lift out the peas and rub them through a sieve or put in the electric blender.

1 oz. *margarine or butter* (25 g.)
1 *egg*
Salt and pepper

Tomato or brown

While the *purée* is still warm, beat in the fat and then the egg and seasoning to taste. Put the mixture in a greased basin, cover, and steam for 1 hr. Turn out and serve with cooked meat such as pork, ham, or bacon, or serve as a separate dish with a sauce such as

Alternative. Use canned pease pudding which simply needs reheating.

POTATOES or *Solanum tuberosum*

A plant introduced from America to Britain in the sixteenth century and now the most important vegetable crop grown.

There are many varieties of potato and they are classified according to the time of year when they mature.

EARLY POTATOES

Arran Pilot. A kidney-shaped potato at its best when used before August. Later it is suitable for chips.

Epicure. A round potato with white flesh and very deep eyes. Popular in the north.

Duke of York. A kidney-shaped potato with a distinctive yellow flesh.

Home Guard. Are regular in shape and round-oval.

MAIN CROP POTATOES

Arran Banner. A white round potato with medium to deep eyes. Good for baking in the winter.

Golden Wonder. Dry mealy potatoes with nutty flavour, mainly in Scotland and rarely in England.

Kerr's Pink. Round with pink skin and white flesh and mealy texture. Favourite in Scotland.

King Edward. Red markings on skin, creamy flesh, large regular shape, shallow eyes.

Majestic. White flesh, kidney shape, very good for chips.

Waxy Potatoes. These are best for salads and certain other special potato dishes. New potatoes are waxy but after that the Dutch imported potato is usually the only one available unless you grow your own.

Preserved potatoes are available in a number of forms. Canned potatoes are not particularly good but the dehydrated varieties such as potato flakes and powder make a very good emergency supply for dishes needing mashed potatoes. Dried chips in packets are fairly new and can be very good. Frozen chips are not so successful but potato crisps (game chips) are good and very popular.

PREPARING POTATOES

Scrub them well to remove loose dirt. For peeling, use a potato peeler or a small sharp vegetable knife. Peel as thinly as possible. If a mechanical peeler is used, only leave the potatoes in as long as needed to remove the minimum of skin. This is for the sake of flavour and economy of potato and food value. Sometimes it is convenient to prepare them in advance but they should then be covered with plenty of cold water to prevent discoloration. Except when making chips do not cut the potatoes before soaking as the greater the cut surfaces the greater the losses will be to the water.

BOILED POTOES

Cooking Time 20–40 mins., depending on size and condition.
Quantities Allow 5–8 oz. or more per person (150–250 g.).

Select potatoes of uniform size so that they will all cook in the same time. If that is not possible, cut the large ones in halves or quarters. Scrub off the dirt, peel thinly, and remove eyes and damaged parts. Sound potatoes can be boiled without peeling and served in their jackets or peeled before serving. This way gives the best flavour and food value. If the potatoes are peeled in advance of cooking cover them with cold water to prevent discoloration.

Put about 2 in. (5 cm.) of water in the pan with 1 tsp. salt to each pound of potatoes. Bring the water to the boil, add the potatoes, cover the pan, and bring back to the boil. Reduce the heat to keep the potatoes just below boiling until they are almost tender. Actual boiling gives faster cooking but the floury type of potato is more likely to break. Rapid boiling causes very bad breaking. Drain the water away, return the potatoes to the pan, and keep over a gentle heat with the lid tilted for a few minutes to dry them off and finish cooking. Serve at once, sprinkled with chopped parsley, or use to make mashed potatoes or potato *purée*.

MASHED POTATOES

Quantities for 3–4.

1 Tbs. hot milk	1 lb. freshly boiled potatoes ($\frac{1}{2}$ kg.)
Salt and pepper	Chopped fresh herbs
	1 oz. butter or margarine (25 g.)

Mash the hot potatoes, or rub them through a sieve. Beat in the milk, fat, and flavourings and continue beating until well blended and quite smooth. Keep the pan over a gentle heat to make sure the potatoes remain hot. Serve at once.

NEW POTATOES

Imported new potatoes begin arriving in Britain towards the end of the winter. The flavour is best if they are boiled in their skins. Simply wash and cook as for boiled potatoes, but the time required will be only 15–20 mins., depending on the size. Serve in their jackets or skin them and toss in a little melted butter and sprinkle with chopped parsley. People who are fond of mint, cook a sprig with the potatoes, and remove it before serving. New potatoes can be used in any recipe not needing mashed potatoes. They are the best for potato salads.

ROAST POTATOES

There are different methods of roasting potatoes, but the best ones use a hot oven.

Cooking Time ¾ hr.   *Temperature E.450° (230°C), G.8.*

Peel the potatoes and roll them in flour. Heat some fat in a baking tin and roll the potatoes in this. Then put near the top of the oven and turn once or twice during cooking.

Alternative methods are to put the potatoes round the joint and baste them occasionally. If the meat is being cooked at a low temperature the potatoes probably will not brown and in this case it is better to cook them separately but give them plenty of time. Alternatively, par-boil the potatoes, increase the heat in the oven for the last 30 mins, and cook the potatoes quickly near the top.

SAUTÉ POTATOES

> Boiled potatoes   Fat or oil for frying
> Chopped parsley or other green herbs

Cut the potatoes into ¼ in. (6 mm.) slices. Heat the fat and fry the potatoes until they are golden brown turning once during frying. Serve on a hot dish sprinkled with parsley or green herbs.

Alternative Method. Sprinkle the potatoes with grated cheese and heat gently until it begins to melt. Fried chopped bacon and/or onion can be added for extra flavour.

POTATO CHIPS

Cooking Time 8–10 mins.   *Frying Temperature* 390°F (200°C).
Quantities 6–8 oz. raw potato per portion (150–250 g.).

Majestic are the best of the ordinary potatoes but a waxy variety is even better as it soaks up less fat. Use large potatoes, wash and peel them. A potato chipping device is a time saver, if you make chips often. Otherwise slice the potatoes lengthwise about ⅜ in. (9 mm.)

thick and then again the other way to make the chips. Cover with cold water and soak for about 1 hr. Drain and dry thoroughly on a clean towel. Fry until golden brown and tender. Drain well on absorbent paper, sprinkle with salt, and serve at once.

Alternative Method. Fry the chips at 370–380° (190°C) until they are just beginning to brown at the edges. Remove them from the fat and heat it up to 390° (200°C). Return the chips to finish browning. This often gives a crisper result.

GAME CHIPS (Crisps)

Wash and peel the potatoes. Cut into thin shavings on a vegetable slicer or shredder. Soak in cold water for an hour. Drain, dry, and fry like chips, but they will take only about 1 min.

POTATO RIBBONS

Wash and peel potatoes. Then with a potato peeler or small vegetable knife peel the potato flesh in as long a ribbon as possible. Soak for an hour in cold water and then fry in deep fat in the same way as potato chips but be very careful to drain and dry them well before putting them in the deep fat.

JULIENNE POTATOES (Straw)

Wash and peel large potatoes. Cut into thin strips about the thickness of a match. Some of the mechanical shredders will do this very easily. Soak in cold water for 1 hr, drain, and dry thoroughly. Fry in deep fat as for potato chips but they will only take about 1 min. Usually served with game or poultry or for garnishing purposes.

PARISIAN POTATOES

Cooking Time 10–15 mins.
Quantities Allow 4–6 oz. per portion (125–150 g.).

Cut raw potatoes in small cubes or shape them into balls with a vegetable cutter. Fry them in shallow fat until they are well browned and cooked through. Drain and sprinkle with chopped parsley, salt, and pepper.

POTATO CAKES or RISSOLES or CROQUETTES

Frying Time 2–3 mins. *Fat Temperature* 390°F (200°C).
Quantities for 8 cakes.

2 Tbs. milk	1 lb. boiled potatoes (½ kg.)
1 tsp. salt	¼ tsp. ground mace or nutmeg
Pinch of pepper	2 Tbs. chopped parsley
	1 tsp. onion juice or grated onion

Mash the potatoes and beat in the milk and flavourings. Leave to become almost cold. Mould into flat cakes, balls, or cylinders according to taste.

Fresh breadcrumbs   1 egg   Oil or fat for frying

Beat the egg with a little cold water. Put the crumbs in a paper bag. Brush each cake with egg and then shake it in the crumbs until it is well coated. Fry in deep fat until golden brown.

Alternative Cooking Methods

Grilling. Put in the grill pan with a knob of fat on each and grill until brown on both sides.

Sauté. Fry in a little shallow fat until brown on both sides.

Baked. Put on a baking tray with a small knob of fat on each cake. Bake in a hot oven for 15–20 mins. or until heated through and brown.

BAKED JACKET POTATOES

Cooking Time 45 mins. or longer, depending on the size.
Temperature E.400–450° (200–230°C), G.6–8.
Quantities Allow 1 potato per portion.

Potatoes can be baked at lower temperatures for very much longer times but then they do not have the tasty skins and floury insides of those baked faster.

Choose potatoes without blemishes and scrub well. Dry in paper towels and rub the skins well with a greased paper or oil them. This is not essential but gives a nicer skin for eating. Put on a baking sheet or tin or straight on the grid shelves and bake until one feels soft when squeezed gently in a cloth. They should then be pricked to let the steam out and keep them floury otherwise they become soggy on cooling. Prick a cross on top of each using a table fork.

Gently squeeze the potato at the bottom with both hands and the cross will open out into four leaves. Put in some salt and pepper and a knob of butter and serve at once.

BAKED STUFFED POTATOES

Bake the potatoes as in the previous recipe. Cut a piece off one of the flat sides of the cooked potato or cut large ones in half. Use a small spoon to scoop out most of the inside, leaving just enough to keep the skin in shape. Put the potato in a hot basin and mash with one of the flavourings given below. Pile back into the shells, and return to a hot oven for a few minutes to brown the top.

Quantities for 1 potato

1–2 Tbs. hot milk   ½ tsp. butter or margarine

Salt and pepper to taste

Beat these into the potatoes and then add one of the following:

1 Tbs. chopped parsley or watercress or mixed fresh herbs
1 Tbs. chopped cooked meat, game, or poultry
1 Tbs. chopped or flaked, cooked or canned fish, fresh or smoked
1 Tbs. chopped fried mushrooms

Or, return part of the potato to the shell, break in a raw egg. Pipe remaining potato round the egg and cook in the oven for 10–15 mins. or until the egg is set.

DUCHESS POTATOES

These are chiefly used for garnishing purposes. They are twice-cooked potatoes and the flavour is never as good as that of fresh potatoes and the vitamin C content may easily be practically nil.

Cooking Time 40–45 mins. (including boiling the potatoes).

Temperature E.450° (230°C), G.8.

Quantities for 4.

1 lb. potatoes (½ kg.)

1 oz. butter or margarine (25 g.)   1 egg or 2 yolks

Boil the potatoes and sieve them while hot.

Return them to the pan and dry them over a gentle heat or in the oven.

Beat in the fat. Beat the egg and add it, beating again to mix thoroughly.

208

Hot cream or milk

Beat in to make the mixture soft enough to use in a forcing bag.

Pinch of grated nutmeg   Salt and pepper

Add seasoning to taste. Put in a forcing bag with a large rosette nozzle and pipe into rosette pyramids or other shapes. Pipe on to baking trays or flat tins.

Beaten egg or melted butter

Brush the potato with one of these and bake until lightly browned and heated through. Use to garnish meat or fish dishes.

POTATO PATTIES

Use the Duchess Potato recipe and put the mixture in a forcing bag fitted with a star tube. Force on to a greased tray in coils to form a case. Brush with egg or melted butter and bake in a hot oven until brown. Serve hot, filled with meat, fish, game, or poultry in a well-seasoned sauce.

ANNA POTATOES

Cooking Time 1 hr.   *Temperature* E.425° (220°C), G.7.
Quantities for 3–4.

1 lb. new or waxy potatoes ($\frac{1}{2}$ kg.)

Peel, wash, and dry the potatoes and if they are uneven sizes trim them to match. Cut in very thin slices, about $\frac{1}{8}$ in. (3 mm.) or thinner. Grease a 6 in. (15 cm.) cake tin and put a circle of greased paper at the bottom. Arrange the potatoes in overlapping circles beginning from the outside.

Salt and pepper   2–4 oz. butter (50–125 g.)

Melt the butter and sprinkle each layer of potatoes with salt and pepper and a little butter. Press each layer down well. When all the potatoes are in, put a layer of buttered paper on top, and cover with a lid. Bake until the potatoes are brown all through. If they appear to become dry during cooking, add some more butter. Drain off any excess butter before serving them. Turn the cake out on a hot dish and cut in wedges.

POTATO RAGOUT

Cooking Time 45 mins. *Quantities for* 4.

16 *small potatoes*	3 *large onions*
1 *oz. fat* (25 *g.*)	2 *Tbs. flour*

Peel the potatoes and onions and cut them into quarters.

Heat the fat in a large pan and stir in the flour. Stir and cook until it begins to turn yellow.

Add to the flour and stir until it boils.

1 *pt. stock* (½ *l.*)	
Salt and pepper	1 *bay leaf*
2 *sprigs parsley*	1 *sprig thyme*

Add these to the pan together with the potatoes and onions. Cover and boil gently for 45 mins. or until the vegetables are tender. Serve hot as a supper or high-tea dish to accompany sausages or cold meat.

PUMPKIN or Cucurbits or Winter Squash

A trailing plant belonging to the same family as marrows and gourds. There are several varieties of edible pumpkin, most of them large, round, and deep yellow to orange in colour. They need plenty of sun to mature and ripen with a good flavour. To prepare pumpkin for cooking, cut it in pieces, remove the seeds, and pulp and the tough outer skin, though this is sometimes removed after cooking and when the skin is very tough this is the simpler method.

Pumpkin seeds are edible and contain a fair amount of protein, fat, and B vitamins.

BAKED OR ROAST PUMPKIN

Cooking Time 45–60 mins.
Temperature E.375–400° (190°–200°C), G.5–6.
Quantities for 4.

2 *lb. pumpkin* (1 *kg.*)	*Salt and pepper*
Melted butter, margarine, or oil	

Cut the pumpkin in about 8 pieces, removing seeds and skin. Put in a baking tin or dish and brush with the fat or oil. Sprinkle with salt and pepper and bake until tender and brown. It may also be cooked round roast meat.

210

BOILED PUMPKIN

Cooking Time 20–30 mins.   *Quantities for 4.*

2 *lb. pumpkin* (1 kg.)   1 *oz. butter* (25 g.)
Salt and pepper

Cut the pumpkin in pieces and remove seeds and skin. Then cut the pieces in 1 in. (2½ cm.) cubes. Boil about 1 in. water with 1 tsp. salt, add the pumpkin, cover, and boil until it is tender. Drain well, and mash with the butter and plenty of pepper.

SALSIFY or Purple Goat's Beard or *Tragopogon porrifolius*

A biennial plant cultivated for its tap root which is used as a vegetable. It is ready in the early autumn and is stored in sand for later use. Sometimes it is called the 'oyster plant' because of its flavour, though this is not always strong enough to justify the name. The roots are washed, scraped, and soaked in a solution of 1 Tbs. vinegar to 1 qt. (1 l.) water. They are cooked and served in the same way as Jerusalem artichokes, though, unless cut in small pieces, they may take very much longer to cook. Allow about 1 lb. (½ kg.) for 3 portions.

SAMPHIRE or *Crithmum maritimum*

A plant growing on shingle and on steep cliffs by the sea. It is boiled and served as a vegetable with butter and seasoning or else it is pickled like cucumber or gherkins.

SAUERKRAUT

A preparation of cabbage widely used in Germany and northern Europe. It is made from very large white cabbages which are shredded, seasoned with salt, and maybe with juniper berries or caraway seeds or other flavourings. The cabbage is weighted heavily and left to ferment, during which time lactic acid is produced and this acts as a preservative as well as giving a characteristic sharp taste to the cabbage. It is definitely an acquired taste. *Sauerkraut* is served with sausages, smoked meats such as ham and bacon, and with boiled salt beef. During the fermenting process some vitamin C is formed as well as some lost to the liquid. When cooked, *Sauerkraut* has about a third of the vitamin C content of an equivalent amount of fresh-cooked cabbage.

Sauerkraut is sold by the pound in some shops in Britain and is also available in tins.

It is cooked by putting it in a pan with a little cold water and boiling for about ½ hr., drain, and serve hot. Alternatively, cook with some butter and white wine to moisten.

SEAKALE or *Crambe maritima*

A seaside plant which grows wild amongst sand and shingle. The blanched stems are eaten and look like smooth celery. They are cooked and served like asparagus. It is sometimes on sale in greengrocers during the winter.

Cooking Time 20–30 mins.

Quantities allow 1 lb. (½ kg.) for 3 people.

Prepare the seakale by cutting off any discoloured leaves and peeling the stump. To cook, tie in bundles, put in boiling salted water, and cook until tender.

Serve with Hollandaise sauce or thicken the cooking liquid to make a sauce.

SEAKALE BEET or *Beta vulgaris var. Cicla.* Also known as Swiss Chard and Silver Beet.

This is a plant belonging to the same family as the beetroot and sugar beet. It has large handsome leaves with very broad white stems. Leaves and stems can be cooked together (stems cut up), or the two cooked separately, the green part like spinach and the white stem like celery. It is a very delicious vegetable but not often on sale in shops as the green part wilts very quickly.

SHALLOT or *Allium cepa var. ascalonicum*

A small onion with a mild flavour, used for pickling and as a vegetable (see *Onions*).

SORREL or *Rumex*

A plant related to the dock, which grows wild, but is also cultivated for use as a vegetable. The leaves are stripped from the stalks and boiled in a little water for about 20 mins. Then it is sieved to give a *purée*, seasoned, and mixed with a little butter and served with eggs, meat, or fish. It is also used to make a soup or as a salad vegetable.

SPINACH or Spinacia

There are two varieties, *S. oleracea* or 'prickly seeded' or 'winter' spinach, and *var. inermis* or 'rough-seeded' or 'summer' spinach. New Zealand spinach is a different species, *Tetragonia expansa*, but the leaves are used in the same way as the others.

For Silver Beet see *Seakale Beet*. Perpetual spinach or spinach beet is a large pale-leaved plant used like spinach, but belonging to the same family as Seakale Beet. It is in season for most of the year and is one of the varieties frequently available in shops.

Spinach needs very thorough washing, especially the small-leaved varieties which grow close to the ground and usually in sandy soil. Pick over, removing any decayed leaves and weeds, and wash in several changes of water until the last water is clean. Lift the spinach out each time to allow the sand to collect in the water. Let the water away, run in fresh, and add the spinach. Drain in a colander.

BOILED SPINACH

Cooking Time 10–15 mins.
Quantities Allow ½ lb. (¼ kg.) per person.

Wash the spinach. Drain and put in a large pan. Add 1 tsp. salt per lb. (½ kg.), cover, and bring to the boil (no water needed). Boil until tender. Drain in a colander, pressing to remove the moisture. Put back in the pan with a knob of butter or margarine and mix and heat until all free water has evaporated. If liked, add a pinch of pepper and ground mace or nutmeg.

CREAMED SPINACH

Cooking Time 20 mins.   *Quantities* for 4.
                        2 *lb. spinach* (1 *kg.*)

Boil the spinach as above. Drain well and rub through a sieve or put in an electric blender.

2 *oz. butter or margarine* (50 *g.*)   *Salt and pepper*
Pinch of grated nutmeg   *Squeeze of lemon juice*

Melt the fat in the pan used for cooking the spinach. Add the spinach and other ingredients. Heat gently until it thickens. Serve at once.

213

SPINACH AU GRATIN

Cooking Time 15–20 mins.   *Quantities for 4.*

2 *lb. spinach* (1 kg.)

Prepare and boil the spinach. See *Boiled Spinach*. Drain and chop it.

1 *oz. butter or margarine* (35 g.)

Heat in the pan and then add the spinach, cooking quickly until all the water is dried from it.

3 *oz. grated cheese* (¾ *c. or* 75 g.)   *Pinch of pepper*

Add to the spinach and mix well. Put in a greased fireproof dish.

1 *oz. melted butter* (25 g.)   1 *oz. grated cheese* (25 g.)

Sprinkle these over the top and put in a hot oven or under the grill for the cheese to melt and brown.

SWEDE or *Napobrassica*

A large root vegetable with a cream-purple outside and a yellow inside, turning orange when cooked. It is not a universally popular vegetable possibly because it is so seldom prepared in an appetising form. It is a cheap winter vegetable and has a useful content of vitamin C at a time when the amount in potatoes is at its lowest.

BOILED SWEDES

Cooking Time 20–30 mins.

Quantities Allow 6–8 oz. per portion (150–250 g.).

Wash off any dirt and peel the swedes thickly to remove the outer skin. Cut the flesh in chunks or thick slices. Boil a little salted water, add the swedes, and cook until they are tender. Drain well and then mash with a generous piece of butter and season with plenty of pepper. Serve very hot.

SWEET PEPPERS or *Capsicum annuum*

These belong to the same family as the chilli, paprika, and cayenne peppers. See *Capsicum*.

Sweet peppers are a very mild variety (except for the hot seeds), and are used as a vegetable. Most of those sold in Britain are the green or unripe variety but sometimes the ripe red and yellow ones are also available. These last two are preserved by pickling and canning and are available all the year round.

When in good condition, sweet peppers have a smooth shiny skin and are firm with no soft patches. If soft, wrinkled, and stale, they can be very hot and bitter so it is wise to taste a small piece before serving them.

To prepare them for serving and cooking, wash, dry, cut in half, scrape out all the seeds, and cut out the white pithy parts. They can then be used raw, for salads or *hors-d' œuvre*, or cooked as flavouring for casseroles, rice dishes, fish sauces, or to make a dish on their own.

SAUTÉ SWEET PEPPERS

Cooking Time 8–10 mins.   *Quantities for 4.*

4 *sweet peppers, green or red*

Wash, cut in half, remove seeds and pithy white bits. Cut in small pieces.

2 *Tbs. oil*

Heat the oil, add the peppers, cover, and cook over a gentle heat until the peppers are almost tender but not soft. Season with salt and pepper and serve as a garnish for meat, fish, or poultry.

STEWED GREEN PEPPERS WITH TOMATOES (to use as a vegetable)

Cooking Time about 20 mins.   *Quantities for 4.*

2 *or 3 green peppers*

Wash, cut in half, remove seeds and white pith. Cut in strips.

3 *large tomatoes*   1 *small onion*

Skin and slice both these

1 *oz. lard or oil (25 g.)*

Heat the fat and fry the onion in it until brown. Add pepper and tomatoes, cover, and cook for 15 mins. or until almost tender. Season to taste with salt. Serve hot with meat, fish, or omelets.

STUFFED BAKED SWEET PEPPERS

Cooking Time 35 mins. for cooked peppers, 45–60 mins. if raw peppers used.
Temperature E. 375° (190°C), G.5.
Quantities Allow 1 pepper per person.

Some prefer to use cooked peppers for this, others the raw. Which is best rather depends on the choice of filling. One which cooks quickly is better put into cooked peppers otherwise it will be over-cooked by the time the peppers are done.

Prepare the peppers either by cutting in half lengthwise or by cutting off the stem end. Scoop out all the seeds in both cases. To pre-cook either steam for about 5 mins. over boiling water or boil for 5 mins. in a little water. Drain. Fill with the stuffing and put them in a shallow baking dish. Either add a little water to moisten the dish or pour a sauce round, e.g. tomato sauce. Serve either as a main dish or as a vegetable according to the filling.

Suitable Fillings Minced raw meat pre-cooked by frying with onion and then binding with sauce; cooked minced meat bound in a sauce; cooked or canned tomatoes seasoned with salt, pepper, and sugar and topped with buttered crumbs.

STUFFED GRILLED SWEET PEPPERS

Prepare the peppers as described above but boil them in a little water for 15 mins. Drain and keep hot. Fill with a hot filling, top with cheese or buttered crumbs, and brown under the grill.

Suitable Stuffings. Hard-boiled eggs and chopped cooked ham in a white or *Béchamel* sauce; cooked ham in a white or *Béchamel* sauce; cooked diced chicken or other poultry in a tomato or other savoury sauce; cooked flaked fish in a cheese sauce.

SWEET POTATOES or *Ipomoea batatas*

These are tubers resembling the potato. They are native to India and grow in most warm countries. They are cooked and served like potatoes and also sometimes used to make sweet dishes.

TOMATO or *Lycopersicon esculentum*

An annual plant bearing red or yellow fruits, used either raw or cooked. Fresh tomatoes are available all the year round.

Canned tomatoes are either canned whole, or as pulp, or concentrated *purée* (paste) or juice. Tomato soups and sauces are canned and also sold dried.

TO SKIN TOMATOES

Plunge the tomatoes into boiling water for a minute or two and then into cold water. The skins will then come off very easily.

BAKED TOMATOES

Cooking Time 20 mins.   *Temperature* E.375° (190°C), G.5.

Wash the tomatoes and prick with a fork. Place in a fireproof dish and bake until tender. If preferred, cut the tomatoes in halves before baking, season, and put a small konb of butter on top of each.

FRIED TOMATOES

Cut in half and dip cut sides in seasoned flour. Fry, cut side down, in hot fat for 5–10 mins.

GRILLED TOMATOES

Cooking Time 10–15 mins.

Cut the tomatoes in halves, season, and grill under a moderate heat until they are tender.

Alternatively, put a small knob of butter on each before grilling.

STEWED TOMATOES

Skin the tomatoes (see above) and cut them into halves or quarters. Cook them gently in a pan without water until they are tender. Season with a little sugar, salt, and pepper.

TOMATO JUICE

Fresh juice can be made by rubbing really ripe tomatoes through a fine sieve, or by using a vegetable press, or an electric juice extractor, or by putting the tomatoes in an electric blender. In this case, it may be necessary to strain out pips. Canned tomato juice has not the flavour of fresh but is a better colour and is useful in cooking and for making cocktails.

STUFFED TOMATOES

Cooking Time 20 mins.   *Temperature* E.400° (200°C), G.6.
Quantities for 4.

1 lb. tomatoes (8 average-sized)

Wash and dry the tomatoes and cut a slice off the stem end. With

217

a small teaspoon scoop the insides into a small sieve and rub through to remove the pips.

| 1 *rasher bacon* | ½ *oz. fat* (15 *g.*) | ½ *small onion* |

Skin and chop the onion. Remove rind and chop the bacon. Heat the fat in a small pan and fry onion and bacon in it until they begin to brown. Add the tomato pulp.

1 *Tbs. grated cheese*	*Pinch of pepper*
1 *tsp. chopped parsley*	*Pinch of sugar*
Pinch of grated nutmeg	½ *tsp. salt*
1½ *oz. fresh breadcrumbs* (½ *c. or 15 g.*)	

Add these to the pan and mix well. Use this to fill the tomato cavities. Put the slices back as lids. Put tomatoes in a baking dish and cook for 20 mins. Serve hot as a separate dish or to accompany meat or fish.

SCALLOPED TOMATOES

Cooking Time 30–35 mins.   *Temperature* E.400° (200°C), G.6.
Quantities for 4.

| | 1½ *lb. ripe tomatoes* (¾ *kg.*) |

Skin the tomatoes (see page 217) or leave the skins on, according to taste. Slice the tomatoes.

| 1 *medium-sized onion* | ½ *oz. dripping* (15 *g.*) |

Skin and chop the onion and fry it in the dripping until it begins to brown.

1 *Tbs. sugar*	1 *tsp. salt*	¼ *tsp. pepper*	*Dripping*
2 *oz. grated cheese* (optional) (50 *g.*)			
3 *oz. fresh breadcrumbs* (75 *g.*)			

If the cheese is to be used, mix it with the breadcrumbs. Put the tomatoes in a fireproof baking dish in layers with the other ingredients, finishing with a layer of crumbs. Dot the top with dripping and bake in a moderate oven for 30–35 mins. or until the tomatoes are tender. Serve as a vegetable or as a separate course.

TOMATOES *AU GRATIN*

Cooking Time 45 mins.   *Temperature* E.350° (180°C), G.4.
Quantities for 4.

| | 4 *large tomatoes* |

Wash and cut in halves.

    1 shallot or small onion   1 Tbs. chopped parsley
                         1 Tbs. oil

Skin and chop the onion. Heat the oil in the bottom of a fireproof baking dish. Add the parsley and shallot and put the tomatoes on top.

        Salt and pepper   1 Tbs. oil
        Fine breadcrumbs (about 4 Tbs.)

Season the tomatoes and cover the tops with breadcrumbs. Sprinkle the oil over the tops and bake until the tomatoes are tender. *Alternative.* If more convenient, bake in a hotter oven for a shorter time.

TRUFFLE or *Tuber*

An underground fungus of which there are black and white varieties. There is a white variety occasionally found in Britain, in beech and oak woods, but the finest truffles come from France and are black. Truffles are very delicious for flavouring in the same way as mushrooms but are very expensive, even the canned ones. They are used for garnishing cold and hot dishes, for flavouring cold dishes like terrines, in sauces, and in stuffings.

TURNIP or *Brassica rapa*

In some parts of Britain swedes are also called turnips, or yellow turnips or swede turnips. See *Swedes.* The turnip is either white or yellow and much smaller and rounder than the swede. They are in season most of the year though towards the end of the winter they get pithy inside and are not much use. Young spring turnips are delicious eaten raw in slices, or grated in salads, or cooked and served whole. The flavour is strong and when they are used with other root vegetables, they should be in the minority or the flavour will predominate. The flavour goes well with lamb and mutton and pork. Young green turnip tops may be cooked like spinach.

BOILED TURNIPS

Cooking Time 15–20 mins.
Quantities Allow 6–8 oz. per person (150–250 g.).

Wash off loose dirt and peel thickly to remove the outer layer of skin. Very young ones may need no peeling at all. Leave small ones whole but cut large ones in thick slices or chunks. Put in a little boiling salted water, cover, and boil until just tender. Avoid over-cooking as they will become watery and unpleasant. Drain and mash well with a knob of butter or margarine and some pepper. If they are to be served without mashing, they look better cut into neat dice before cooking. Then toss in a little melted butter and sprinkle with chopped parsley.

TURNIPS COOKED IN FAT

Cooking Time 15–20 mins.

Quantities Allow 6–8 oz. per person (150–250 g.).

Peel the turnips and cut large ones in pieces. Heat enough dripping or butter to cover the bottom of a stew pan, add the turnips and ½ tsp. salt per lb. (½ kg.). Cover and stew gently until tender, shaking the pan occasionally. Serve, sprinkled with chopped parsley.

TURNIP RAGOUT

Cooking Time 45 mins. *Quantities* for 4–6.

Peel the turnips.

16–20 small young turnips

1 oz. dripping (25 g.)	1 pt. stock (½ l.)
1 oz. flour (3 Tbs. or 25 g.)	1 tsp. salt
Pinch of pepper	1 Tbs. sugar
	Chopped parsley

Melt the dripping in a stew pan and stir in the flour, stirring and cooking until it turns yellow. Remove from the heat and stir in the stock. Return to the heat and stir until it boils. Add the seasonings and the turnips, cover, and cook gently until the vegetables are tender, about 45 mins.

Sprinkle with parsley and serve hot as an accompaniment to lamb or pork.

VEGETABLE MARROW or *Cucurbita pepo*

A trailing plant bearing large green or yellow fruits which are eaten as a vegetable. Very small (2–3 in. or 5–6 cm.) marrows are known as 'courgettes' and are cooked without peeling. Ordinary marrows, picked when they are about 9 in. (22 cm.) long, can be cooked whole, skin and insides too, but larger ones need to be peeled and have the centre pith and seeds removed. They are in season from late summer to late autumn.

VEGETABLE MARROW *AU GRATIN*
See *Vegetables au Gratin*, page 163.

BOILED VEGETABLE MARROW

Cooking Time depends on the age, 10–20 mins. or longer.
Quantities 2–3 lb. (1–1½ kg.) for 4 portions if large, 1–1½ lb. (½–¾ kg.) if small.

Prepare large marrows by peeling, removing the centre pith and seeds and cutting in large pieces suitable for serving. Small marrows, wash and leave whole or cut in large pieces. Boil about ½ in. (1 cm.) water, add salt and the marrow, cover, and boil gently until just tender. Avoid over-cooking or they become very flabby and tasteless. To serve, add a little butter or serve with a well-seasoned white sauce and sprinkle with chopped parsley or chives, or serve with a cheese sauce.

VEGETABLE MARROW IN A CASSEROLE
See *Vegetables in a casserole*, page 163.

VEGETABLE MARROW LYONNAISE

Use 1 large onion to 1 lb. marrow (½ kg.). Cut the marrow in small pieces and boil as above. Skin and chop or slice the onion and fry it in a little fat until tender. Mix the two vegetables and serve hot. Be sure the marrow is not over-cooked, and is well drained.

ROASTED OR BAKED VEGETABLE MARROW
See *Roast Vegetables*, page 163.
Marrow may be roasted with the skin on.

VEGETABLE MARROW STEWED IN FAT
See *Vegetables Stewed in Fat*, page 162.
For young marrows leave the skin on.

VEGETABLE MARROW STEWED WITH TOMATOES

Suitable for large marrows or small ones.

Cooking Time 35 mins.   *Quantities for 4.*

Prepare the marrow and cut it into small pieces. Small ones, simply wash and cut up.

2 *lb. marrow* (1 *kg.*) or	
1–1½ *lb. small marrow or courgettes* (½–¾ *kg.*)	
8 *oz. tomatoes* (¼ *kg.*)	1 *oz. fat* (25 *g.*)
1 *medium onion*	
Salt and pepper	½ *tsp. sugar*
Pinch of mixed herbs	¼ *pt. stock* (1½ *dl.*)
Chopped parsley	

Wash and slice the tomatoes. Skin and chop the onion. Heat the fat in a saucepan and fry tomatoes and onion for about 5 mins. Add the marrow.

Add to the pan, cover, and cook gently until the marrow is just tender.

Turn marrow into a hot dish and sprinkle with chopped parsley.

STUFFED VEGETABLE MARROW

Cooking Time ¾ hr. or more depending on size.
Temperature E.375° (190°C), G.5.   *Quantities for 4.*

1 *medium-sized marrow, about* 2 *lb.* (1 *kg.*)
1 *lb. sausage meat or an equal amount of minced meat, flavoured with herbs and/or onion* (½ *kg.*)
Fat or dripping
Brown sauce or tomato sauce

Peel the marrow and cut a slice off the top. Scoop out the pith and seeds and fill with the stuffing. Tie the top on.

Melt enough to cover the bottom of a baking tin or dish and add the marrow. Cook in a moderate oven, basting often with the fat. Alternatively, wrap the marrow in a parcel with foil but cook in a hot oven (E.450° (230°C), G.8) for a longer time.

Serve the marrow with some of the sauce poured over it.

When raw sausage meat or raw minced meat is used for the stuffing, it is important to make sure it is thoroughly cooked in the middle. Some people prefer partly to cook the meat in a frying pan before stuffing. But do this just before the marrow goes in the oven. If cooked meat is used, add a little sauce or gravy to moisten it.

WATERCRESS or *Nasturtium officinale*

A plant which grows in running water. It is cultivated in beds of clean water. This is important because watercress from polluted streams can be a danger to health. It is in season from autumn to early summer and is sold either tied in bunches, or loose, by the lb. It must be very thoroughly washed in strong salty water and then drained well. It is served for tea with bread and butter or as a sandwich filling. It is a useful salad vegetable for garnishing, either in sprigs or chopped, and for making soups, stuffings, and flavoured butter.

YAMS or *Dioscorea*

A tuber grown in tropical countries and used like a potato. Some varieties grow to an enormous size. They are sold in many greengrocers in Britain. Usually cut in pieces and boiled. Yam flour, a starchy preparation, is made from them.

15 Rice and Pasta as Meat Accompaniments

BOILED RICE

Cooking Time 15–25 mins. *Method 1:* 40 mins. *Method 2.*
Quantities for 4.

> 8 oz. rice (1 c. or 250 g.)   1 tsp. salt
> 1 pt. water or stock (½ l.)

Packet rice should not need washing but it is as well to wash the other kinds. Put the rice in a strainer and run cold water through it. Shake well to remove wet.

METHOD 1

Put into a pan with the salt and water. The rice will increase in volume about four times so use a pan large enough to allow for this (3 pt. or 1½ l.). Bring to the boil and stir once. Cover and simmer for 15 mins. without stirring. This part of the cooking can be done in a double boiler or in a moderate oven. After 15 mins. test a few grains by squeezing them between thumb and finger and if the rice is done there will be no hard core of uncooked starch. By this time all the water should have been absorbed. To produce a dry rice, fluff it with a fork, cover and stand it in a warm place, 5–10 mins. to steam dry but do not have enough heat to continue cooking. Turn into a hot dish and fluff lightly with a fork.

METHOD 2

Put rice and salt in a casserole and add boiling water. Stir. Cover and cook in a moderate oven (E.350° (180°C), G.4) for about 40 mins. Test as before and, if necessary, remove the lid for a few minutes at the end to evaporate all traces of water. Fluff lightly with a fork.

RE-HEATING BOILED RICE

Cold boiled rice keeps well in a covered dish in the refrigerator for up to a week, or in a cold larder for 2–3 days.

To re-heat it, put the rice in a covered saucepan with a few table-spoons of water and stand the pan over a low heat. Shake the pan occasionally and in a few moments the rice will be hot and fluffy and read to serve.

FRIED RICE

Fry a little finely-chopped onion in oil or butter until it is soft and beginning to brown.

Add dry cooked rice and stir and heat until all the fat is absorbed and the rice is beginning to brown. Add chopped green herbs and season to taste. Serve with meat or fish.

Optional Additions

Chopped canned pineapple and chopped salted almonds.

Raisins and chopped almonds.

Fry some chopped green pepper with the onion.

Fry some chopped celery and mushrooms with the onion.

Add chopped raw tomato.

RICE WITH RAISINS AND ALMONDS (to serve with meat and poultry)

Cooking Time 15–25 mins.   *Quantities* for 4.

8 oz. rice (1 c. or ¼ kg.)

Boil the rice. See opposite page.

Small onion   2 oz. almonds (50 g.)

Skin and chop the onion. Skin and slice the almonds.

1 oz. butter (25 g.)

Heat in a pan and cook the onion and almonds in it until they are brown.

2 oz. raisins (¼ c. or 50 g.)

Add to the pan and heat well, adding the cooked rice at the end.

Salt and pepper

Season well and serve hot.

Alternative. Add a little chopped green pepper to the onion and almond mixture and fry together. Pack the mixture into 4 hot moulds and then unmould on to the serving dish.

PASTA

The varieties of pasta most commonly served as an accompaniment to meat are spaghetti, noodles and macaroni, generally either dressed with melted butter or with a tomato sauce. Stuffed cannelloni, and lasagne dishes are useful ways of handling small quantities of fresh or cooked meat.

BOILED *PASTA*

Most of the varieties sold in packets have cooking instructions on the packet and it is advisable to follow these as many of them have been specially prepared for quick cooking and the traditional method which follows will over-cook them. If there are not any special instructions use the following method.

Cooking Time 5–15 mins. depending on the variety, 20 mins. for ravioli.

Quantities Allow 4 oz. or more per person for a main dish (125 g.); 2 oz. if served with other things (50 g.).

For each lb. of pasta ($\frac{1}{2}$ kg.) allow 6–8 pt water (4 l.) and 1 Tbs. salt.

Bring the water to the boil and add a knob of margarine or a tablespoon of olive oil as well as the salt. This prevents the water from boiling over if you want to keep a lid on the pan. When the water is boiling add the *pasta* gradually, keeping the water boiling all the time. If it is a long *pasta* put in one end letting the top protrude above the edge of the pan and as the *pasta* softens the whole will curl down into the water. Boil rapidly until a piece tested is just tender. It should still be firm or have 'bite'. If it is cooked beyond this stage it is pappy and uninteresting to eat and tends to clump together in a sticky mess. Drain well in a sieve or colander.

MACARONI WITH TOMATOES

Cooking Time 45 mins.   *Temperature* E.375° (190°C), G.5.
Quantities for 4–6.

6 oz. macaroni (150 g.)

1 oz. butter or margarine (2 Tbs.)   Salt and pepper
1 lb. sliced tomatoes ($\frac{1}{2}$ kg., fresh or canned)

Boil until just tender and then drain.

Put the macaroni in a baking dish in layers with the ingredients, the margarine being in small pieces.

2 oz. grated cheese (½ c. or 50 g.)

Sprinkle over the top and bake for about 20–30 mins. until the tomatoes are cooked and the cheese browned lightly. Serve hot in place of potatoes with meat or as a separate dish.

FRIED NOODLES

Cooking Time 10 mins. or more.   *Quantities for 4.*

4 oz. noodles (125 g.)   Oil for deep frying

Boil the noodles for 5 mins. Drain, rinse in cold water, and drain again until they are almost dry. This is very important otherwise the oil will bubble and boil over, due to excess water.

Heat the oil to 375° (190°C). Place the noodles in the frying basket and lower them very slowly into the oil. Cook until crisp and golden brown. Drain well and keep hot.

GNOCCHI

Italian dumplings made with egg and either flour, semolina, mashed potato, or potato flour. They are cooked in boiling water and served with a sauce and/or grated cheese.

POTATO GNOCCHI

Cooking Time 45 mins.   *Quantities for 4.*

1 lb. potatoes (½ kg.)

Peel, boil, and mash or sieve.

½ tsp. salt   5 oz. plain flour (1 c. or 150 g.)

Add salt and flour to the potatoes and knead to a smooth dough. Divide the dough into 4 pieces and roll each to a sausage about ¾ in. thick (2 cm.). Cut each roll in ¾ in. pieces (2 cm.), dip in flour, and drop in fast-boiling salted water (1 Tbs, to 1 qt. or 1 l.). Boil rapidly for 10 mins. Drain.

Tomato sauce   Grated cheese

Pour the sauce over the *gnocchi* and hand the cheese separately to be sprinkled on at the table.

ITALIAN TOMATO SAUCE (to serve with spaghetti or other pasta)

Cooking Time 30 mins.   *Quantities* for 1 lb. (½ kg.) spaghetti.

> 2 *medium-sized onions*   2 *Tbs. oil*

Skin and chop the onion finely. Heat the oil and fry the onion in it for 5 mins.

> 1 *small tin concentrated tomato paste* (2½ *oz. or* 75 *g.*)

Add to the onion and stir and cook for a minute or two.

> *Salt and pepper*
> *Pinch of dried thyme*
> 1 *pt. water* (½ *l.*)

Add to the pan, stirring until it boils. Boil gently without covering for about 25 mins., or until it is a creamy consistency. Season to taste and serve hot.

16 Salads

In traditional British cooking it is not usual to serve salads with hot meat, except for orange salad with duck and garnishes of watercress with grills. But today many people follow the continental custom of eating raw salad with, or immediately following, a hot course. This is in place of a second vegetable. Tossed lettuce salad is at present the favourite but any is suitable; a salad of mixed raw or cooked vegetables, or either alone. All are suitable for serving with cold meat.

MAKING SALADS

Details are given in the individual recipes.

All salad vegetables should be crisp. Wash them thoroughly and dry in a salad basket or in paper towels. If prepared in advance, put in a covered dish or polythene bag in the refrigerator to keep them crisp.

Cooked vegetables should be quite cold and well drained of liquid. Cut them in dice or slices, and mix with the dressing. They can be stored in a covered dish in the refrigerator.

Raw vegetables which are too tough to serve whole should be shredded finely or grated coarsely but do not do this until just before they are to be served.

When diced cooked meat is mixed with dressing; this can be done in advance, an hour or so before required, and stored in the refrigerator.

Lettuce and other delicate greens should not be dressed in advance as this makes them become flabby and slimy.

Serve salads either in large flat bowls, on platters, or make individual portions. Their fresh bright appearance can usually be relied on to improve the look of any meal they are served with.

229

HERBS AND FLAVOURINGS

Any green herbs, singly or a mixture. Herb vinegars such as tarragon, or the vinegar from pickled fruits or vegetables. Use a clove of garlic to rub round the salad bowl for flavouring green salads or potato salad; finely chopped raw onion, chopped chives or Welsh onions; small cooked onions dressed with oil and vinegar. Chopped or sliced pickles including gherkins and sweet pickled fruits.

ALPHABETICAL LIST OF SALADS

ARTICHOKES

Use cooked Jerusalem artichokes or cooked or canned globe artichoke bottoms.

JERUSALEM ARTICHOKE SALAD

Quantities for 4–6.

> 8 oz. cold cooked onions or leeks (¼ kg.)
> 1 lb. cold cooked artichokes (½ kg.)
> French or other salad dressing

Arrange the sliced vegetables in layers in a serving dish and pour the dressing over them.

> *Mixed pickles*   8 oz. cooked or canned carrots (¼ kg.)

Decorate the salad with sliced or chopped pickles and carrots.

ASPARAGUS SALAD

Use cold, boiled asparagus, fresh or frozen, or canned asparagus, drained of liquid. Dress with mayonnaise or Vinaigrette Sauce. Serve plain or on a bed of lettuce leaves and decorated with slices of hard-boiled egg.

AUBERGINES

Cooked in any way, dressed and served cold.

BEANS

Any kind of cooked beans, dried, fresh or canned.

230

BEETROOT

Cooked, canned or pickled, including small whole baby beets. Finely grated raw beetroot is decorative and the earthy flavour liked by some.

BEETROOT AND MINT SALAD

Quantities for 4.

1 lb. cooked beetroot (4 medium) ($\frac{1}{2}$ kg.)   French dressing
2 Tbs. chopped mint   1 lettuce

Peel and slice the beetroot. Wash and dry the lettuce and arrange nests of the leaves on each plate or arrange the nests on a large platter. Put the sliced beetroot in the centre of each nest and pour the dressing over it. Sprinkle the chopped mint on the beetroot.

BRUSSELS SPROUTS

Cooked or raw, the latter sliced very thinly are excellent and as tender as lettuce.

BRUSSELS SPROUTS AND CELERY SALAD

Quantities according to appetite but about 2–3 sprouts and a stick of celery per person.

Raw Brussels sprouts, fairly small ones
Raw celery, crisp sticks
Salad dressing, any kind
Slices hard-boiled egg or beetroot to garnish

Wash the vegetables thoroughly and drain well. Slice them finely with a sharp knife and mix them in equal quantities. Combine at once with the salad dressing and decorate with both or one of the suggested garnishes.

CABBAGE

Makes an excellent winter salad but use a firm tender-hearted one, white or red. It must be very finely shredded otherwise it is rather tough and dull to eat. Dress with mayonnaise, a thick salad dressing or yoghurt dressing.

CABBAGE CELERY AND APPLE SALAD

Quantities for 4.

2 sticks celery, chopped   1 carrot, grated
6 oz. very finely shredded raw cabbage (2 c. or 150 g.)
1 dessert apple, peeled and chopped
Salad dressing to moisten

Mix all the ingredients together and serve in a salad bowl.

COLE SLAW SALAD

This is a popular American salad made from very finely shredded raw cabbage mixed with salad dressing or mayonnaise. It can have chopped onion or chopped sweet green peppers as an addition and makes a very good lunch or supper dish if served with plenty of sliced hard-boiled eggs. The cabbage may be prepared in advance and stored in a covered dish in the refrigerator, then dress it just before serving.

MORAVIAN CABBAGE SALAD

Quantities for 4.

1 lb. raw shredded cabbage (½ kg.)   Boiling water

Put the cabbage in a basin and pour over it enough boiling water to cover. Leave for a minute or two and then drain in a colander. Put in a basin.

1 tsp. sugar   1 Tbs. vinegar

Sprinkle this over the cabbage.

1 rasher fat bacon

Remove rind and chop bacon finely. Fry it quickly without added fat, until crisp. Sprinkle the bacon and fat over the salad and serve. An optional extra is a little finely chopped fried onion.

CARROTS

Use cooked, canned, or finely grated raw.

CARROT AND APPLE SALAD

Quantities for 4.

2 c. raw grated carrot   1 lettuce
2 c. raw grated apple   *Salad dressing*
½ c. raisins or other dried fruit

Mix the carrot, apple, and raisins together and combine with a little of the dressing. Wash and drain the lettuce and arrange nests of it on individual plates.

Arrange the carrot mixture in the centre and mask with dressing or hand more dressing separately.

CAULIFLOWER (and Broccoli)

The flower part used raw, sliced or in tiny sprigs, has a pleasant nutty flavour. Cooked sprigs are also good with mayonnaise or French dressing and garnished with anchovy fillets.

CELERY AND CELERIAC

Use celery raw sliced, and celeriac raw grated or cooked. Curled celery is used for garnishing. Cut very thin strips down the length of a stick. Then hold one end, and with a knife in the other hand, pull firmly down along the strip curling as you go. Put in iced water where the curling process will continue. Drain well before using.

RED CABBAGE AND CELERY SALAD

Mix equal quantities of very finely shredded red cabbage (all thick centre ribs removed), with finely chopped celery. Mix with any salad dressing and serve garnished with young celery leaves.

CHICORY SALAD

Quantities Allow ½ lb. chicory (¼ kg.) for 2–3 people.

The simplest way of serving is to slice the chicory across thinly and then dress it with any favourite dressing and combine it with any other salad vegetable.

CHICORY AND BEETROOT SALAD

Quantities for 4.

4 small head chicory   1 medium-sized cooked beetroot

233

Wash the chicory and cut it across in slices. Skin and dice the beet-root, and mix with the chicory.

1 egg, hard-boiled	Salt and pepper
1 Tbs. tarragon vinegar	4 Tbs. yoghurt
Juice of ½ lemon	

Mash the egg yolk and mix it with the other ingredients to make a dressing. Pour it over the salad and decorate with the chopped egg white.

CORN SALAD or Lamb's Lettuce or *Valerianella Locusta* or *V. olitoria*

A useful salad plant available in autumn and winter. It is used in the same way as lettuce although the leaves are very much smaller.

CUCUMBER SALAD

This can be simply peeled or unpeeled thinly sliced cucumber dressed with salt and pepper, vinegar and oil, or the following more elaborate method. The small, fat ridge cucumbers make delicious salads.

Quantities for 4–6.

1¼ lb. cucumbers (1 large or 750 g.)

1 Tbs. salt

Peel the cucumber and slice it as thinly as possible, the thinner the better. Arrange in layers in a shallow dish.

Sprinkle this over the cucumber and leave for 2 hrs. for the moisture to be drawn out by the salt. Pour away the liquid, rinse to remove some of the salt, and drain well.

4 Tbs. vinegar	1–2 Tbs. sugar
1 Tbs. water	¼ tsp. pepper

Mix these and pour over the cucumber.

2 Tbs. chopped parsley

Sprinkle with chopped parsley just before serving.

ENDIVE or *Cichorium endivia*

A salad vegetable like a flat lettuce in shape but the centre is bleached. It is in season in late autumn and winter. The leaves are tougher than lettuce and have a slightly bitter flavour likely to be rather pronounced if the bleaching is incomplete. It is used in the same way as lettuce.

FRUIT

Any fresh or dried fruits and also firm canned fruits such as peaches, pineapple, pears, grapefruit, mandarin oranges and cherries.

GRAPEFRUIT AND BEETROOT SALAD

Quantities for 4.

2 *large grapefruit*

Peel and remove all pith. Divide into segments or slice into circles, removing pips.

2 *medium-sized cooked beetroots*

Skin and slice.

1 *lettuce*

Wash and dry and use it to line a salad bowl or flat dish. Arrange on it alternately the grapefruit and beetroot.

French dressing

Pour it over the fruit just before serving.

LEEKS

Finely sliced raw used for flavouring and garnishing. Cooked, by themselves, or with other cooked vegetables.

LEEKS *VINAIGRETTE*

Boil leeks in the usual way, cutting large ones in half. Drain very thoroughly and allow to cool to lukewarm. Dress with French dressing or with *vinaigrette* sauce. Serve as an *hors-d'œuvre* or salad. They may be served quite cold but are nicest slightly warm.

LETTUCE SALAD

There are many varieties of lettuce but they may be roughly divided into two main groups, the round or cabbage lettuce and the long or cos lettuce. The latter has coarser leaves with thick ribs but is very crisp and usually has more flavour than cabbage lettuce. Most people only use lettuce for salads but it may be cooked, usually stewed or braised. Lettuce leaves are also cooked with green peas and used in mixed vegetable soups.

235

When preparing it, wash the lettuce carefully under running water and then dry in a salad basket and store it in a plastic box in the refrigerator to keep it crisp. A plain lettuce salad is usually dressed with French dressing and flavoured with chopped fresh herbs, or the salad bowl is first rubbed with a cut clove of garlic which is sufficient to impart a faint aroma to the lettuce. The lettuce is turned or tossed in the dressing until each leaf is well coated and then it must be served quickly or the dressing will make the leaves flabby and sodden.

MUSHROOM SALAD

Raw button mushrooms make very delicious salads. Wash them and dry thoroughly. Slice them thickly and dress lavishly with French dressing using lemon juice in place of vinegar. Sprinkle with chopped parsley and, if liked, a very little garlic.

NASTURTIUM

This is the botanical name for watercress (*Nasturtium officinale*). See *Watercress*. The flowering plant usually known as 'nasturtium' is *Tropaeolum*. The leaves have a slightly peppery taste and are used in salads and sandwich fillings. The green seeds are sometimes pickled in vinegar and used as a substitute for capers. The flowers are edible too and are wonderful for garnishing salads and other cold foods.

ONIONS. See *Herbs and Flavourings*, page 230

ORANGE SALAD for serving with meat or poultry
Quantities for 4.

4 *oranges*

Chopped fresh tarragon and chervil

Sprinkle over the oranges.

2 *Tbs. olive oil*   1 *Tbs. vinegar*

2 *tsp. lemon juice*

Peel the oranges and remove all pith. Slice into thin rounds, removing the pips.

Mix these and pour them over the oranges. Leave to stand for a while.

Watercress

Serve the salad on individual plates garnished with watercress.

ORANGE, APPLE, AND CELERY SALAD

Quantities for 4.

3–4 *oranges*

Peel the fruit, removing all pith. Either slice into rounds or divide into segments. Remove all pips.

1 *lettuce, washed and dried*

Arrange the lettuce on individual plates and put the oranges in the centre of each.

1 *or* 2 *dessert apples*   *A few stalks crisp celery*

Peel and chop the apples. Wash and chop the celery to give about the same amount. Mix these and cover the orange with them.

1 *Tbs. chopped nuts*

Sprinkle them over the top.

Mayonnaise or French dressing

Serve this separately or, if preferred, mix the apples and celery with the dressing before putting the mixture on top of the oranges.

PEAS

Some like eating very young green peas raw; otherwise use cooked or canned, usually mixed with other vegetables, or as a garnish.

POTATO SALAD

Use either new potatoes or the waxy Dutch kind. Floury potatoes do not keep a good shape. If they are the only ones available, boil them in their skins until just tender, and allow to become quite cold before peeling. Canned potatoes make a useful substitute.

Quantities for 4.

1½ *lb. boiled potatoes* (¾ *kg.*)   1 *Tbs. chopped green herbs*
¼ *pt. mayonnaise or vinaigrette sauce* (1½ *dl.*)
1 *Tbs. finely-chopped onion or chives*

If new or waxy potatoes are used, dress them while warm. Cut the cooked potatoes in cubes and mix with the onion and dressing. Serve with the green herbs sprinkled on top.

RADISH or *Raphanus sativus*

There are a number of varieties grown, the most common being either the small round or large oval ones. Radishes need to be grown quickly with plenty of moisture if they are to be crisp and juicy. Tired old ones are not worth having. To keep them fresh, wash, drain, put in a polythene bag, and keep in a cold place but if they are kept in the refrigerator, bring them out an hour or so before serving. The green tops are usually trimmed to about 2 in. (5 cm.) and the roots cut off. They are usually served for an *hors-d'œuvre* (sometimes with 2 or 3 slices of salami or other sausage), or they are served with cheese. In either case serve salt with them.

For purposes of garnishing, they are either cut into fine rings or into 'roses'. To do this, use a sharp pointed knife and carve the petals from root end to within ¼ in. (1 cm.) of the stem end. Lever up the red skin away from the white to free the petals. Put in ice water until required.

Black Radish is either grated or else sliced very thinly to be used in salads or eaten with cheese. It is a large winter radish with a black skin and white flesh. Large ones can be cooked and used in the same way as turnips.

SORREL

Small quantities of fresh young leaves add an astringent quality to other vegetables.

SPINACH

The young, tender, raw leaves can be added to other salad greens, either whole or shredded.

SWEET PEPPERS

Raw sliced, or cooked or canned; cold stuffed peppers are also suitable, see *Vegetables*, page 215.

SWEET PEPPER SALADS

Slice the peppers very finely and dress with French dressing and a little chopped onion. These are served as a salad or *hors-d'œuvre*.

Some people do not like completely raw peppers and prefer to grill them until they can be skinned easily and then to slice and dress them as before.

They may also be mixed with some sliced raw tomatoes, about half and half. Sprinkle this salad with chopped parsley.

SWEDES

Raw and finely grated, they are decorative and sweet tasting.

TOMATO SALAD

Wash and dry the tomatoes and slice them. Dress with French dressing containing a good pinch of sugar (or sprinkle tomatoes first with a little sugar). Sprinkle the salad with chopped fresh parsley or tarragon and serve at once.

TURNIPS

Raw or cooked, see *Vegetables*, page 219.

WATERCRESS SALADS

Watercress goes with any salad vegetables, the following being good mixtures: watercress, cucumber, and spring onions; watercress and beetroot; watercress and chicory; watercress and potato salad. Also serve as a salad garnish, with grilled and fried meat and fish.

MAIN DISH SALADS

CHICKEN AND ALMOND SALAD

Quantities for 4.

6 oz. seedless raisins (150 g.)

Put the raisins in a small pan, cover with cold water, bring to the boil and leave to stand at the side of the stove for 5 mins. to make the raisins plump up. Strain them and run cold water through to cool them quickly.

4 oz. shelled almonds (125 g.)

Blanch the almonds and toast them in a hot oven or under the grill until they are well browned. Chop coarsely.

12 oz. cooked chicken (375 g.)

Dice the chicken.

1 Tbs. grated onion   4 Tbs. French dressing
1 Tbs. chopped parsley   Lettuce
           Sliced cucumber

Mix raisins, almonds, chicken, onion, and parsley together and moisten with dressing. Make a nest or bed of lettuce leaves and serve the salad on this. Garnish with sliced cucumber.

CHICKEN AND CUCUMBER SALAD

Quantities for 4.

> 8 oz. diced cooked chicken (1 c. or ¼ kg.)
> 8 oz. coarsely chopped walnuts (1 c. or ¼ kg.)
> 8 oz. cooked or canned green peas (1 c. or ¼ kg.)
> 1 medium cucumber, diced
> *Salad dressing*

Combine all the ingredients with enough dressing to moisten.

> *Lettuce*

Arrange lettuce leaves to line the salad bowl or make individual nests on serving plates and arrange the salad mixture in the centre.

> *Tomato or paprika pepper to garnish*

DRESSED CHICKEN SALAD

Quantities for 4.

> *4 portions of cooked chicken*

Dressing

> 1 oz. butter (25 g.)   ¼ pt. chicken stock (¼ l.)
> 1 oz. flour (3 Tbs. or 25 g.)   2 egg yolks
>
> Vinegar   Salt and pepper
> Mustard   ½–1 Tbs. sherry
> Sugar

Melt the butter in a small pan and add the flour, stirring and cooking until crumbly. Remove from the heat and gradually stir in the stock. Return to the heat and stir until it boils. Boil for 5 mins. Remove from the heat and stir in the egg yolks. Leave to become cold, stirring occasionally as it cools.

Add these to the sauce, to taste, and pour the dressing over the pieces of chicken. Garnish with

> *Cooked peas, small cooked potatoes, and lettuce*

HAM-AND-CHEESE SALAD

Quantities for 4.

> 4 oz. rice (125 g.)

Boil and leave to become cold. See *Rice.,* page 224

4 oz. ham (125 g.)   *1 pickled cucumber*
4 oz. cheese (125 g.)   *2 oz. cooked or canned green peas (50 g.)*
2 tomatoes   *4 Tbs. French dressing*

Cut the ham and cheese in strips. Slice the tomato and chop the cucumber. Mix all the ingredients together.

1 lettuce

Wash and dry and use to line the salad bowl. Pile the rice mixture in the centre.

HAM-AND-ORANGE SALAD

Serve rolls of cooked ham with Orange and Lettuce Salad.

SAUSAGE SALAD

Quantities for 4.

3 pork sausages (about ½ lb. or ¼ kg.)
4 medium-sized potatoes   *1 medium-sized onion*

Cook the sausages by any method and leave to become cold.

Boil the potatoes and allow to become cold. If raw onion is disliked, boil it too. Slice both these.

6 pickled gherkins   *1 small lettuce*
French dressing or salad cream   *Tomatoes or radishes*

Wash and shred the lettuce, slice the gherkins. Mix all the ingredients together. Serve the dressing separately or mix with the salad, as preferred. Garnish with tomato or radishes.

PARISIAN SALAD

Quantities for 4.

8 oz. cold boiled beef or other meat (250 g.)

Trim off any skin, gristle or fat and cut the meat in strips.

4 diced cold potatoes   *2 small blanched onions*
2 hard-boiled eggs   *4 tomatoes*

Chop the onions, dice or slice the eggs and tomatoes. Mix all with the meat.

French dressing   *Lettuce*
Chopped parsley

241

Add enough dressing to moisten the mixture. Add 4 large lettuce leaves torn in pieces, or to taste, and then mix in the parsley.

TONGUE SALAD

Quantities for 4.

6 oz. cooked or canned tongue (150 g.)   1 apple
4 hard-boiled eggs   1 medium-sized beetroot

Peel the beetroot and apple and cut all the ingredients into small pieces, reserving two of the egg yolks for the dressing.

Pinch of pepper   *¼ tsp. salt*
½ tsp. mustard   *2 Tbs. vinegar*
2 Tbs. single cream or evaporated milk

Mash the egg yolks and seasoning and mix smoothly with first the vinegar and then the cream. Mix this into the salad.

Lettuce or chicory leaves

Serve the salad in a nest of leaves.

17 Sauces and Salad Dressings

Most people enjoy a well-made sauce which can very much improve many dishes, but if it is badly made the original food would probably be better without anything. Some people actually prefer dry food and dislike all sauces and gravies.

The purpose of a sauce is to add to the appearance and flavour of a food, not to cover up its deficiencies.

There are many short cuts to sauce-making. Quickest of all are the ready-prepared sauces, packet or canned. Some are very good indeed but they are not cheap. Concentrated canned soups are used as sauces but discretion is needed here as they can be too salty and strong in flavour for the accompanying meat. They are at their best when used for making quick casseroles.

Almost as quick as these are sauces made in an electric blender or liquidiser and I have included the basic method for these.

If you have a freezer, most sauces can be made in advance and frozen until required. It is a good plan to make double the recipe whenever you want a sauce and then to freeze the surplus.

Another device for speeding up sauce-making is to keep a stock of roux in the refrigerator or freezer and this then only needs to be dropped into hot liquid, and stirred until it melts and thickens.

Most sauces can safely be made in advance and kept hot in a *bain marie*, or double boiler. Give an occasional stir to sauces liable to form a skin, or give them a second in the blender to smooth them out before serving.

ROUX (to make and store)

A mixture of flour and fat used for thickening purposes. Also used for thickening stews and casseroles after cooking and before serving.

Equal quantities of fat and flour are the usual proportions though opinions differ on this matter, some preferring more fat. A white *roux* consists of fat and flour cooked and stirred together until they look crumbly and a deep cream colour, used for thickening white sauces and stews. A brown *roux* is achieved by cooking the fat and flour together for a long time until the mixture turns a light brown. It needs slow cooking and frequent stirring and is most simply done in a moderate oven in a wide pan or tin.

A properly cooked *roux* will keep well in a jar in a refrigerator and it is useful to make up about a pound at a time and keep ready for use as wanted.

Pieces of this sort of *roux* are dropped into the hot liquid which is to be thickened, and whisked and boiled for a few minutes.

If it is to be stored in the freezer, divide the finished *roux* into 1–2 oz. (25–50 g.) pieces, wrap each in foil and put the lot in a polythene bag. It is then a simple matter to take out the amount required.

Proportions for 1 pint liquid (½ l.)

Thin sauce	2 oz. *roux* (50 g.)
Medium sauce	3 oz. *roux* (75 g.)
Thick sauce	4 oz. *roux* (125 g.)

These quantities need adjusting for smaller amounts of sauce than 1 pt. because the rate of evaporation is greater proportionately with small quantities. Either use less thickening or add more liquid.

If eggs are added this is done after the sauce is cooked and just before serving. The sauce should not be allowed to boil. Sometimes extra butter is added at the end of cooking and just before serving. If cream is used this goes in at the end too. Undiluted evaporated milk can be substituted for cream in most recipes.

THE BLENDER METHOD

Heat the liquid in a saucepan and put it in the blender goblet with the flour, fat and flavourings. Blend until smooth, return to the saucepan and stir until it boils. Cook for 3 mins., or longer over hot water.

THE ONE-STAGE METHOD

Use soft fat or warm it in the saucepan. Add the flour and liquid and heat until it boils, beating well with a rotary beater or electric beater. Continue beating and heating for 2–3 mins. and then add the flavourings. Unless you have a non-stick pan it is wise to cook this sauce over a gentle heat or the mixture may stick and burn.

244

THICKENING WITH CORNFLOUR OR POTATO STARCH

These make thicker sauces than flour does so use about two-thirds the amount to get the same thickness as with flour.

USING OIL

Make the sauce in the usual way using 1 Tbs. of oil to replace 1 oz. (25 g.) of fat.

Note. The recipes which follow use the conventional method of making sauces but they can equally well be made by one of the quicker methods described above.

BÉCHAMEL SAUCE (WHITE SAUCE)

A standard French 'white sauce', well worth the small amount of extra time and trouble involved in making it. The difference between this and a plain white sauce is that the milk is first infused with vegetables, herbs, and spices to flavour it, and cream is added just before serving.

Cooking Time 15–20 mins.

1 pt. milk (½ l.)
1 shallot or onion
Piece of carrot
Piece of celery
1 bay leaf
10 *peppercorns*

Peel the onion or shallot and clean the other vegetables Put all ingredients in a pan and bring to the boil. Remove from the heat and leave to infuse for 5 mins. Then strain.

1 oz. butter or margarine (25 g.)   *Salt*
1 oz. flour (3 Tbs. or 25 g.)   4 Tbs. single cream

Melt the butter or margarine and stir in the flour. Cook gently until crumbly looking. Remove from the heat and add the strained milk, whisking until quite smooth. Return to the heat and stir until boiling. Boil gently for a few minutes, or cook over hot water. Season to taste and add the cream just before serving.

BROWN SAUCE

Cooking Time about ½ hr.   *Quantities for 1 pt.*

2 onions   2 small carrots
2 oz. fat (50 g.)

Peel the onions and carrots, and slice or chop into small pieces. Heat the fat and fry the vegetables in it until they are lightly browned.

1½ oz. flour (4½ Tbs. or 45 g.)

Add the flour and mix well, cook stirring occasionally, until the flour turns brown, about 15–20 mins.

1 pt. stock (½ l.)   Sprig of parsley
¼ bay leaf   Salt and pepper

Add the stock and herbs and stir until it boils. Boil gently for ½ hr. Strain, reheat, and season to taste adding gravy browning if you want a darker sauce.

ESPAGNOLE SAUCE

Cooking Time 2 hrs.   Quantities for 6 or more.

2 oz. butter (50 g.)   2 oz. chopped ham or bacon (50 g.)

Heat butter and fry ham or bacon in it for a few minutes.

1 medium onion   1 small carrot

6 mushrooms or equivalent in stalks

Peel onion and scrape carrots, chop them. Wash and chop the mushrooms. Add all to the pan and continue frying until the vegetables begin to brown.

1 oz. flour (3 Tbs. or 25 g.)

Sprinkle into the pan and stir and cook until the flour begins to brown.

1 pt. brown stock (½ l.)   2 Tbs. tomato paste

Add to the pan and stir until it boils. Boil gently for 1 hr., adding more water or stock if it seems to need it. Strain the sauce through a fine sieve.

4 Tbs. sherry or madeira   Salt and pepper

Add the wine, season to taste and re-heat.

GRAVY

A sauce made from the juices which escape when meat is roasted.

Thin Gravy. Remove the meat to a hot dish. Tilt the pan to make the drippings flow down to one corner. Wait a few moments for the sediment to settle and then pour off the fat very gently leaving the juices behind. Add stock and seasoning, bring to the boil, and stir to incorporate all the brown pieces stuck to the pan. Strain into a hot gravy boat.

Thick Gravy. Pour off the fat as before, except for about 2 Tbs. Add 2 Tbs. flour or 1 Tbs. cornflour, mix well, and cook until it begins to brown. Add ½ pt. stock (¼ l), stir until it boils, cook for a few minutes, season, and strain into a gravy boat.

APPLE SAUCE

Cooking Time ¼ hr.   *Quantities for 4.*

  1 lb. cooking apples (½ kg.)   2 oz. sugar (¼ c. or 50 g.)

Peel, core, and slice the apples and cook them in a saucepan with just enough water to prevent burning. Cook to a pulp. If a smooth sauce is wanted, rub through a sieve or put in the electric blender. Add the sugar and reheat. Serve hot.

BASIC BARBECUE SAUCE

  1 tsp. dry mustard   2 Tbs. vinegar
  2 tsp. Worcester sauce   3 Tbs. oil or melted butter
                                 or margarine

All are mixed together and used to baste the food several times during grilling. To this basic mixture can be added herbs and crushed garlic.

CURRY BASTING SAUCE

Use a normal sauce made with stock and not too thick.

WINE BASTING SAUCE

Equal quantities of oil and wine infused for several hours with a little chopped marjoram, or thyme or rosemary, crushed garlic cloves, and bay leaf. The wines used are red and white, sherry, or vermouth.

See also *Barbecue Chicken,* page 139.

BREAD SAUCE

Cooking Time 25 mins.   *Quantities for 4.*

  1 onion   4 cloves

  ½ pt. milk (¼ l.)

247

Peel and slice the onion and heat with the other ingredients for about 10 mins. or until the milk is well flavoured. Strain.

> 2 oz. fresh breadcrumbs (1 c. or 50 g.)

Add crumbs to the milk and heat slowly without boiling until the crumbs swell.

> 1 oz. butter or margarine (25 g.)   Salt and pepper

Add the fat, season well, and serve hot.

BROWN BUTTER SAUCE

Cooking Time a few minutes.   *Quantities for 4.*

> 2–4 oz. butter (50–125 g.)

Heat in a small saucepan until it turns nut brown.

> 1–2 tsp. chopped parsley   1–2 tsp. vinegar

Add parsley and cook for a few seconds, then add the vinegar and pour quickly over the food. This is a sauce which must be made at the last minute so the accompanying food must be cooked first.

CAPER SAUCE

Cooking Time 10–15 mins.   *Quantities for 4.*

> 2 oz. butter or margarine (50 g.)
> 2 oz. flour (6 Tbs. or 50 g.)

Melt the fat and add the flour, stirring and cooking until it looks crumbly. Remove from the heat.

> 1 pt. stock (½ l.)

Add the stock, stir until it boils, and boil for 5 mins.

> 2 Tbs. capers, chopped   Salt and pepper to taste
> 1½ Tbs. vinegar from the capers

Add these to the sauce and serve hot.

CHEESE SAUCE

> 1½ oz. butter or margarine (45 g.)   Pinch of dry mustard
> 1½ oz. flour (4½ Tbs. or 45 g.)

Melt the fat in a saucepan and add the flour and mustard. Stir and cook until it looks crumbly.

> 1 pt. milk (½ l.)

Add the milk and stir until it boils. Boil for 5 mins.

3–4 oz. grated cheese (75–125 g.)   Salt and pepper
                                Pinch of ground mace or nutmeg

Add the cheese and heat, without boiling, until the cheese is melted. Season to taste and serve at once.

CHEESE SAUCE   Quick Method

¼ pt. evaporated milk (1½ dl.)   A little made mustard
4 oz. processed cheese (125 g.)   Salt and pepper to taste

Dice the cheese and put all the ingredients into a saucepan. Heat gently until the cheese melts, and the sauce thickens. Season to taste and serve at once.

CRANBERRY SAUCE

Can also be purchased ready-made in jars and tins.

Cooking Time 10 mins.   Quantities for 4.

8 oz. cranberries (¼ kg.)   ¼ pt. water (1½ dl.)

Boil the cranberries in the water, crushing them with a spoon during cooking. When they are quite tender rub them through a sieve or cool and put in the blender.

4 oz. sugar (½ c. or 125 g.)

Add the sugar, reheat, and stir until it dissolves. If required cold, pour into a small mould and leave at least 12 hrs. before using. If to be served as a hot sauce, thin down with hot water to make it about the consistency of a thick sauce. The cold sauce can be served in a small dish or turned out like a mould. For garnishing a dish of cold turkey the sauce could be set in a number of very small dariole moulds or egg cups and then unmoulded.

EGG SAUCE

Cooking Time 10 mins.   Quantities for 4.

1½ oz. butter or margarine (45 g.)
1½ oz. flour (4½ Tbs. or 45 g.)
1 pt. chicken stock or milk (½ l.)

249

Melt the fat and add the flour, stir, and cook until crumbly. Stir in the liquid and stir until it boils. Boil gently for 5 mins.

> Pinch of nutmeg   2–3 hard-boiled eggs
> Salt and pepper   Chopped parsley or chervil, optional

Shell and chop the eggs and add to the sauce together with season-ings to taste. Heat thoroughly and serve at once. An alternative method of adding the eggs is to separate yolks and whites and add the chopped whites to the sauce. The yolks are then put through a potato ricer or a coarse sieve and used as a garnish for the dish which has been coated with the sauce.

FENNEL SAUCE

Add finely-chopped fennel leaves to a white sauce or to a sauce made with mutton stock. Add the fennel just before serving so as to maintain the maximum flavour. Use plenty.

HOLLANDAISE SAUCE   Method 1

> 4 oz. butter (125 g.)   2 egg yolks
> 1 Tbs. lemon juice

Divide the butter into 3 portions and put one in a small pan with the egg yolks and the lemon juice. Cook over hot water, stirring with a wire whisk until the butter is melted. Add the second piece of butter and whisk and heat until the sauce begins to thicken slightly. Add the third piece of butter.

> 2–3 Tbs. boiling water   ¼ tsp. salt
> Few grains cayenne pepper

Add the boiling water to give the desired consistency (it is meant to be thin), and heat for 1 min. more. Add the seasoning. Remove from the heat at once.

If the mixture should curdle add 2 Tbs. double cream or 2 Tbs. boiling water drop by drop, beating hard all the time.

If the sauce is not to be served at once keep it warm, not hot.

HOLLANDAISE SAUCE (for the electric blender)   Method 2

> ¼ pt. tepid water (1½ dl.)   2 Tbs. lemon juice
> 1 oz. melted butter (25 g.)   2 sprigs parsley
> 3 egg yolks   Salt and pepper

Put all the ingredients in the goblet and blend at full speed for 1 min. Pour into a saucepan and heat gently until it thickens, stirring all the time. Serve at once.

HORSERADISH SAUCE (cold)

Quantities for 4.

Pinch of paprika pepper   *2 tsp. dry mustard*
4 Tbs. grated horseradish   *1 tsp. wine vinegar*

Mix these together until they are well blended.

4 Tbs. yoghurt or double cream

Add this to the first mixture and blend well. Beat until creamy. Serve cold.

HORSERADISH SAUCE (hot)

Quantities for 4–6.

1½ oz. margarine or butter (45 g.) *1½ oz. flour (4½ Tbs. or 45 g.)*
1 pt. stock or milk (½ l.)   *2 tsp. dry mustard*

Melt the fat and add the mustard and flour, stir and cook for a few minutes. Add the milk. Stir until it boils and boil for 5 mins.

1 tsp. salt   *1 tsp. sugar*   *6 Tbs. vinegar*
3 oz. grated horseradish (1 c. or 75 g.), more if liked

Add to the sauce and serve hot.

LEMON SAUCE

Quantities for 3–4.

2 egg yolks   *Juice of 1 lemon*

Beat these together until thick.

½ pt. warm stock (¼ l.)

Add the stock and put the mixture over hot water. Continue to whisk and cook until it is light and fluffy.

Salt and pepper

Season to taste and serve at once.

MINT SAUCE

Quantities for 4.

4 Tbs. *chopped fresh mint*   1 Tbs. *sugar*

$\frac{1}{4}$ *pt. wine or malt vinegar* (1$\frac{1}{2}$ *dl.*)

Mix all together, stirring until the sugar dissolves. Cover and leave to infuse for at least 2 hrs. before serving with hot or cold roast lamb or as a dressing for salads to go with lamb.

MUSHROOM SAUCE

Quantities for 4 or more.

1 *pt. brown sauce* ($\frac{1}{2}$ *l.*)   1 *doz. button mushrooms*

If making the brown sauce specially for this add the chopped mushroom stalks to it. Wash and chop the mushrooms and simmer them in the sauce for 5 mins.

ONION SAUCE

Cooking Time 10–15 mins.   *Quantities for 4.*

8 *oz. onions* (250 *g.*)   2 *oz. fat or oil* (50 *g.*)

$\frac{1}{2}$ *oz. butter or margarine* (15 *g.*)

$\frac{1}{2}$ *pt. milk* ($\frac{1}{4}$ *l.*)

$\frac{1}{2}$ *oz. flour* (1$\frac{1}{2}$ *Tbs. or* 15 *g.*)

Skin and slice the onions. Heat the fat in a saucepan and add the onion. Cook slowly with the lid on the pan until they are tender but not brown.

Melt the fat in another pan and add the flour, stirring and cooking until crumbly. Add the milk and stir until it boils. Boil for 5 mins.

Salt and pepper   *Pinch of ground mace or nutmeg*

Pinch of sugar

Season the sauce to taste and add the cooked onions.

Alternative Method. Boil the onions instead of frying them. Chop them up small. Make the sauce with half milk and half onion water and add the onions.

PARSLEY SAUCE

Add 2 Tbs. chopped parsley to 1 pt. ($\frac{1}{2}$ *l.*) of white or *Béchamel* sauce.

TARRAGON SAUCE

Mix finely-chopped fresh tarragon leaves with melted butter, lemon juice, and seasoning to taste. Serve hot. Do not add the tarragon until just ready to serve the sauce.

TOMATO SAUCE

Cooking Time 35 mins.

    1½ oz. fat (45 g.)   1 onion   2 or 3 bacon rinds

Skin and chop the onion. Heat the fat and fry the onion and bacon rinds in it until the onion begins to brown.

    1 oz. flour (3 Tbs. or 25 g.)   ½ pt. stock (¼ l.)
    ½ pt. tomato juice (¼ l.) or 1 lb. fresh ripe tomatoes (½ kg.)

Add the flour and stir in, cooking for a few minutes. Stir in the liquids, and stir until it boils.

    ½ bay leaf   ½ tsp. sugar

Add to the sauce and boil gently for 30 mins.

    Salt and pepper

Strain the sauce and reheat, seasoning to taste. Serve hot.

SAUCE FOR VEGETABLES (using the cooking liquid)

    1 oz. fat (25 g.)   1 oz. flour (3 Tbs. or 25 g.)
    1 pt. vegetable stock and/or milk (½ l.)

Melt the fat and stir in the flour, cook and stir until it looks crumbly. Add the liquid and stir until it boils. Boil for at least 5 mins.

    Salt and pepper   *Chopped parsley or other fresh green herbs.*
        See *Herbs in Meat Cookery,* page 20

Season to taste but be careful with the salt because the vegetable water should have some in it. Add the sauce to the vegetables and serve them sprinkled with the parsley.

When canned vegetables are used the liquid from the can should be made into a sauce and the vegetables heated gently in it.

VINAIGRETTE SAUCE

    4 Tbs. salad oil   Salt and pepper
    2 Tbs. tarragon vinegar   ½ tsp. made mustard
    1 tsp. each of finely chopped gherkin, shallot, and parsley

Mix all the ingredients together. Stir before serving.

COMPOUND BUTTERS OR SAVOURY BUTTERS

These are used to serve with grilled meats, to dress vegetables, for baked potatoes, and many other uses.

To make them, the butter should be softened but not melted and the ingredients beaten together until creamy and smooth. For use on grills or vegetables, shape the mixture into small pats and chill. Put on the hot food just before serving.

The mixture can be made in advance and stored for some time in covered containers in the refrigerator or freezer. Alternatively freeze pats of the mixture with layers of freezer paper between, or form into a small roll and wrap in foil; slices can then be cut off as required (thaw a little first).

Maître d'hôtel or Parsley Butter
4 oz. butter (125 g.), 2 Tbs. chopped parsley, lemon juice to taste.

Watercress Butter
As above, substituting watercress for the parsley.

Garlic and Parsley Butter
4 oz. butter (125 g.), 2 Tbs. single cream, ¼ tsp. garlic salt, chopped parsley.

Curry Butter
4 oz. butter (125 g.), 1 tsp. curry powder, salt and pepper, onion juice to taste (or use onion salt).

MAYONNAISE AND SALAD DRESSINGS

MAYONNAISE

2 *egg yolks*	*Pinch of cayenne pepper*
¼–1 *tsp. salt*	1 *Tbs. vinegar*
	½ *tsp. mustard*

Mix these to a smooth paste in a small basin.

½ *pt. salad or olive oil* (¼ *l.*)

Use a wooden spoon or a small wire egg whisk and stir the mixture vigorously and continuously, adding the oil drop by drop from a

254

spoon. Have the oil at room temperature, not hot or very cold. Wait until each addition of oil has been blended in before adding the next. When half the oil has been added begin adding it a spoonful at a time but always mixing it in before adding more.

1 Tbs. vinegar or to taste

When all the oil has been added, mix in vinegar or lemon juice to taste and to dilute to the thickness required.

Mayonnaise sometimes curdles and this is usually because the oil has been added too quickly, or there is too much oil for the egg yolks to emulsify. If this does happen, put another egg yolk in a basin and beat the curdled mayonnaise gradually into it.

ELECTRIC-BLENDER MAYONNAISE

Manufacturers recommend a variety of recipes for their blenders but the above recipe can also be used, allowing the oil to trickle through the hold in the lid provided for the purpose.

It is possible to make mayonnaise with a whole egg and this makes it lighter with a bigger volume for the oil used.

1 egg
2 Tbs. lemon juice
1 tsp. French mustard
Pinch of sugar
Pinch of salt
¼-½ pt. oil (1½-2½ dl.)

Put all except the oil in the goblet of the blender. Turn the speed to the fastest number and add the oil through the hole provided in the lid. Continue mixing until the mayonnaise is of the desired consistency.

JELLIED MAYONNAISE (for masking cold meat)

To half of either of the above recipes add gradually 6 Tbs. of melted aspic jelly which is quite cold.

FRENCH DRESSING
Quantities for 4.

1½ Tbs. olive oil
Pinch of pepper
½ Tbs. vinegar (wine, cider, tarragon, or other flavour)
or 1 Tbs. lemon juice
Pinch of dry mustard
¼ tsp. salt

Mix the oil and seasonings and add the vinegar. Use at once or stir well before using. A larger amount may be mixed and stored in a covered jar. Shake it well before using.

SOUR CREAM DRESSING

2 *hard-boiled eggs*	¼ *tsp. pepper*
1 *tsp. salt*	1 *tsp. mustard*
¼ *pt. sour or cultured cream* (1½ *dl.*)	

Separate the yolks and whites and mash the yolks with salt and pepper and a little mustard. Gradually work in the cream. Use the egg whites to garnish the salad.

YOGHURT DRESSING

Quantities for 4.

1½ *Tbs. lemon juice*	*Pinch of pepper*
¼ *tsp. made mustard*	¼ *tsp. salt*
¼ *pt. yoghurt* (1 *small jar or* 1½ *dl.*)	

Mix the lemon and seasonings together and slowly stir in the yoghurt. Blend thoroughly and chill for ½ hr. before serving.

18 Stuffings

STUFFINGS

These are used to add flavour (and sometimes bulk) to meat, poultry and vegetables. They usually have a cereal or starch base such as bread, potato, chestnuts, cornflakes, oatmeal or rice. To these are added flavourings such as fresh or dried herbs, lemon rind and juice, onions or garlic, and many other flavouring ingredients. Beaten egg is the usual mixing and binding ingredient, although some wine may be used for moistening and flavouring.

Breadcrumbs are usually made from stale bread and the quickest method is in the electric blender when fresh herbs may be chopped with the bread. Alternatively use pieces of bread soaked in water and squeezed dry before mashing. Cornflakes can be purchased as crumbs or made in the blender or crushed with a rolling pin. Chestnuts are shelled and skinned and then cooked. Rice is usually cooked first.

Stuffings should be mixed so that they are dry enough to keep their shape, but not be stodgy. Sometimes the mixture is made into small balls which are cooked round the joint, or cooked separately. They can also be used as a garnish for soups and other savoury dishes.

Stuffed meat and poultry should always be thoroughly cooked because they have been handled during boning and stuffing and any contamination in the middle can grow to dangerous proportions if the meat is not well-cooked. If the stuffing is prepared in advance of cooking time, store it separately from the meat and poultry, in a refrigerator or cold larder.

CHESTNUT STUFFING

Quantities for a 12–14 lb. turkey (5–6 kg.).

2 lb. chestnuts (1 kg.).

Wash the chestnuts and cut a slit in the shell on the flat sides. Grill until the skin loosens, or bake about 20 mins. in a hot oven. Remove the shells and the skins should come away too. They are easier to shell while still hot so do not heat them all at once.

Stock

Barely cover the shelled nuts with stock and bring to the boil. Cover, and cook slowly until they are tender and almost dry. Rub through a sieve or blend in several lots to make a purée. While fresh chestnuts have the better flavour either canned purée or dried chestnuts may be used instead (1 lb., ½ kg.). The latter need to be cooked like the fresh chestnuts, but using more stock or water.

6 oz. breadcrumbs (175 g.)	1 Tbs. chopped parsley
1 lb. sausage meat (½ kg.)	3 tsp. salt
Stock to moisten	¼ tsp. pepper
4 oz. melted butter or dripping (125 g.)	

Add these to the chestnuts and mix thoroughly, adding just enough stock to moisten well.

LEMON STUFFING

Quantities for 1 small chicken.

2 oz. melted butter (50 g.)	Juice of ½ lemon
Grated rind of ½ lemon	2 Tbs. chopped parsley
Pinch of salt and pepper	1 small egg or ½ large one
2 oz. fresh breadcrumbs (¾ c. or 50 g.)	
Pinch of dried thyme and marjoram	

Mix all ingredients thoroughly.

MINT OR WATERCRESS STUFFING (for lamb or mutton)

Quantities to stuff a shoulder.

4 Tbs. chopped onion	
3 oz. margarine or dripping (75 g.)	

Fry the onion in a little of the fat. When it is cooked, add the rest of the fat and leave to melt.

8 oz. breadcrumbs (2½ c. or ¼ kg.)	1 tsp. salt
3 Tbs. chopped parsley	1 Tbs. sugar
Pinch of pepper	
½ c. chopped fresh mint or 1½ c. chopped watercress	

Mix all these with the melted fat and onion.

OATMEAL STUFFING (for chicken)

Quantities for a 3–4 lb. chicken (1½–2 kg.).

2 oz. onion (50 g.)

Skin and chop

2 oz. grated suet (⅓ c. or 50 g.)

Take about ½ oz. of this and melt it in a small pan. Fry the onion in it until brown.

4 oz. medium oatmeal (⅓ c. or 125 g.)

Spread the oatmeal out in a shallow tin and toast it in a hot oven for a few minutes. Add this and the rest of the suet to the fried onion.

¼ tsp. salt   Pinch of pepper

Add to the oatmeal mixture, mix well, allow to cool, and stuff the bird just before cooking.

PRUNE AND APPLE STUFFING (for roast goose)

Quantities for 1 goose.

1 lb. prunes (½ kg.)

Soak overnight in cold water to cover. Next day remove the stones.

2 lb. apples (1 kg.)

Peel, core, and slice.

1 oz. butter or margarine (30 g.)   1 Tbs. water

3 oz. sugar (6 Tbs. or 75 g.)

Put all the ingredients in a pan and cook very gently for 2–3 hrs. until the mixture is the consistency of jam. Stir frequently.

Variation. Use equal quantities of prunes and fresh or dried apple rings. Soak the prunes in warm water for 5 mins. and then remove the stones. Chop prunes and apples roughly and stuff the bird three-quarters full, allowing room for fruit to swell.

RICE STUFFING (for lamb)

Quantities for a shoulder.

3 oz. rice (6 Tbs. or 75 g.)

Boil the rice by any of the methods. See *Rice*, page 224.

4 *rashers bacon*	½ *tsp. grated lemon rind*
1 *sheep's kidney*	*Salt and pepper*
2 *oz. sultanas* (⅓ *c. or 50 g.*)	1 *egg or 2 yolks*
½ *tsp. chopped fresh or dried rosemary*	

Remove the rinds and chop the rashers. Remove core and skin and chop the kidney. Mix all ingredients with the cooked rice and use at once.

SAGE AND ONION STUFFING (for goose, duck or pork)

Quantities for 1 small goose or 2 ducks.

4 *large onions*

Skin, and boil in a little salted water for 5 mins. Drain.

10 *fresh sage leaves or 1 tsp. dried sage*

Dip fresh sage leaves in boiling water for a minute. Dry. Chop or mince the sage and onions.

1 *oz. melted butter or margarine* (30 *g.*)	2 *tsp. salt*
4 *oz. breadcrumbs* (1⅓ *c. or 125 g.*)	½ *tsp. pepper*

Mix all the ingredients together.

VEAL FORCEMEAT OR STUFFING

Quantities for a small chicken.

2 *oz. fresh breadcrumbs* (⅔ *c. or 50 g.*)	½ *tsp. grated lemon rind*
2 *oz. grated suet* (6 *Tbs. or 50 g.*)	1 *Tbs. chopped parsley*
Pinch of ground mace or nutmeg	½ *tsp. salt*
1 *tsp. dried thyme or savory or*	⅛ *tsp. pepper*
2 tsp. fresh	*Milk to mix*
1 *egg*	

Mix all the ingredients together. If the stuffing is to be used for poultry, the liver, chopped and fried in a little fat, may be added.

WALNUT STUFFING (for pheasant)

Quantities for 1–2 birds.

8 *oz. chopped lean pork* (250 *g.*)	1½ *oz. butter* (45 *g.*)

Melt the butter and fry the pork in it.

1 oz. breadcrumbs (½ c. or 25 g.) 1 tsp. chopped thyme
2 oz. chopped walnuts (¼ c. or 50 g.) 2 Tbs. chopped parsley
Pinch of pepper 2 Tbs. red wine
1 tsp. salt ½ egg

Mix all ingredients together and use at once.

INDEX